Kazakhstan and the New International Politics of Eurasia

D1127562

Richard Weitz

Johns Hopkins University-SAIS, 1619 Massachusetts Ave. NW, Washington, D.C. 20036
Institute for Security and Development Policy, V. Finnbodav. 2, Stockholm-Nacka 13130, Sweden
www.silkroadstudies.org

"Kazakhstan and the New International Politics of Eurasia" is a Silk Road Paper published by the Central Asia-Caucasus Institute and the Silk Road Studies Program. The Silk Road Papers Series is the Occasional Paper series of the Joint Center, and addresses topical and timely subjects. The Joint Center is a transatlantic independent and non-profit research and policy center. It has offices in Washington and Stockholm and is affiliated with the Paul H. Nitze School of Advanced International Studies of Johns Hopkins University and the Stockholm-based Institute for Security and Development Policy. It is the first institution of its kind in Europe and North America, and is firmly established as a leading research and policy center, serving a large and diverse community of analysts, scholars, policy-watchers, business leaders, and journalists. The Joint Center is at the forefront of research on issues of conflict, security, and development in the region. Through its applied research, publications, research cooperation, public lectures, and seminars, it functions as a focal point for academic, policy, and public discussion regarding the region.

ISBN: 978-91-85937-33-2

Printed in the United States of America

Distributed in North America by:

The Central Asia-Caucasus Institute
Paul H. Nitze School of Advanced International Studies
1619 Massachusetts Ave. NW, Washington, D.C. 20036
Tel. +1-202-663-7723; Fax. +1-202-663-7785
E-mail: caci2@jhu.edu

Distributed in Europe by:

The Silk Road Studies Program
Institute for Security and Development Policy
V. Finnbodavägen 2, SE-13130 Stockholm-Nacka
E-mail: info@silkroadstudies.org

Editorial correspondence should be addressed to Svante E. Cornell, Research and Publications Director, at either of the addresses above (preferably by e-mail.)

Table of Contents

Preface

During the past half-decade Kazakhstan has accomplished something which no other state formed from the ruins of the USSR has achieved: beginning as a largely rural country with a small but politically powerful urban elite, it has emerged with a large and growing middle-class that increasingly seeks to make its voice heard in national affairs. Oil has been the engine of this change, but Kazakhstan is now working hard to diversify the sources of its wealth. Under any circumstances, such progress as has occurred would not have been possible without prudent reforms and innovative legislation. Nor could it have happened without a foreign policy that assured the country's security without tying it to any one outside power.

In 2008, the Central Asia-Caucasus Institute & Silk Road Studies Program Joint Center undertook a review of Kazakhstan's progress and current status in three areas: social evolution, political reform, and international security. This has already resulted in two monographs issued by the Joint center as *Silk Road Papers*: John C. K. Daly's *Kazakhstan's Emerging Middle Class* and Anthony Clive Bowyer's *Parliament and Political Parties in Kazakhstan*. With this paper by Richard Weitz, we conclude the series. Dr. Weitz, a Senior Fellow and Director for Program Management at the Hudson Institute, offers a detailed overview of Kazakhstan evolving role in regional security and economic relations, as well as its relationship with major international organizations and powers. Indeed, Dr. Weitz shows how Kazakhstan's cautious and multi-vector foreign policy has contributed to strengthening the country and making it an increasingly independent power-house in Eurasia, with balanced and positive relations with all major and regional powers. We hope readers find this of interest.

S. Frederick Starr
Chairman

Executive Summary

Thanks to its large territory and population, vast energy wealth, relative political and ethnic stability, and skillful diplomacy, Kazakhstan has emerged as a leader of efforts to promote regional economic and political integration in Eurasia. Under President Nursultan Nazarbayev, Kazakh officials have pursued a "multi-vector" foreign policy that has sought to maintain good relations with the most important external great powers and multinational institutions engaged in the region. Furthermore, Kazakh officials have sought for over a decade to strengthen ties among the countries of Central Asia and the Caspian Basin region—areas that define Kazakhstan's "extended neighborhood." In addition to their recurring proposals for a Eurasian union, Kazakh representatives have promoted concrete cooperation regarding a range of specific economic, political, and security areas.

Kazakhstan plays a prominent role in Eurasia's most important international institutions, either as a participant in their decisions or as a partner in their programs:

- The Kazakh government has remained a loyal if frustrated supporter of the Commonwealth of Independent States (CIS), and was a founding member of the Collective Security Treaty Organization (CSTO);

- Kazakh officials have been leading advocates of strengthening the Eurasian Economic Community (Eurasec), especially in the areas of water management and standardization of members' customs and tariff policies;

- The Kazakh government has sought to strengthen the Shanghai Cooperation Organization (SCO) while preventing that institution from becoming overtly anti-American;

- Kazakhstan has developed closer ties with the North Atlantic Treaty Organization (NATO) than any of the other former Soviet republics of Central Asia;

- The European Union (EU) has identified Kazakhstan as a key partner in Central Asia due to its energy resources and Kazakh support for regional integration efforts;

- In 2010, Kazakhstan will become the first Eurasian country to assume chairmanship of the Organization for Security and Co-operation in Europe (OSCE).

Kazakh officials have pursued several initiatives independent of these institutions to enhance the security of Central Asia and the Caspian region from diverse threats:

- Kazakh officials have worked directly with Russia, the United States, and other countries to eliminate the weapons of mass destruction Kazakhstan inherited following the disintegration of the Soviet Union;

- Kazakhstan has promoted and signed the Treaty of Semipalatinsk, which established a Central Asian Nuclear-Weapon-Free Zone;

- Astana has joined Moscow, Washington, and other governments in supporting multilateral initiatives aimed at averting nuclear terrorism or illicit trafficking in nuclear materials;

- Kazakh authorities have participated in diverse bilateral and multilateral counterterrorist initiatives;

- The Kazakh government has strengthened the country's armed forces to enhance Astana's ability to contribute to regional security initiatives and international peacekeeping missions;

- Kazakh officials and security experts have been the driving force behind the Conference on Interaction and Confidence-Building in Asia process, which seeks to extend OSCE-like security enhancements throughout Asia.

In line with President Nursultan Nazarbayev's stated objective of making Kazakhstan a "transcontinental economic bridge" and a "regional locomotive" of economic development, Kazakh officials have promoted closer commercial integration among Eurasian nations at multiple levels, with priority given to:

- Improving regional transportation, pipeline, and communication networks;

- Reducing customs and other manmade barriers to trade;

- Encouraging tourism and other nongovernmental exchanges while strengthening regulations governing labor mobility in Eurasia;

- Promoting Kazakh private investment in other Eurasian economies, especially through joint ventures.

The strong Kazakh support for greater regional integration results in part from a recognition that Kazakhstan would strongly benefit from enhanced ties among Eurasian countries:

- Kazakhstan and its neighbors would achieve greater room to maneuver among the great powers active in the region, reducing the risks of their coming under the control of a great power condominium or becoming overly dependent on any single supplier, customer, investor, or market;

- Economic, political, and security problems in one Eurasian country could easily adversely affect neighboring countries, either through direct spill-over or by discouraging external investors;

- Kazakhstan's ability to realize its potential as a natural crossroads for east-west and north-south commercial linkages depends on reducing manmade political and economic obstacles to the free flow of goods and people among Eurasian nations;

- The increase in regional prosperity that economists predict would ensue from greater regional integration would help Kazakhstan expand its economic activities into new horizontal and vertical markets.

Kazakhstan's ability to realize its regional objectives will depend on several factors. Its transition to a post-Nazarbayev generation of political leaders, the effectiveness of Astana's stewardship of the OSCE, and the state of the Eurasian economies will all play crucial roles in determining Kazakhstan's success. Also important will be the policies of other countries engaged in Central Asia and the Caspian region—China and Russia above all, but also the United States.

Introduction

The disintegration of the Soviet Union in December 1991 ushered in a novel era in the international relations of Eurasia. The newly independent states of the region confronted the problem of achieving the twin goals of establishing their national independence while retaining beneficial relations with other former Soviet republics. One technique these countries have used is to deepen their ties with China, Europe, and the United States as well as the other major powers active in the region to balance Russia's continuing preeminence. Another approach has been to promote cooperation among regional states, in a manner independent of, though not in conflict with, the great powers. Kazakhstan has emerged as a natural leader in these latter endeavors due to the size of its territory, its vast energy wealth, its relative political and ethnic stability, its early and sustained decision to transition from a command to a market-based economy, and its skillful diplomacy.

Kazakhstan's geography has allowed it to exercise decisive influence in two of Eurasia's most important subregions—Central Asia and the Caspian Sea. These areas are sometimes referred to as "Greater Central Asia," but from Astana's perspective might be termed "Kazakhstan's extended neighborhood." At a minimum, analysts traditionally include Kazakhstan, Kyrgyzstan, Tajikistan, Turkmenistan, and Uzbekistan in "Central Asia." This approach may reflect the practice of Soviet ethnographers and political leaders, who divided the region into these five republics during the 1920s.[1] In contrast, the "Caspian Basin region" typically includes Armenia, Azerbaijan, Georgia, Turkmenistan, Kazakhstan, as well as parts of Iran and Russia. The past decade has made clear that other nearby countries also decisively affect political, economic, and security developments in these regions—notably Afghanistan, Iran, India, Mongolia, Pakistan, and Turkey.

---

[1] Pauline Jones Luong, *Institutional Change and Political Continuity in Post-Soviet Central Asia: Power, Perceptions, and Pacts* (Cambridge: Cambridge University Press, 2002), pp. 55, 64-65.

All of these countries help shape the international politics of Eurasia. Their independence has made regional relations much more complex than during the original "great game" between Russia and Great Britain in the 19th century, when St. Petersburg and London could largely ignore or control local actors in their bipolar struggle for mastery of Eurasia. The involvement of so many external actors in the region, with their changing mixture of common and diverging interests, also has complicated the international politics of Eurasia, especially by expanding the local states' room to maneuver.[2] Although Russia, China, Europe, and the United States substantially affect regional developments, they cannot dictate outcomes the way imperial governments frequently did a century ago.

Yet, since the USSR's collapse, the local nations have found it difficult to cooperate with one another. These states share unresolved disputes over borders, trade, visas, transportation, illegal migration, and natural resources such as water and gas. The Eurasian governments closed ranks behind the Uzbek government after the May 2005 anti-regime violence in Andijan, accepting the need for solidarity despite misgivings about the regional policies and domestic practices of Uzbek President Islam Karimov.[3] Even so, the poor state of their mutual relations has meant that these countries regularly enjoy closer ties with external actors (through bilateral and multilateral mechanisms) than with each other.

Under President Nursultan Nazarbayev, who has been in office since independence, Kazakhstan has remained committed to a "multi-vector" foreign policy that seeks to maintain good relations with Russia, China, Japan, the United States, and the European Union as well as other countries with important economic, political, or other roles in Eurasia. Nazarbayev and his team have managed to stand largely aloof from the quicksand of regional great power diplomacy, which has ensnarled rival Uzbekistan, while eschewing the extreme isolationism of the government of Turkmenistan under former President Saparmurat Niyazov. In 2004, Foreign Minister

---

[2] Matthew Edwards, "The New Great Game and the New Great Gamers: Disciples of Kipling and Mackinder," *Central Asian Survey*, vol. 22, no. 1 (March 2003), pp. 83-102.
[3] Shirin Akiner, *Violence in Andijan, 13 May 2005: An Independent Assessment* (Washington, DC: Central Asia-Caucasus Institute and Silk Road Studies Program, 2005), pp. 39-40.

Kasymzhomart Tokayev justified Kazakhstan's "balanced and multi-dimensional policy" as "an objective necessity." The policy's application has sometimes annoyed Moscow (regarding Kazakhstan's Trans-Caspian initiatives) as well as Washington (regarding Astana's dealings with Tehran). Yet, it is hard to disagree with Tokayev's explanation that, "Limiting ourselves to certain countries and regions could do serious harm to our national interests."[4]

As early as March 1994, Nazarbayev proposed the establishment of a Eurasian Union, but the plan failed to gain support among the other newly independent states that had only just rid themselves of a different (Soviet) type of union and were not eager to try another.[5] Nazarbayev has subsequently reaffirmed his commitment to a union, launching a new initiative in April 2007 that focused on borders and water management, issues that had long complicated relations among Central Asian states but which they could clearly manage more effectively together than in isolation.[6] A union of Central Asian states would represent a logical culmination of Kazakh efforts to strengthen regional autonomy and deepen local integration processes. Although the union would be independent of the CSTO, SCO, and other regional groups, and would exclude Russia, China, and other great powers from membership, the Eurasian grouping would not be directed against these institutions or countries. In fact, Nazarbayev's union proposal effectively presumes that the great powers would remain sufficiently engaged in regional security issues to balance one another and thereby allow Kazakhstan and other Central Asian countries room to maneuver.[7]

Kazakh experts consider the deeper integration of Central Asian countries a natural process that, although often impeded by man-made obstacles, accords

---

[4] Cited in Ibragim Alibekov, "While Russia Watches, Kazakhstan and Azerbaijan Explore New Ties," Eurasia Insight, March 3, 2004,
http://www.eurasianet.org/departments/business/articles/eav030304.shtml.

[5] Konstantin Syroezhkin, "Kazakhstan's Security Policy in the Caspian Sea Region," in Gennady Chufrin, ed., *The Security of the Caspian Sea Region* (Oxford: Oxford University Press, 2001), pp. 213-214.

[6] Timur Dadabaev, "Central Asian Regional Integration: Between Reality and Myth," *Central Asia-Caucasus Institute Analyst*, May 2, 2007,
http://www.cacianalyst.org/?q=node/4604.

[7] Syroezhkin, "Kazakhstan's Security Policy in the Caspian Sea Region," p. 233.

with the genuine national interests of these nations, which share historical and cultural ties as well as common borders and economic incentives for collaboration. To realize these advantages, proponents of greater unity argue that effective integration should entail the sharing of water and energy resources; additional improvements in the region's transportation infrastructure; the establishment of common customs and trading tariffs; mechanisms to respond collectively to environmental threats and natural disasters; and support for region-wide tourist networks. More generally, supporters envisage a process of evolution from a free trade zone to a customs union to an economic union with ancillary political and other institutions.[8]

Another economic factor, with political implications, inducing Kazakh leaders to promote regional integration is the belief that instability in neighboring countries could easily spill across state borders, either directly through imitative popular protests and refugee flows or indirectly by discouraging international capital markets from investing in the region. Despite recent Kazakh efforts to diversify their economic partners, Kazakhstan's economy remains heavily dependent on foreign companies for capital and technology.[9]

Kazakh and foreign experts argue that greater cooperation is required to resolve these disputes and better exploit the natural resources and pivotal location of Central Asia and the Caspian as natural transit routes for commerce between Europe and Asia. Enhanced collaboration is especially needed, they maintain, to counter transnational terrorist and criminal groups as well as exploit the economic comparative advantages enjoyed by Kazakhstan and neighboring states. By reducing inter-regional tensions and promoting deeper economic integration, these countries will become more

---

[8] L. M. Muzaparova, "Economic Cooperation in Central Asia: Problems and Prospects," Kazakhstan Institute for Strategic Studies, November 27, 2007, http://www.kisi.kz/site.html?id=1788.

[9] Mevlut Katik, "Kazakhstan Entertains Grand Economic Development Plan," Eurasia Insight, April 6, 2006, http://www.eurasianet.org/departments/business/articles/eav040606.shtml.

attractive to foreign investors and enhance their collective leverage with external actors.[10]

Since 2006, Nazarbayev has repeatedly proclaimed the goal of transforming Kazakhstan into one of the world's 50 most competitive developed countries.[11] Kazakh leaders believe that strong regional cooperation—ideally with a degree of integration that would both help harmonize regional economic policies and promote political, security, and other forms of collaboration—is essential for realizing this objective. Above all, it would allow Kazakh businesses to access new markets and exploit superior economies of scale from the resulting increase in labor, capital, and other factors of production. The Kazakh government has also sought to develop extensive security, economic, cultural, and other international links to enhance the country's autonomy by limiting Kazakhstan's dependence on any single supplier, customer, investor, or market.

At an October 22, 2007 conference in Washington, D.C., Erlan Idrissov, Ambassador of Kazakhstan to the United States, told the audience that, since independence, Kazakhs had resolved "not to take as a curse" their country's landlocked status, but instead to "turn it into an opportunity and a benefit" by leading the drive for regional integration. In its foreign policies, Idrissov added, Kazakhstan operates on the principle that "one cannot prosper without being surrounded by prosperous countries." [12]

Furthermore, Kazakhs realized that their country's large population of ethnic Russians and other ethnic communities makes it unlikely that Kazakhstan

---

[10]V. N. Sitenko, "ShOS i Problemy Bezopastnosti v Tsentral'noy Azii: Znacheniye dlya Kazakhstana," *Kazakhstan-Spektr*, no. 1 (2008), http://www.kisi.kz/site.html?id=5369. Many reports of the International Crisis Group have identified inadequate regional cooperation as a source of Eurasian economic, political, and other problems; for a list see http://www.crisisgroup.org/home/index.cfm?id=1251&l=1.

[11] Nazarbayev reaffirmed this goal in his latest state-of-the-nation address, delivered on February 6, 2008, available at http://www.akorda.kz/www/www_akorda_kz.nsf/sections?OpenForm&id_doc=0793 D9432423DDE5062573EC0048005B&lang=en&L1=L2&L2=L2-22.

[12] Conference on "Integrating Central Asia into the World Economy: Perspectives from the Region and from the U.S.," co-hosted by the Carnegie Endowment for International Peace and the Wolfensohn Center for Development at the Brookings Institution.

could remain unaffected by developments in neighboring countries.[13] At independence, the country's titular nationality actually constituted less than half the population. According to the 1989 Soviet census, ethnic Kazakhs comprised 39.5% of the population: Russians, 37.7%, Ukrainians, 5.4%; and Belorussians, 1.1% (i.e., ethnic Slavs amounted to 44.2% of the republic's population). National identity, bilingualism, and dual citizenship emerged as especially important issues during the first few years of Kazakhstan's independence. Some observers thought that the northern provinces, with their Slavic majorities, might seek unification with Russia.

The salience of these concerns subsequently declined due to the emigration of many ethnic Slavs, the higher birth rate of ethnic Kazakhs, the return of many exiled ethnic Kazakhs to their homeland (or that of their ancestors), the government's tolerant language and ethnic practices, and the country's booming economy, which has benefited large numbers of ethnic Slavs as well as ethnic Kazakhs. The decision of Kazakhstan's leaders to stress loyalty to the state rather than any particular national identity was also essential in decreasing ethnic tensions.[14] According to a 1999 census, 53.4% of the country's population consisted of ethnic Kazakhs, 30% Russians, 3.7% Ukrainians, 2.5% Uzbeks, 2.4% Germans, 1.7% Tatars, 1.4% Uighurs, and 4.9% belonged to other ethnic groups.[15] As of January 2007, Kazakhstan's population consisted of 15,396,600 people—59.2% ethnic Kazakhs, 25.6% ethnic Russians, 2.9% ethnic Ukrainians, 2.9% ethnic Uzbeks, 1.5% Uighurs, 1.5% Tartars, and 1.4% ethnic Germans.[16]

Although two of six million ethnic Russians have left Kazakhstan since its independence, the four million Russians that have remained have contributed considerably to the country's economic development, educational

---

[13] Rafis Abazov, "Kazakhstan's Security Challenges in a Changing World," in Michael Intriligator, Alexander Nikitin, and Majid Tehranian, eds., *Eurasia: A New Peace Agenda* (Amsterdam: Elsevier, 2005), pp. 229-231.

[14] Sally N. Cummings, *Kazakhstan: Centre-Periphery Relations* (London: Royal Institute of International Affairs, 2000), pp. 46-47; and Luong, *Institutional Change and Political Continuity*, pp. 152-154.

[15] John C. K. Daly, *Kazakhstan's Emerging Middle Class* (Washington, D.C.: Central Asia-Caucasus Institute, March 2008), pp. 20-21.

[16] Embassy of Kazakhstan in the USA and Canada, "Population Grows to 15.4 Million, More Births, Less Emigration Are Reasons," Kazakhstan News Bulletin, April 20, 2007, http://www.kazakhembus.com/042007.html.

achievements, and other socioeconomic advances. Many belong to Kazakhstan's middle class, but this stratum encompasses many ethnic Kazakhs as well, including young professionals who have thrived as entrepreneurs under the government's pro-business policies. This diverse composition has meant that no one ethnic group predominates in Kazakhstan's middle class.[17]

The November 2007 decision to award Kazakhstan chairmanship of the Organization for Security and Co-operation in Europe (OSCE) in 2010 recognizes the country's growing importance in Eurasia. Kazakh officials are characterizing this long-sought status as an endorsement of their country's successful economic and political reforms, their leading role in Europe and Central Asia, and their contribution as a bridge between the former Soviet republics and other OSCE members. While acknowledging problems with Kazakhstan's adherence to the principles of liberal democracy as practiced in the European Union and the United States, other governments hope that the OSCE chairmanship will encourage movement towards those standards in Kazakhstan as well as bolster the OSCE's influence in the former Soviet bloc. The Kazakh government has launched a "Road to Europe" reform program to prepare the country for the economic and political challenges and opportunities the OSCE chairmanship will present.[18]

In addition to skillful diplomacy, Kazakhstan's emergence as the most important driver of regional integration within Central Asia and the Caspian Sea region has been attributed to the country's powerful but not overwhelming attributes of state power. Kazakhstan possesses more energy resources than its less endowed neighbors. It also enjoys the region's most dynamic economy and capital markets. Yet, Kazakhstan lacks the economic and military foundations to aspire for regional hegemony, especially given that its power and influence is dwarfed by that of Russia and China.

The remainder of this paper is divided into four sections that present different perspectives on Kazakhstan's role in its "extended neighborhood."

---

[17] Daly, *Kazakhstan's Emerging Middle Class*, pp. 5-6.
[18] Embassy of Kazakhstan to the USA and Canada, "President Nazarbayev Delivers Annual State-of-the-Nation Address, Announces Kazakhstan's 'Road to Europe'," News Bulletin, February 8, 2008, http://www.kazakhembus.com/NBSpecialIssue_3_020808.html.

The first chapter considers how the most significant international institutions shaping regional politics relate to Kazakhstan. Astana plays an important role in all of them—either as a major partner in their programs or as a participant in their decision making. The next section analyzes the manner in which Kazakh leaders have sought to promote security and stability throughout Central Asia and the Caspian region as well as contribute to countering global nonproliferation and other threats. Kazakh officials recognize that adverse regional security developments could present both direct threats to Kazakhstan's security as well as indirect damage to the country's economic and political aspirations by deterring foreign investment, disrupting Eurasian trade and tourism, and generally making Kazakhstan's environs less pleasant. The third chapter discusses Kazakhstan's potential to become a regional energy and economic leader as well as various obstacles to the realization of this objective. The second and third sections are intimately linked in that security is essential for the continued energy and economic development of Kazakhstan and its neighborhood. To take but one example, Central Asian governments will remain reluctant to relax their border controls, which impede regional commerce, if they fear that transnational criminal organizations will exploit the opportunity for illicit purposes. The final section of the paper surveys Kazakhstan's bilateral relationships with its immediate neighbors in order to provide yet another view on how Kazakhstan is responding to the challenges and opportunities presented by the new international politics of Eurasia.

The Institutional Framework

The following section reviews Kazakhstan's relations with the major multinational political, economic, and security institutions active in Eurasia. Kazakhstan also belongs to other organizations. These include universal bodies like the United Nations as well as institutions that have members in Eurasia but either are not very active (e.g., the Economic Cooperation Organization) or whose main efforts focus outside the region (such as the Organization of the Islamic Conference, which Kazakhstan joined in 1995[19]). The ones below, however, most affect Kazakhstan's relations with its Eurasian neighbors.

Commonwealth of Independent States

The Commonwealth of Independent States (CIS), consisting of all the former Soviet republics except for the Baltic countries, initially represented Kazakhstan's most important regional institution after the USSR's disintegration. Kazakhstan and eight other members signed a CIS Collective Security Treaty (CST) at their May 15, 1992, summit in Tashkent. According to its provisions, they pledged to refrain from joining other alliances directed against any other CST signatory. The CST signatories also agreed to cooperate to resolve conflicts between members and cooperate in cases of external aggression against them. The main effect of the Tashkent Treaty was to help Russia legitimize its continued military presence in many CIS members. The CST did not, however, fulfill Kazakhstan's objective of establishing a system of collective security in the former Soviet Union.[20]

---

[19] Organisation of the Islamic Conference, "Member States, 2008," http://www.oic-oci.org/oicnew/member_states.asp.

[20] Konstantin Syroezhkin., "Kazakhstan's Security Policy in the Caspian Sea Region," in Gennady Chufrin, ed., *The Security of the Caspian Region*, (Oxford: Oxford University Press, 2001), pp. 213-214.

The CIS itself initially played a useful role in facilitating a "civilized divorce" among its members. Compared with the chaos that arose in the former Yugoslavia, another communist-dominated multinational state that had failed to resolve its underlying ethnic divisions, the disintegration of the Soviet Union occurred with surprisingly little violence, with the notable exception of the Caucasus region. For the most part, the leaders of Kazakhstan and the other newly independent former Soviet republics accepted the USSR's administrative boundaries as their new national borders.[21] Russian President Vladimir Putin has praised the organization for "clearly help[ing] us to get through the period of putting in place partnership relations between the newly formed young states without any great losses and play[ing] a positive part in containing regional conflicts in the post-Soviet area."[22]

After its first few years, however, the CIS ceased having a great impact on its members' most important polices. For example, the agreement establishing a collective air defense network, which began to operate in 1995, had to be supplemented by separate bilateral agreements between Russia and several important participants such as Ukraine. Georgia and Turkmenistan withdrew from the system in 1997.[23] The influence of the CIS reached nadir in 1999, when Russia withdrew its border guards from Kyrgyzstan and its military advisers from Turkmenistan, while three members (Azerbaijan, Georgia, and Uzbekistan) declined to renew their membership in the CST.[24] Despite the CST, CIS governments proved unable to collaborate sufficiently to end the civil war in Tajikistan or establish a common front regarding the Taliban and related terrorist threats emanating from Afghanistan, exposing the weakness

---

[21] Ministry of Foreign Affairs of Kazakhstan, "Aktual'nye Voprosy Vneshney Politiki Kazakhstana: Delimitatsiya i Demarkastsiya Gosudarstvennoy Granitsy," http://portal.mfa.kz/portal/page/portal/mfa/ru/content/policy/issues/delimitation.

[22] Vladimir Putin, "Annual Address to the Federal Assembly of the Russian Federation," May 10, 2006, http://www.kremlin.ru/eng/speeches/2006/05/10/1823_type70029type82912_105566.shtml.

[23] Marcin Kaczmarski, "Russia Creates a New Security System to Replace the C.I.S.," December 21, 2005, http://www.pinr.com/report.php?ac=view_report&report_id=416&language_id=1.

[24] Jim Nichol, *Central Asia: Regional Developments and Implications for U.S. Interests*, (Washington, D.C.: Congressional Research Service, December 1, 2005), p. 4.

of the Tashkent Treaty at the time it was most needed.[25] It was only in March 2000 that Kazakhstan, Kyrgyzstan, Russia, and Tajikistan finally announced the establishment of the long-discussed CIS antiterrorist center.[26]

The CIS historically has had difficulties securing implementation of many of the economic, political, and security agreements its member governments have signed. Although the institution does provide opportunities for dialogue among its members, especially among government ministries and agencies dealing with common problems such as customs and migration, and legislatures through the CIS Parliamentary Assembly, the lack of effective enforcement or oversight mechanisms severely limits effective cooperation. According to President Nazarbayev, of the 1,600 agreements formally adopted by the CIS, its members had signed and implemented fewer than 30% of them.[27] Even Russian lawmakers ratify only a small percentage of CIS accords, making it hard to reconcile members' conflicting legislation and policies.

The problems of achieving consensus among twelve governments with increasingly divergent agendas, combined with the organization's weak, opaque, and inefficient institutions for making and implementing decisions, have led to its stagnation and steady decline relative to the other major multinational institutions with a presence in Central Asia. Perennial plans to reform its ineffective decision making structures have failed to achieve much progress.

Besides its structural weaknesses, policy differences among CIS members also have called into question the institution's viability. Major frictions between Russia and other members have arisen over a number of issues. For example, they disagree over the appropriate prices for Russian energy and

---

[25] Maulen Ashimbaev and Murat Laumulin, "The Role of the Central Asian Countries in Providing Security in Asia," *Central Asia's Affairs*, no. 2(2005).

[26] Konstantin Syroezhkin., "Kazakhstan's Security Policy in the Caspian Sea Region," in Gennady Chufrin, ed., *The Security of the Caspian Region*, (Oxford: Oxford University Press, 2001), p. 226.

[27] "CIS Summit Brings No Progress on Post-Soviet Borders, Reform," RIA Novosti, November 28, 2006, http://en.rian.ru/world/20061128/56131971.html.

Russia's restrictions on labor mobility.[28] Plans to establish a CIS free trade zone have been repeatedly postponed due to the disparities among its members in terms of economic policies and attributes. At present, many members trade more with Western countries than they do with each other. Similar divergences are evident in the desire of some but not all members to move closer to seemingly rival Western institutions like the European Union and NATO. The wave of color revolutions a few years ago has widened divergences among the members' political systems, with certain countries seeking to establish European-style liberal democracies and other regimes committed to preserving their authoritarian status quo.

Ironically, a core weakness permeating the CIS—its inability to reduce the differences in goals, policies, and values of its members—also probably will prevent its complete disintegration. Much more than the EU, the CIS encourages its members to pursue "multi-speed integration" arrangements in which the pace of integration varies by issue and the participants. Since, it exercises so few limits on their freedom of action, these governments lack a strong reason to break with inertia and formally leave the organization. Instead, the CIS likely will persist, but as a decreasingly influential institution as its members redirect their attention and resources elsewhere.[29]

President Nazarbayev has been pushing for years for a major restructuring and strengthening of the organization. At the July 2006 informal summit of CIS leaders in Moscow, he offered a comprehensive program for reforming the CIS that proposed concentrating reform efforts in five main areas: migration, transportation, communications, transnational crime, and scientific, educational, and cultural cooperation.[30] Nazarbayev also suggested several cost-cutting measures that would have allowed for the more efficient use of the organization's resources.[31] At the November 2007 meeting of CIS

---

[28] Sergei Blagov, "The CIS: End of the Road?," *Eurasia Insight*, August 29, 2005, http://www.eurasianet.org/departments/insight/articles/eav082905.shtml.
[29] Oskana Antonenko, "Assessing the CIS," February 14, 2006, http://www.russiaprofile.org/international/2006/2/14/1035.wbp.
[30] Ministry of Foreign Affairs of Kazakhstan, "Kazakhstan i integratsionnyie protsessy: SNG: Sodruzhestvo Nezavisimyx Gosudarstv," http://portal.mfa.kz/portal/page/portal/mfa/ru/content/policy/inegration/CIS.
[31] RIA Novosti, "CIS Summit Brings No Progress on Post-Soviet Borders, Reform," November 28, 2006, http://en.rian.ru/world/20061128/56131971.html.

Prime Ministers in Ashgabat, Kazakh Prime Minister Karim Masimov called for the establishment of a common CIS food marketing and pricing policy. Masimov stated that "food prices have been growing lately so ... our governments should draft specific measures and take specific steps for lifting administrative and other non-market barriers in food deliveries." The CIS leaders decided to create a group of CIS agricultural ministers to develop a food market development strategy."[32]

In most cases, however, other CIS leaders have ignored Nazarbayev's reform proposals. The leaders of Georgia and Ukraine still see the organization primarily as a mechanism for consultations with fellow CIS leaders, a concept derisively referred to as a "presidential club" by its critics. Even such close CIS allies as Russia and Belarus are divided over key issues like whether to adopt a common currency and over the price other CIS members should pay for Russia's oil and gas.[33] In October 2007, the member governments did agree to establish a special CIS body to supervise migration among their countries, but other organizations have assumed the lead role in promoting regional integration regarding most other issues.[34]

Collective Security Treaty Organization

Soon after becoming president, Vladimir Putin launched a sustained campaign to re-channel the CIS by enhancing cooperation among a core group of pro-Russian governments and reorienting it from a collective-defense organization towards one directed against transnational threats such as drug trafficking, arms smuggling, and especially terrorism, a more pressing concern to most of its participating governments. In 2001, the CIS members authorized the formation of a Collective Rapid Deployment Force (CRDF). Although the CRDF was designed primarily to provide for a collective response to terrorist attacks or incursions, it initially was not a standing force. Instead, it consisted of earmarked battalions based in Kazakhstan,

---

[32] "CIS: Rejuvenation or Disintegration," November 27, 2007, http://www.newscentralasia.net/Articles-and-Reports/196.html.

[33] Yuri Filippov, "CIS—Unembellished Results of the Year," RIA Novosti, December 19, 2006, http://en.rian.ru/analysis/20061219/57216450.html.

[34] "CIS Leaders Agree to Form Body Controlling Migration—Putin," RIA Novosti, October 6, 2007, http://en.rian.ru/world/20071006/82769544.html.

Kyrgyzstan, Russia, and Tajikistan.[35] More importantly, on May 14, 2002, the presidents of Kazakhstan, Kyrgyzstan, Russia, and Tajikistan (with Armenia and Belarus) agreed to transform the CIS CST into a Collective Security Treaty Organization (CSTO).[36] They established an ad hoc group composed of deputy ministers of defense and other senior government representatives to draft the main regulations for the CSTO, a process completed on November 1, 2002.[37]

Since the formal inauguration of the CSTO the following year, when all its member states ratified its founding documents, the organization has developed a more defined legal basis, including a charter committing members to coordinate their foreign, defense, and security policies. It also has established several standing bodies: a Foreign Ministers Council, a Defense Ministers Council, the Committee of Security Council Secretaries, a secretariat in Moscow, and a CSTO staff group stationed in Bishkek. The most authoritative organ is the CSTO Collective Security Council, which consists of the members' heads of state. The member governments' national presidents chair the Council in succession. The CSTO Permanent Council coordinates CSTO activities between sessions of the Collective Security Council. A CSTO Parliamentary Assembly Council also exists. It seeks to harmonize security-related legislation—such as in the areas of terrorism, narco-trafficking, and illegal migration—among member governments.

The CSTO provides for the mobilization of larger multinational military formations in the event of external aggression. Two such groups presently exist: an East European group (between Russia and Belarus) and a Caucasian group (between Russia and Armenia). Kazakhstan, Kyrgyzstan, Russia, and Tajikistan are currently in the Southern group of forces, which in wartime would come under the command of the standing combined headquarters.[38]

---

[35] Oksana Antonenko and Kathryn Pinnick, "Russia's Foreign and Security Policy in Central Asia: The Regional Perspective," The International Institute for Strategic Studies, 2003, p. 6.

[36] V. Nikolaenko, "Collective Security Treaty: Ten Years Later," *International Affairs* (Moscow), vol. 48, no. 3 (2002), p. 186.

[37] Rafis Abazov, "Kazakhstan's Security Challenges in a Changing World," in Michael Intriligator, Alexander Nikitin, and Majid Tehranian, eds., *Eurasia: A New Peace Agenda* (Amsterdam: Elsevier, 2005), p. 236.

[38] "CSTO to Create Central Asia Military Group," Interfax, February 7, 2006.

The CSTO also assumed control of the CRDF and transformed it into a standing force with a small multinational staff and a mobile command center. At present, the CRDF comprises 10 battalions of about 4,000 troops in total. Russia and Tajikistan each provide three battalions; Kazakhstan and Kyrgyzstan have each allocated two battalions to the force. CRDF units, joined by other military formations from CSTO member states, have engaged in several major exercises on the territory of its Central Asian members. These have included the rapid deployment anti-terrorist exercise *Rubezh-2004* ("Frontier 2004") in August 2004, and *Rubezh-2005* in April 2005, which involved some 3,000 troops.[39] The CSTO members also have largely taken over development of the CIS collective air defense network, with Russia alone paying for 80% of its maintenance costs.[40] The other CIS governments either send observers to these CSTO military activities or do not participate at all. (Thus far, Armenia and Belarus have also proved less active CSTO members than Russia and the Central Asian countries.)

The governments of Kazakhstan and other CSTO members stress that the organization represents more than just a military bloc, and can contribute to meeting a range of regional security problems. For example, countering narcotics trafficking and terrorism within Central Asia have become CSTO priorities. Since 2003, their intelligence, law enforcement, and defense agencies have jointly conducted annual "Kanal" ("Channel") operations to intercept drug shipments from Afghanistan through the region's porous borders to markets in the former Soviet republics and Western Europe. Azerbaijan, Iran, Uzbekistan, and other non-CSTO members have participated in these exercises. The CSTO has established a working group on Afghanistan to strengthen its government law enforcement and counter-narcotics agencies. The CSTO member governments have agreed to coordinate their nonproliferation and export control policies, paying

---

[39] For a description of the 2004 exercise see Erica Marat, "CSTO's Antiterrorist Exercises 'Rubezh-2004' Score High Rating among Member-States," *Central Asia-Caucasus Analyst*, August 25, 2004, http://www.cacianalyst.org/view_article.php?articleid=2614. For the 2005 exercises see "'Counter-Terrorist Exercise 'Rubezh-2005' to End in Tajikistan Soon," RIA Novosti, April 6, 2005, http://www.globalsecurity.org/military/library/news/2005/04/mil-050406-rianovosti09.htm.
[40] "CIS Air Defense to Hold Command-and-Staff Exercise in October," RIA Novosti, August 21, 2006, http://en.rian.ru/russia/20060821/52872338.html.

particular attention to the need to prevent illegal shipments of weapons of mass destruction (WMD), WMD-related materials, and their means of delivery.[41] CSTO law enforcement and internal security officials regularly exchange information about regional terrorist threats. CSTO governments also update their partners about their basing arrangements, weapons sales, and other security ties with other countries. For example, Kyrgyz representatives have kept their partners abreast of the negotiations concerning the renewal of their Manas base agreement with the United States.[42]

In June 2005, CSTO members signed agreements to enhance joint military training, including by exchanging students at their military education establishments and by compiling a list of testing sites and target ranges for use during joint exercises. They also created a commission to promote closer ties between their defense industries. Its responsibilities encompass establishing more joint ventures and research and development projects, defining common standards for military equipment, ensuring sufficient production of spare parts and other defense items, and helping implement the "program for military-technical cooperation for 2006-2010."[43] In December 2005, Russian Defense Minister Sergey Ivanov announced that he and his CSTO colleagues had agreed to coordinate their defense programs relating to nuclear, biological, or chemical security against terrorist attacks.[44] CSTO planners have made strengthening members' special forces a priority due to their superior effectiveness in combating terrorists and drug traffickers.[45] The CSTO governments subsequently devoted much attention to refining the technical, financial, and organizational issues raised by their decision to create a mechanism to deploy a collective peacekeeping force.

---

[41] "CSTO Experts Discuss Export Control Issues and Adopt List of Terrorist Organizations," *International Export Control Observer*, no. 6 (April 2006), pp. 25-26.

[42] "CSTO Should Be Briefed on U.S.-Kyrgyz Base Talks-Lavrov," Interfax, June 7, 2006.

[43] "Putin: CSTO to Establish Anti-Drug Structure," RIA Novosti, June 23, 2005, http://en.rian.ru/world/20050623/40751672.html.

[44] Maria Danilova, "Putin Calls for Strengthening Security Pact of Ex-Soviet Nations," Associated Press, November 30, 2005, http://www.accessmylibrary.com/coms2/browse_JJ_T282-200511_1801_1875.

[45] Anatoly Klimenko, "Russia and China as Strategic Partners in Central Asia: A Way to Improve Regional Security," *Far Eastern Affairs*, vol. 33, no.2 (2005), p. 5.

The Russian government has adopted a policy of allowing CSTO members to purchase Russian-made military equipment and supplies at the same prices paid by the Russian armed forces, avowedly for the purpose of facilitating the arming of their CRDF contingents. Although delays have occurred due to the need to develop effective control mechanisms against unauthorized re-exports, and Central Asian militaries have adopted some NATO standards and procedures, they still rely heavily on Russian-manufactured hardware. The Russian Ministry of Defense also heavily subsidizes the costs of training officers from CSTO states, whose senior commanders were trained at Soviet academies, at its professional military education institutions. Whereas the United States, China, and other countries typically offer short-term courses, Russian training curriculum often last for years.[46] Russian diplomats led the successful effort to secure formal observer status for the CSTO in the U.N. General Assembly in December 2004. They also have been pressing NATO to develop formal ties with the organization.

The CSTO has developed into a stronger institution than the CIS. The threat perceptions of the CSTO governments overlap more than those of the larger, more diverse CIS—some of whose members want to join NATO whereas others see the alliance as a major threat. In contrast, CSTO leaders jointly focus on "terrorists" and other groups perceived as seeking to overthrow them. Their attention concentrates on Afghanistan, which they also see as the main source of narcotics trafficking in Central Asia. CSTO members have shown some interest in providing the institution with economic functions. In August 2006, the CSTO member governments formally began reviewing a package of documents aimed to strengthen the legal basis for military and economic cooperation under CSTO auspices.[47] The CSTO also has been developing ties with the Eurasian Economic Community and the International Organization for Migration.

Kazakhstan has been a very active participant in CSTO activities. In August 2006, for instance, the CSTO held its largest military exercises of the year in

---

[46] Roger N. McDermott, "Tajik Military Weary of NATO," Eurasia Daily Monitor, April 4, 2006, http://www.jamestown.org/edm/article.php?article_id=2370946.
[47] Roger McDermott, "Boucher Visit to Bishkek Reveals Widening Gap in U.S.-Kyrgyz Relations," Eurasia Daily Monitor, August 15, 2006, http://www.jamestown.org/edm/article.php?article_id=2371382.

Kazakhstan. *Rubezh-2006* ("Frontier-2006") involved some 2,500 defense personnel as well dozens of armored vehicles, artillery pieces, and warplanes from CSTO member governments Kazakhstan, Kyrgyzstan, Tajikistan, as well as Russia. All the CSTO's major command components—its standing joint headquarters, permanent joint staff, and secretariat—participated in the exercise, which occurred on Kazakhstan's Caspian coastline, about 30 kilometers northwest of the Kazakh town of Aktau.

From Kazakhstan's perspective, however, the CSTO presents the problem of enshrining Russian military dominance in Central Asia. For example, Moscow justified establishing the Kant airbase, offered rent-free by the Kyrgyz government, on the grounds that it provided air support "for the whole of the Collective Security Pact right up to the Afghan border."[48] Putin himself described Russia's newly legal military base in Tajikistan as a CSTO facility that, "along with the air base at Kant, Kyrgyzstan, will be an important part of the united system of collective security for the region."[49]

In addition, involvement with the CSTO imposes some clear constraints on Kazakhstan's security policies. For example, in October 2005, Russia's Defense Minister argued that if Kazakhstan or any other CSTO member was considering hosting foreign military bases, "they should take into account the interests of Russia and coordinate this decision with our country."[50]

Eurasian Economic Community

At Nazarbayev's initiative, some of the former Soviet republics established a Eurasian Economic Community (Eurasec; or EEC) on October 10, 2000. Nazarbayev made his proposal after the CIS proved unable to make adequate progress in the pursuit of economic integration and the customs union then

---

[48] Olga Dzyubenko, "Kyrgyzstan: US Forces Can Stay—If They Pay More," Reuters, September 21, 2005, http://go.reuters.com/newsArticle.jhtml?type=topNews&storyID=9716375&src=rss/topNews.

[49] Cited in Bruce Pannier, "Central Asia: Russia Comes on Strong (Part 2)," November 17, 2004, http://www.rferl.org/featuresarticle/2004/11/ffdd150c-4daa-4577-9d8a-893ff8613e82.html.

[50] Radio Mayak, Radio Free Europe/Radio Liberty Newsline, October 11, 2005, cited in Stephen J. Blank, *U.S. Interests in Central Asia and the Challenges to Them* (Carlisle, PA: Strategic Studies Institute of the U.S. Army War College, March 2007), p. 8.

existing between Kazakhstan, Belarus, Kyrgyzstan, Russia, and Tajikistan seemed equally ineffective. (The economic crisis experienced by Russia and Kazakhstan in the late 1990s led them to levy heavy tariffs on each other's imports.) Eurasec's main function is to promote economic and trade ties among countries that formed a unified economic system during the Soviet period by reducing custom tariffs, taxes, duties, and other factors impeding economic exchanges among them. Its stated objectives include creating a free trade zone, a common system of external tariffs, coordinating members' relations with the World Trade Organization and other international economic organizations, promoting uniform transportation networks and a common energy market, harmonizing national education and legal systems, and advancing members' social, economic, cultural, and scientific development and cooperation.[51]

In 2005, Eurasec absorbed the Organization of Central Asian Cooperation, whose members included Kazakhstan, Kyrgyzstan, Russia, Tajikistan, and Uzbekistan. Besides Kazakhstan, its membership roster now includes Belarus, Kyrgyzstan, Russia, Tajikistan, and most recently Uzbekistan. Armenia, Moldova, and Ukraine enjoy observer status. With its smaller number of members, all favorably disposed toward Moscow's leadership, Eurasec (like the CSTO) represents a logical alternative to the more unwieldy and contentious CIS. Eurasec's members account for approximately three-fourths of all foreign commercial transactions occurring among CIS members.

Given the difficulties that Belarus and Russia alone have had in negotiating a possible currency union, Eurasec's members have lost enthusiasm for creating a currency union. In recent years, the organization has strengthened ties with the CSTO. Since the CSTO contains the same members as Eurasec, plus Armenia, their leaders often hold sessions of both organizations when they assemble at regional summits.

Kazakhstan has been a leading advocate of strengthening the Eurasec. At the Eurasec summit of August 2006, Nazarbayev said he "was always ready to

---

[51] Ministry of Foreign Affairs of Kazakhstan, "Kazakhstan i Integratsionnyi Protsessy: Evraziyskoe Ekonomicheskoe Soobshchestvo,"
http://portal.mfa.kz/portal/page/portal/mfa/ru/content/policy/inegration/EEC.

discuss questions concerning integration within the EEC framework."[52] A recent Kazakh priority has been to promote cooperative initiatives within Eurasec to assess how to regulate Central Asia's unevenly distributed water resources and exploit the region's potential to generate hydroelectric power.

Analysts working with Eurasec have proposed a general set of principles for members' consideration. These include determining a suitable fuel and energy balance for the countries, restoring Soviet principles of irrigation for downstream states, promoting joint investment in building power stations, removing barriers for electricity companies in a common market for member states, and establishing multinational regulatory bodies.[53] The International Crisis Group (ICG) and other institutions have long warned that the continued lack of an effective region-wide mechanism for managing water supplies could engender further conflicts among Central Asian countries. For example, a May 2002 ICG report warns that, "Tensions over water and energy have contributed to a generally uneasy political climate in Central Asia. Not only do they tend to provoke hostile rhetoric, but they have also prompted suggestions that the countries are willing to defend their interests by force if necessary."[54]

During the Soviet period, Kyrgyzstan and Tajikistan would store excess water in winter and then release it in summer to the downstream countries of Kazakhstan, Turkmenistan, and Uzbekistan. According to the Soviet economic plan, these latter countries would use the water to support agriculture and cotton harvesting, receiving fossil fuels in return for winter heating. The break-up of the USSR has made it easier for Kyrgyzstan and Tajikistan, despite complaints by the other three countries, to use more water for hydropower to generate electricity for their own uses.[55] In January 2006, Russia and Kazakhstan created a Eurasian Development Bank, with a

---

[52] Sergei Blagov and Igor Torbakov, "EEC Summit Focuses on Energy, Security and Free Trade," Eurasia Insight, August 17, 2006, http://www.eurasianet.org/departments/insight/articles/eav081706.shtml.

[53] Lillis, "Central Asia: Water Woes."

[54] International Crisis Group, "Central Asia: Water and Conflict," May 30, 2002, p. ii, http://www.crisisgroup.org/library/documents/report_archive/A400668_30052002.pdf.

[55] Joanna Lillis, "Central Asia: Water Woes Stoke Economic Worries," Eurasia Insight, April 28, 2009, http://www.eurasianet.org/departments/insight/articles/eav042808.shtml.

subscribed capital base of $1.5 billion. [56] Its purpose is to help finance infrastructure and development and private sector activities in Central Asia. Analysts believe it could become an important instrument in enhancing Eurasec's effectiveness. [57] The current Eurasec Secretary General, Tair Mansurov, was governor of North Kazakhstan region and a former Kazakh ambassador to Russia. In late 2007, he replaced Grigory Rapota, from Belarus, who had served as Secretary General since October 2001, almost its entire history. [58]

The members' diverging status with respect to the World Trade Organization (WTO) remains a major factor complicating their efforts to establish a customs union. Whereas Kyrgyzstan has been a WTO member since 1998, Belarus has not even begun formal accession negotiations. Russia, Kazakhstan, and Tajikistan are negotiating their terms of entry. Russia's efforts to join the WTO remain blocked by several unresolved disagreements with the United States, which Moscow and Washington proved unable to resolve at bilateral meetings during the July 2006 G-8 summit in St. Petersburg. Economics Minister German Gref, presidential aide Sergey Prikhodko, and other Russian officials have made statements suggesting that they see a Eurasec customs union as an alternative, at least for a while, to WTO membership.

At an October 6, 2007 session of the Eurasec Intergovernmental Council in Dushanbe, Presidents Nazarbayev, Putin, and Alexander Lukashenko of Belarus signed agreements to accelerate formation of a customs union among their three countries. Putin predicted that the customs union would become operational within three years. [59] As of April 2008, the three governments had

---

[56] "Russia to Contribute Another $600 mln to Eurasian Bank," RIA Novosti, January 14, 2008, http://en.rian.ru/russia/20080114/96607471.html.

[57] Johannes F. Linn, "Central Asia: A New Hub of Global Integration," November 29, 2007,
http://www.brookings.edu/articles/2007/1129_central_asia_linn.aspx?emc=lm&m=210508&l=50&v=105274.

[58] "Tajikistan to Hold Rotating Presidency in Eurasec in 2008," RIA Novosti, October 6, 2007, http://en.rian.ru/world/20071006/82768497.html.

[59] "Russia, Belarus, Kazakhstan Sign Agreement Moving Closer to Customs Union," Associated Press, October 6, 2007,

signed over a dozen documents defining the legal basis for the union.[60] Only Kazakhstan, Belarus, and Russia would commit to a Eurasec customs union because they alone have made substantial progress towards harmonizing the relevant legislation—a development that may foreshadow the evolution of a multi-speed Eurasec in which a core group of countries, including Kazakhstan, achieve deeper and more rapid economic integration than most members.

In any case, Nazarbayev has made clear that he does not want to rely exclusively on the CIS, Eurasec, or other Russian-dominated institutions. Within Eurasec, Russia enjoys a 40% share in the voting and financial rights, whereas Kazakhstan, Belarus, and Uzbekistan only have 15% each while Kyrgyzstan and Tajikistan control merely 7.5% each.[61] At the October 2007 Eurasec meeting, Nazarbayev expressed unease at Russia's domination of Eurasec and other former Soviet institutions, which he argued should function very differently than during the Moscow-dominated Soviet period: "Of course Russia is the biggest economy and we cooperate smoothly. But although the special role of France and Germany is taken into account in the European Union, they cannot make decisions without smaller member states."[62] At this Dushanbe summit, Nazarbayev repeated his longstanding call for the creation of a union of Central Asian countries that would "allow the region of 50 million people to create a self-sufficient market using both economic and political means."[63] At a Eurasec meeting the following January, Kazakh Prime Minister Karim Masimov proposed convening a major business forum in Astana to consider creating a Eurasian Economic Union as

---

http://www.iht.com/articles/ap/2007/10/06/asia/AS-GEN-Tajikistan-Ex-Soviet-WT.mc_id=rssap_news.

[60] "Eurasec Deputy PMs to Discuss Customs Union in Moscow," RIA Novosti, April 24, 2008, http://en.rian.ru/russia/20080423/105680383.html.

[61] Sergei Blagov, "Moscow Signs Series of Agreements within Eurasian Economic Community Framework," Eurasia Daily Monitor, February 5, 2008, http://www.jamestown.org/edm/article.php?article_id=2372777.

[62] "Unhappiness with Moscow Sours CIS Summit," Moscow Times, October 8, 2007, http://www.moscowtimes.ru/stories/2007/10/08/011.html.

[63] "Unhappiness with Moscow Sours CIS Summit."

well as establishing a Eurasian scientific club and a Eurasian bank devoted to promoting new technologies.[64]

Shanghai Cooperation Organization

Russia's overwhelming preeminence in the CSTO has led Kazakhstan and other Central Asian governments to cultivate military ties with additional regional security institutions, especially the Shanghai Cooperation Organization (SCO), which is not dominated by a single country like the CIS or CSTO. In the words of an unnamed Central Asian diplomat, "With the Chinese in the room, the Russians can't resort to their usual tricks."[65] Despite the possible emergence of a Sino-Russian condominium, this condition presumably reduces fears of external subordination and gives them more room to maneuver. Kazakh leaders cite the contribution of the SCO to preserving the national sovereignty of its members as one of the main reasons they value the organization.[66]

Another reason for the SCO's popularity in Kazakhstan is that it allows Central Asian governments to manage Beijing's growing presence in their region multilaterally, backstopped by Russia, rather than deal with the China colossus directly on a bilateral basis. For example, when Kazakhstan conducted its August 2006 "Tianshan-I" exercise with China, which the Chinese *People's Daily* termed a "joint anti-terrorism drill"—though it involved only some 1,000 law enforcement and special forces personnel, including some cavalry units—it did so "within the SCO framework.[67] The first phase occurred in eastern Kazakhstan Almaty region; the second in

[64] Sergei Blagov, "Moscow Signs Series of Agreements within Eurasian Economic Community Framework," Eurasia Daily Monitor, February 5, 2008, http://www.jamestown.org/edm/article.php?article_id=2372777.

[65] Cited in Martha Brill Olcott, *Central Asia's Second Chance* (Washington, DC: Carnegie Endowment for International Peace, 2005), p. 198.

[66] Yerzhan Kh. Kazykhanov, "On Kazakhstan," *American Foreign Policy Interests*, vol. 28, no.3 (July 2006), p. 190.

[67] "China, Kazakhstan Hold Anti-Terror Drill," People's Daily Online, August 25, 2006, http://english.people.com.cn/200608/25/eng20060825_296744.html.

China's Xinjiang Uygur Autonomous Region, where the other SCO members sent over 100 observers.[68]

The SCO arose from arose from a border delimitation and arms control process between China and its new post-Soviet neighbors. During the 1990s, Kazakhstan, China, Russia, Kyrgyzstan, and Tajikistan negotiated several confidence-building and disarmament measures limiting their permissible military deployments and holdings along their mutual frontiers. After Uzbekistan joined this "Shanghai Five" process, the member governments transformed their dialogue into a formal international organization. Since then, they have undertaken a number of initiatives within the SCO framework.

The title of the "Shanghai Convention on Combating Terrorism, Separatism, and Extremism"—signed at the organization's founding summit in June 2001—aptly highlights the SCO's security priorities. Cooperation against "terrorism" (broadly defined to include the two other "evil forces" of ethno-separatism and political "extremism") resulted in the creation of the Regional Anti-Terrorism Structure (RATS) in Tashkent. Since it officially began operations in June 2004, the RATS has coordinated studies of Eurasian terrorist movements, exchanged information about terrorist threats, and provided advice on counterterrorist policies. It also has coordinated exercises among SCO security forces and organized efforts to disrupt terrorist financing and money laundering. In July 2005, the SCO governments formally pledged not to extend asylum to any individual designated as a terrorist or extremist by a SCO member. The resulting accord, entitled "Concept of Cooperation Between SCO Member States on Combating Terrorism, Separatism, and Extremism," provided for enhanced cooperation under the auspices of the RATS against terrorist financing and terrorist efforts to acquire weapons of mass destruction (WMD) and their means of delivery.[69] For several years, SCO members have undertaken numerous joint initiatives to combat narcotics trafficking and organized crime. In late 2005,

---

[68] "China Kicks off Second Phase of Joint Anti-Terror Drill," Xinhua, August 26, 2006, http://news.xinhuanet.com/english/2006-08/26/content_5009293.htm.

[69] Matthew Oresman and Zamir Chargynov, "The Shanghai Cooperation Summit: Where Do We Go from Here?," *CEF Quarterly: The Journal of the China-Eurasia Forum* (July 2005), pp. 5-6, http://www.chinaeurasia.org/files/CEF_Quarterly_August_2005.pdf.

they signed an agreement providing for mutual assistance to manage the consequences of natural disasters and other emergencies. Their national emergency management agencies are now developing enhanced modalities of cooperation.[70]

Since the SCO's establishment, member governments have conducted increasingly ambitious military exercises under the SCO's auspices. In October 2002, China and Kyrgyzstan conducted the first bilateral anti-terror exercise within the SCO framework, involving joint border operations by hundreds of troops. It marked the first instance of joint maneuvers by the Chinese People's Liberation Army (PLA) with another country's armed forces. In August 2003, the militaries from all the member governments, with the exception of Uzbekistan, participated in the first formal SCO-sponsored combined exercise (*Cooperation 2003*). It involved over 1,000 troops engaging in several counterterrorism scenarios in eastern Kazakhstan and the bordering Xinjiang region of China.[71] During the unprecedented Russian-Chinese military exercises of August 2005, all six SCO defense or deputy defense ministers attended as observers. Representatives from the United States and other Western countries were not invited. In early March 2006, Uzbekistan affirmed its elevated commitment to the SCO by hosting a multilateral exercise under its auspices, *East-Antiterror-2006*. Representatives from the member governments' special services and law enforcement agencies practiced rescuing hostages and defending critical infrastructure from terrorists.[72]

The SCO's activities also have expanded to encompass bilateral and multilateral projects in the areas of economics, energy, culture, and other fields. In September 2003, the SCO prime ministers adopted a Multilateral

---

[70] Interview with Russian Deputy Foreign Minister Alexander Alexeyev, Interfax, January 3, 2006, http://www.interfax.com/17/118163/interview.aspx.

[71] For descriptions of these exercises see Roger N. McDermott and William D. O'Malley, "Countering Terrorism in Central Asia," *Jane's Intelligence Review*, vol. 15, no. 10 (October 2003), pp. 16-19; Robert Sae-Liu, "China Looks Outward with its Exercise Programme," *Jane's Defence Weekly* (September 24, 2003); and Jing-dong Yuan, "Anti-Terror Exercises Only a First Step," *Moscow Times*, August 14, 2003.

[72] "SCO Member-States Hold Anti-terrorism Exercises in Uzbekistan," UzReport.com, March 10, 2006,
http://jahon.mfa.uz/modules.php?op=modload&name=News&file=article&sid=2202&mode=thread&order=0&thold=0&POSTNUKESID=1a2788d7b8af4f13ae1ee52d22602e6c.

Economic and Trade Cooperation Program that established several general economic objectives. For example, the participants pledged to facilitate trade and investment among themselves while working towards the free movement of goods, services, capital, and technology by 2020. At a September 2004 meeting in Bishkek, Kyrgyzstan, the prime ministers considered over one hundred cooperative projects in such sectors as customs, communications, and public health.[73] In 2005 and 2006, the SCO governments established a series of institutions to help implement the Program and these cooperative projects. The Development Fund, the Business Council (also known as the Entrepreneurs' Committee), and the Inter-Bank Agreement aim to encourage investment in regional projects by promoting collaboration among members' state enterprises, private businesses, and government agencies responsible for foreign economic ties. In November 2005, China hosted a Eurasian Economic Forum under the joint auspices of the SCO Secretariat, the United Nations, and the China Development Bank. It involved about 1,000 political and business leaders from many countries, including from several non-SCO members such as Japan and South Korea.

President Nazarbayev attended the SCO's founding meeting in St. Petersburg in June 2001, along with representatives of China, Kyrgyzstan, Russia and Tajikistan. At the session, he stated that the new organization "could contribute to security, economic prosperity and closer relationships between our peoples and countries." [74] The Kazakh government plans to organize a conference on cultural exchanges within the SCO.[75] Some Kazakh experts have become attracted to the idea of creating an "energy club" within the SCO. In August 2007, Nazarbayev himself proposed creating a SCO energy agency to maintain an oil-and-gas database as well as another SCO

---

[73] Shanghai Cooperation Organization, "Speech by SCO Secretary General Zhang Deguang at the Press Conference of the Eurasian Economic Forum," September 6, 2005, http://www.sectsco.org/news_detail.asp?id=513&LanguageID=2.

[74] Rafis Abazov, "Kazakhstan's Security Challenges in a Changing World," in Michael Intriligator, Alexander Nikitin, and Majid Tehranian, eds., *Eurasia: A New Peace Agenda* (Amsterdam: Elsevier, 2005), p. 236.

[75] Erica Marat, "The SCO and Foreign Powers in Central Asia: Sino-Russian Differences," *Central Asia-Caucasus Institute Analyst*, May 28, 2008, http://www.cacianalyst.org/?q=node/4867.

body to manage energy transactions among member countries.[76] Within this framework, oil and gas exporters such as Kazakhstan as well as Iran, Russia, and Uzbekistan would provide reliable energy supplies to China, India, Kyrgyzstan, Pakistan, Mongolia and Tajikistan.[77]

Astana hosted the July 2005 heads of state summit that made the SCO infamous in many Western circles. The attending SCO governments issued a statement asking the United States and other members of the Operation Enduring Freedom (OEF) coalition to establish a deadline for vacating their temporary military bases in Central Asia "considering the completion of the active military stage of antiterrorist operation in Afghanistan."[78] Although all SCO members signed the declaration, they appear to have done so for different reasons. Uzbekistan seems to have seen the statement as a useful mechanism to eliminate a large NATO military presence that it no longer welcomed after Western governments refused to support the Uzbek security crackdown in Andijan. Moscow and Beijing appear to have sought to reaffirm their expectation that NATO would eventually reduce its substantial military footprint in Central Asia. Kyrgyzstan employed the declaration as leverage to extract greater rent payments from Washington in exchange for continuing to host the U.S. military base at Manas International Airport. Finally, some signatories might have used the statement to signal their displeasure with certain Western policies in the region. For example, they may have hoped to galvanize the United States and NATO into more vigorously combating the terrorist and narcotics threats emanating from nearby Afghanistan. SCO members have repeatedly complained about the alliance's failure to undertake this responsibility, which they believe NATO assumed upon occupying the country.

Whatever their motives, that only Uzbekistan eventually proceeded to expel most NATO forces from its territory—ending in particular American use of

---

[76] "Kazakhstan Proposes Establishing Oil and Gas Regulator, Exchange," RIA Novosti, August 16, 2007, http://en.rian.ru/world/20070816/71834663.html.

[77] See for example G. Rakhmatulina, "Economic Integration in the Framework of the EEC and SCO—The Most Important Priority of the Foreign Policy of Kazakhstan," June 12, 2007, http://www.kisi.kz/site.html?id=1509.

[78] SCO Secretariat, "Declaration of Heads of Member States of Shanghai Cooperation Organisation," July 5, 2005, http://www.sectsco.org/news_detail.asp?id=500&LanguageID=2.

the Kharshi-Khanabad airbase—suggests that most SCO leaders, upon reflection, realized that any major Western military withdrawal from Central Asia under current conditions would substantially worsen their security given the probable inability of Russia, China, or any other country or multilateral group to stabilize Afghanistan as effectively. Kazakhstan has continued to allow U.S. and other NATO warplanes to overfly its territory on a regular basis in support of its operations in Afghanistan. In addition, Kazakh leaders have repeatedly cited, as a positive attribute, that the SCO is not an anti-Western bloc. In June 2006, Nazarbayev listed one of the organization's achievements that, "The SCO is neither a military bloc nor an exclusive alliance targeting [a] third party."[79]

Kazakh security experts and government officials value the contribution the SCO makes to countering regional terrorism, narcotics trafficking, and other illegal transnational activities that would prove difficult to manage on a national level.[80] In supporting the agreement on establishing a database for the SCO RATS, the deputy head of Kazakhstan's National Security Committee, Vladimir Bozhko, said that information exchanged through the RATS had already enhanced the government's regional threat awareness.[81] The Kazakh government also backed the Russian initiative to establish a SCO crisis response mechanism.[82] Yet, Kazakhs also want the SCO members to deepen their cooperation in such areas as education, culture, and commerce. In a 2006 interview, Nazarbayev urged the SCO to "pay attention to the development of trade and economic cooperation."[83]

Kazakhstan presently enjoys a unique position within the SCO. China and Russia enjoy the most influence within the organization, but their differences, and the considerable attention they need to devote to other

---

[79] Xinhua, "Interview: Kazakh President Underlines SCO's Great Achievements," People's Daily Online, June 8, 2006.
http://english.peopledaily.com.cn/200606/09/eng20060609_272308.html.
[80] V. N. Sitenko, "ShOS i Problemy Bezopastnosti v Tsentral'noy Azii: Znacheniye dlya Kazakhstana," *Казахстан-Спектр*, no. (2008), http://www.kisi.kz/site.html?id=5369.
[81] "Kazakh Parliament Votes for Regional Antiterror Database," Interfax-Kazakhstan News Agency, March 6, 2006,
http://www.eurasianet.org/resource/kazakhstan/hypermail/200603/0015.shtml.
[82] Valery Agarkov and Oral Karpishev, "Kazakhstan Backs Russia's Bid to Work Out SCO Anticrisis Mechanism," TASS in English, February 25, 2005.
[83] "Interview: Kazakh President Underlines SCO's Great Achievements."

regions, have prevented the emergence of a genuine duopoly within the organization. The other Central Asian states enjoy substantially less influence within the SCO, appearing most often as objects of SCO policies determined by Beijing and Moscow. Due to its economic development and other advantages, Kazakhstan occupies an intermediate position between the two great powers and the four other Central Asian states. Observers speculate that this consideration probably dampens Astana's interest in expanding the SCO's membership further since the entry of India, Iran, or Pakistan would dilute its influence by incorporating another middle power, with a larger population and stronger military than Kazakhstan, into the organization.[84]

North Atlantic Treaty Organization

Kazakhstan has also sought to balance off Russia's military preeminence and China's emerging economic dominance of Central Asia by cultivating enduring ties with Western institutions. NATO had developed some contacts with Kazakhstan and the other Central Asian republics before September 2001. With the exception of Tajikistan, which until 2002 was preoccupied with domestic reconstruction following its civil war, Central Asian representatives have participated in NATO's Euro-Atlantic Partnership Council (EAPC) and its related Partnership for Peace (PFP) program since the mid-1990s.[85] In December 1995, Kazakhstan, Kyrgyzstan, and Uzbekistan even organized a short-lived Central Asian peacekeeping battalion (CENTRASBAT) under the aegis of NATO and the United Nations. Although Central Asian governments initially expressed interest in participating in international peacekeeping missions, the subsequent increase in local terrorism resulted in their focusing their military resources to counter threats closer to home.

Two events led NATO's interests and activities in Central Asia to soar. First, the alliance decided on a controversial second wave of expansion to offer membership to several other countries besides Turkey that border the Caucasus/Central Asia—and are therefore very concerned about developments in the area. After most East European countries became

---

[84] Stephen Blank, "Russia Tries to Expand the SCO's Membership," *Central Asia-Caucasus Institute Analyst*, March 5, 2008, http://www.cacianalyst.org/?q=node/4807.

[85] Tajikistan joined the PFP in February 2002.

NATO members, in effect graduating from PFP, the program shifted focus towards promoting military reform and cooperation in Central Asia and the Caucasus (as well as the western Balkans). Second, the 9/11 terrorist attacks and the subsequent Operation Enduring Freedom in Afghanistan resulted in a substantial increase in NATO's military presence there. When then NATO Secretary General George Robertson visited the region in 2003, he said that the events of September 11, 2001, had led the alliance to appreciate "that our security is linked closely to security in remote areas. Central Asia is now going to be very much part of NATO's agenda."[86] By taking charge of the International Security Assistance Force (ISAF) in Afghanistan in August 2003, NATO has become engaged in a protracted project of promoting long-term stability and security in Central Asia. In line with its enhanced role, alliance representatives have sought military transit agreements, secure lines of communication, and other supportive arrangements from the Central Asian governments.

At their June 2004 Istanbul summit, the NATO heads of government affirmed the increased importance of Central Asia by designating it, along with the Caucasus, as an area of "special focus" in their communiqué.[87] They also decided to station a liaison officer there. The primary mission of the first incumbent, Tugay Tunçer, was to improve implementation of NATO's cooperation and assistance programs in the region. The decision to locate his headquarters in Almaty signifies the importance NATO governments ascribe to Kazakhstan in their regional strategy.[88] The summit participants also established a Secretary General Special Representative for the Caucasus and Central Asia. Besides explaining to Central Asian governments what activities and programs NATO has available and how they can best use them, the incumbent, Ambassador Robert F. Simmons, has strived to inform their

---

[86] Cited in Vladimir Socor, "Heroin Hunting and Security for Tajikistan," *Wall Street Journal Europe*, August 22, 2003.

[87] North Atlantic Treaty Organization, "Istanbul Summit Communique," Istanbul, June 28, 2004, http://www.nato.int/docu/pr/2004/p04-096e.htm.

[88] Aynur Khasenova, "NATO Dobralos' do Turkestana," *Nezavisimaya Gazeta*, October 7, 2005, http://www.ng.ru/cis/2005-10-07/1_nato.html.

publics about the alliance's positive contributions to regional security, such as in Afghanistan.[89]

The disintegration of NATO's ties with Uzbekistan after the government's military crackdown at Andijan in May 2005 precipitated a sharp collapse in the alliance's influence in the region. NATO's North Atlantic Council issued a statement condemning "the use of excessive and disproportional force by the Uzbek security forces."[90] The alliance also cancelled some cooperative programs with Uzbekistan and scaled back others. In response, the Uzbekistan government told all European NATO members except Germany in late November 2005 to cease using Uzbek airspace or territory to support peacekeeping operations in Afghanistan. (Germany was allowed to continue using the Termez airbase and even develop it further).[91]

As a result, the alliance refocused its security cooperation with other countries, especially Kazakhstan. Kazakhstan began participating in NATO's Partnership for Peace Planning and Review Process (PARP) in 2002, becoming the first Central Asian country to enter the program, which aims to improve the ability of its armed forces to work with NATO.[92] In 2003, Kazakhstan joined NATO's Maintenance and Supply Agency and, in January 2004, began a 19+1 relationship with NATO in the area of discussions on interoperability.[93]

Another sign of Kazakhstan's importance to NATO is that only Astana among the Central Asia governments has negotiated an Individual Partnership Action Plan (IPAP) with the alliance. This agreement came into

---

[89] North Atlantic Treaty Organization, "Cooperation with the Caucasus and Central Asia, Video Interview with Robert Simmons,"
http://www.nato.int/docu/speech/2004/s040910b.htm.
[90] Gleb Bryanski, "Russia Says UN, NATO Calls for Uzbek Probe 'Unfair'," Swiss Radio International, May 27, 2005,
http://www.rusnet.nl/news/2005/05/27/currentaffairs03.shtml.
[91] Alyson J. K. Bailes, ed., *SIPRI Yearbook 2006: Armaments, Disarmament and International Security* (Oxford: Oxford University Press, 2006), pp. 61-62.

[92] North Atlantic Treaty Organziation, "NATO's relations with Kazakhstan," February 29, 2008, http://www.nato.int/issues/nato-kazakhstan/practice.html.
[93] Roger McDermott, "Kazakhstan's Emerging Role in the War on Terror" Terrorism Monitor, May 20, 2004,
http://www.jamestown.org/terrorism/news/article.php?articleid=236741.

force on January 31, 2006.[94] An IPAP provides for more extensive dialogue and specifically tailored cooperation between the alliance and the signatory. It typically specifies detailed military and political objectives and the relative contribution of both parties in achieving them. The agreement provides additional opportunities for the partner to cooperate with alliance experts, receive military training, and participate in NATO activities in such areas as defense reform, managing emergencies, and projects related to science and the environment.

The Kazakh government has assisted NATO to realize its Partnership Action Plan on Terrorism (PAP-T). This initiative aims to share intelligence within NATO and with other allied organizations, develop and maintain national counter-terrorism capabilities, and improve border security.[95] The Kazakhstan Peacekeeping Battalion (KAZBAT) under development is scheduled to become fully operational in 2011. The Kazakh government plans to make the unit available for use by NATO, the United Nations, and other multilateral security institutions.[96] Kazakhstan has also deployed a small number of engineers (approximately 30 de-mining specialists) to Iraq "to express solidarity and support of the U.S. efforts to build democracy and civil society there."[97]

NATO's close ties with Kazakhstan have helped the alliance maintain an important presence in Central Asia despite its deteriorating relationship with Uzbekistan. At the same time that Uzbekistan was curtailing NATO's use of its territory, Kazakhstan ratified a framework agreement regarding its involvement with NATO's PFP. The Kazakh government also ignored the

---

[94] For details of the NATO-Kazakh IPAP see Embassy of Kazakhstan to the USA and Canada, "Kazakhstan and NATO Approve Individual Partnership Plan," Kazakhstan News Bulletin, February 16, 2006, http://www.homestead.com/prosites-kazakhembus/021606.html.

[95] North Atlantic Treaty Organization, "NATO's Relations with Kazakhstan," February 29, 2008, http://152.152.94.201/issues/nato-kazakhstan/practice.html.

[96] Roger N. McDermott, "Kazakhstan's Partnership with NATO: Strengths, Limits and Prognosis," China and Eurasia Forum Quarterly, vol. 5, no. 1 (2007), p. 13, http://www.silkroadstudies.org/new/docs/CEF/Quarterly/February_2007/McDermott.pdf.

[97] Kassymzhomart Tokaev, "Kazakhstan: The Democratic Path for Peace and Prosperity," Heritage Foundation WebMemo no. 877, October 7, 2005, http://www.heritage.org/Research/RussiaandEurasia/wm877.cfm.

SCO's call to impose a timetable for the coalition's withdrawal from its Central Asian military bases. Kazakh officials kept their troops in Iraq, despite popular disapproval of the deployment. In September 2005, Kazakhstan established a new military language institute in Almaty in September 2005 to enhance the Kazakh military's regional area expertise and language skills in English, French, and other predominately NATO foreign languages.[98] In June 2006, Kazakhstan held its first "NATO Week" during which Almaty hosted three NATO-organized scientific symposiums that addressed issues of concern for Central Asia: radiological risks, information security, and improved trans-border water management.[99] In September 2006, Kazakhstan hosted the latest NATO Steppe Eagle exercise. These annual exercises have been held since 2003 to improve compatibility between Kazakh and NATO units and also practice anti-terror missions. The second NATO week occurred April 7-11, 2008, and coincided with a visit by NATO Special Envoy Simmons to Kazakhstan. Simmons met Kazakh government leaders and delivered several public speeches that included a ceremony marking the opening of the NATO depository at the National Library of Kazakhstan.[100]

At the June 2007 meeting of the Euro-Atlantic Partnership Council, Kazakhstan's Deputy Minister of Defense, General Bulat Sembinov, reaffirmed his government's commitment to help achieve stability in Afghanistan by allowing coalition aircraft continued use of Kazakh air space. According to Sembinov, over 5,200 aircraft have overflown Kazakhstan in support of OEF since 2003 and more than 80 aircraft have made emergency landings at Kazakhstan airfields. NATO has reciprocated by continuing to assist Kazakhstan to reform and strengthen its military. For example, the alliance is working to bring the country's rapid deployment forces to NATO's standards.[101]

---

[98] "Kazakhs Open Center to Boost NATO Ties," September 15, 2005, United Press International, http://www.washingtontimes.com/upi/20050915-010222-7627r.htm.
[99] "NATO Week to Inaugurate New Cooperation Level, Assistant General Secretary," June 19, 2006, http://www.inform.kz/showarticle.php?lang=eng&id=142780.
[100] "NATO-Kazakhstan Week to be Held in Kazakhstan on 7-11 April," Trend News Agency, April 8, 2008,
http://news.trendaz.com/index.shtml?show=news&newsid=1171602&lang=EN.
[101] Embassy of Kazakhstan to the USA and Canada, "NATO and Kazakhstan to Expand Ties," February 7, 2007, http://www.kazakhembus.com/020807.html.

In recent months, Uzbek President Islam Karimov has signaled his interest in renewing ties with NATO. Karimov attended the April 2-4, 2008 alliance summit in Bucharest, where he offered to allow expanded use of Uzbek territory to support NATO operations in Afghanistan. [102] Even so, Kazakhstan will probably remain an important regional security partner for NATO as long as the Afghan campaign continues. Kazakh and NATO officials are presently discussing how the alliance might be able to transship goods from Russia to Afghanistan through Kazakhstan as well as across Uzbekistan. The Kazakh leadership intends to remain involved in NATO projects, while recognizing that the alliance's priorities still focus elsewhere (especially in the Balkans, the South Caucasus, and in managing relations with the EU in the west and Russia in the east).

European Union

Several factors have led to Central Asia's assuming a prominent place on the EU's agenda. First, continued friction with Russia over energy issues has increased European interest in importing oil and natural gas from the Caspian countries as well as in promoting these states' independence from Moscow. Second, some EU members, such as Germany, have substantial commercial interests in Central Asian countries that extend beyond their energy trade. Third, the deteriorating security situation in Afghanistan, which has seen a resurgence of both the Taliban insurgency and drug cultivation, has stimulated EU efforts to bolster neighboring states against terrorism and narcotics trafficking. Fourth, the general importance that EU governments assign to promoting political and economic reforms has led these states to press for such reforms in Central Asia. For example, EU leaders only endorsed Kazakhstan's bid to chair the OSCE after Kazakh officials pledged to expand political and economic freedoms. Finally, the EU's eastward expansion, even if it has not encompassed Turkey, has made these and other issues increasingly prominent from the perspective of many EU members. In the words of the European Commission, "EU enlargement and development of the European Neighborhood Policy are bringing Central Asia closer to the

---

[102] "Uzbekistan: Karimov Approves Overland Rail Re-Supply Route for Afghan Operations," *Eurasia Insight*, April 7, 2008, http://www.eurasianet.org/departments/insight/articles/eav040708a.shtml.

EU. Important security and economic interests argue for a higher profile of this region in European external policy."[103]

Kazakhstan's importance to the EU in this context is undeniable. The country is the EU's largest trade partner in Central Asia. The volume of trade between the EU member states and Kazakhstan amounted to EUR 14.287 billion euros in the first three quarters of 2007.[104] The EU's bilateral trade with Kazakhstan exceeds in volume the organization's combined trade with the four other Central Asian states.[105] When Benita Ferrero-Waldner, EU Commissioner for External Relations and European Neighborhood Policy, visited Kazakhstan in October 2006, she praised Kazakhstan's economic achievements and progress towards democratization, and noted that the EU views Kazakhstan as a prospective partner in combating terrorism, the drug trade, and other forms of transnational crime.[106] When the senior EU officials involved in Central Asia assembled in Astana in March 2007, Ferrero-Waldner said they chose the Kazakh capital as their venue because "Kazakhstan has a special importance for us as the first pillar in this region, and we talked about our desire to have special relations, special partnership with Kazakhstan, at the same time that we maintain intensive cooperation with the entire region."[107] In addition, the EU has signed other agreements with Kazakhstan concerning textiles, steel, and nuclear safety.

The EU interacts with Kazakhstan primarily within the framework of its Partnership and Cooperation Agreement (PCA), which the two parties signed in 1995.[108] Since it entered into force in 1999, the PCA has established a

---

[103] "Commissioner Ferrero-Waldner to Visit Kazakhstan 19/20 October," Europa, October 18, 2006, http://europa.eu.int/rapid/pressReleasesAction.do?reference=IP/06/1420&format=HTML&aged=0&language=EN&guiLanguage=en.

[104] German Foreign Office, "Kazakhstan," March 2008, http://www.diplo.de/diplo/en/Laenderinformationen/01-Laender/Kasachstan.html.

[105] "The EU's Relations with Kazakhstan," Europa, http://ec.europa.eu/comm/external_relations/kazakhstan/intro/index.htm.

[106] "EU to Strengthen Relations with Kazakhstan: EC Commissioner," Asia Pulse, October 24, 2006, p. 70.

[107] Embassy of Kazakhstan to the USA and Canada, "Europeans Focus on Central Asia in Key Astana Meeting," Kazakhstan News Bulletin, March 29, 2007, http://www.kazakhembus.com/032907.html.

[108] The European Union and the Republic of Kazakhstan, "Partnership and Cooperation Agreement," http://ec.europa.eu/external_relations/ceeca/pca/pca_kazakhstan.pdf.

legal foundation for negotiating more specific trade, investment, energy (including nuclear safety and nuclear power) and other agreements between Kazakhstan and the EU.[109] The latter typically commits to hold a sustained dialogue on democracy, human rights, economic development, the rule of law, and other issues. An EU-Kazakhstan Republic Cooperation Council, consisting of annual meetings at the ministerial level, supervises the PCA's implementation. More frequent exchanges occur between civil servants, policy experts, and legislators within committees or subcommittees focusing on trade, investment, energy, transport, justice, and other issue areas. Two of the most important are the Subcommittee on Trade and Investment and the Subcommittee on Justice and Home Affairs.

The EU's main areas of concern in Kazakhstan's neighborhood are developing the region's energy and transportation routes, expanding opportunities for trade and investment, and promoting political, economic, and social reforms. For at least a decade, the European Union has sought—especially through its TRACECA (Transport Corridor Europe, Caucasus, Asia) and the INOGATE (Interstate Oil and Gas Transport to Europe) programs—to redirect some commercial and energy flows from the traditional north-south pattern to new east-west corridors connecting from Central Asia, the Caucasus, and Europe. Launched in 1993 and subsequently expanded, TRACECA aims to construct highways, ports, and railways in the Black Sea and Caspian Sea regions.[110] INOGATE seeks to facilitate the export of oil and gas from these regions to Europe.

The EU sees Kazakhstan as a vital element in realizing these programs' objectives. For example, the February 13, 2007 meeting of the Cooperation Council "underlined the importance of regional cooperation in Central Asia as an effective means of conflict prevention and economic development in the region and welcomed the increasingly active role Kazakhstan is playing in different regional initiatives."[111] The EU's security agenda in Central Asia

---

[109] European Commission's Delegation to Kazakhstan, Kyrgyzstan, and Tajikistan, "EU Relations with Kazakhstan," November 7, 2006, http://delkaz.ec.europa.eu/joomla/index.php?option=com_content&task=view&id=24 &Itemid=36.
[110] Additional information is available at http://www.traceca-org.org.
[111] Council of the European Union, "Ninth Meeting of the Cooperation Council between the European Union and Kazakhstan, Brussels, 13 February 2007," Press

also includes working with Kazakhstan and other governments to stabilize the situation in Afghanistan and curb the flow of drugs, weapons, and other illegal activities throughout the region and into Europe.

Kazakh officials have endorsed the EU's vision for developing their country's potential as an energy supplier to Europeans and a key transit country between Europe and Asia.[112] At an international conference on "Kazakhstan-2030" held in 2007, President Nazarbayev declared that his government "is aware of its responsibility for providing global energy balance and security in the world. We will rank among top ten hydrocarbon exporters by 2017, and this will determine Kazakhstan's economic role in the dynamically changing global economic system in the 21st century to a large extent. We count on close cooperation with the European Union in this respect."[113]

The focus of much recent European attention has been on securing access to Kazakhstan's oil supplies. Recent energy confrontations as well as oil and gas delivery cutoffs involving Russian government-controlled firms have reminded European leaders of the desirability of limiting their growing double dependency on Russian natural gas and Russian-controlled pipelines by diversifying their sources of supply. Russia currently sells the entire EU approximately 40% of its natural gas imports, accounting for some 25% of its aggregate demand. Some former Soviet bloc states now in the EU import a much higher share of their energy from Russia. Experts forecast the overall dependency to increase to 60% of all EU gas imports by 2030 unless European governments radically change their energy policies.[114]

In addition to gaining access to Kazakhstan's oil, the European Commission is also negotiating an agreement for peaceful nuclear cooperation with

---

Release 6294/07, http://delkaz.ec.europa.eu/joomla/index.php?option=com_content&task=blogcategory &id=14&Itemid=90.
[112] Embassy of Kazakhstan to the USA and Canada, "Europeans Focus on Central Asia in Key Astana Meeting," *Kazakhstan News Bulletin*, March 29, 2007, http://www.kazakhembus.com/032907.html.
[113] Embassy of Kazakhstan to the USA and Canada, "Kazakhstan Seeks Diversification of Routes for Energy Supplies—President Nazarbayev," *Kazakhstan News Bulletin*, October 17, 2007, http://prosites-kazakhembus.homestead.com/NB12-101707.html.
[114] "Geopolitics of EU Energy Supply," July 18, 2005, http://www.euractiv.com/Article?tcmuri=tcm:29-142665-16&type=LinksDossier.

Kazakhstan, which possesses the second-largest reserves of uranium in the world. Of the five Central Asian countries, only Kazakhstan and Uzbekistan have their own nuclear power programs.[115] Joint civilian nuclear projects and technological exchange might be included in an EU-Kazakh uranium deal.[116]

To enhance its presence and effectiveness in the region, the EU in July 2005 appointed Jan Kubis as its first Special Representative for Central Asia.[117] In October 2006, French diplomat Pierre Morel assumed the position.[118] The EU also operates Commission Delegations in several Central Asian capitals as well as in nearby Kabul. In addition, a Europa House exists in Tashkent. The near doubling of the number of EU member countries has substantially increased the number of EU-affiliated embassies and diplomats in the region.[119] To exploit synergies, the EU tries to coordinate its policies towards Central Asia with other international institutions (especially the OSCE) and the United States. According to a February 2005 Department of State fact sheet, Brussels and Washington work together "to support democratic and economic transition, protection of human rights, promoting good governance/rule of law, increased regional trade, and humanitarian and human development. We also cooperate in the effort to combat trade in opium and heroin from Afghanistan."[120]

---

[115] Bruce Pannier, "Central Asia: Region Pledges to Remain Free of Nuclear Weapons," Radio Free Europe/Radio Liberty, September 8, 2006, http://www.rferl.org/featuresarticle/2006/9/FA5076CE-85DF-46DF-879D-AE78DBA16429.html.

[116] Institute for War & Peace Reporting, "Europeans to Buy Kazakh Uranium," News Briefing Central Asia, October 30, 2006, http://iwpr.net/?p=bkz&s=b&o=324938&apc_state=henh.

[117] Khiromon Bakoeva, "Central Asia: New EU Envoy a Familiar Face in the Region," Radio Free Europe/Radio Liberty, July 19, 2005, http://www.rferl.org/featuresarticle/2005/07/d85d610a-9322-4c4f-953b-3e812b8834e6.html.

[118] "EU Appoints New Point Man for Central Asia," News Central Asia, October 17, 2006, http://www.newscentralasia.com/modules.php?name=News&file=article&sid=1912.

[119] "Patton Speech on 'The EU and Central Asia'," March 15, 2004, http://europa-eu-un.org/articles/et/article_3297_et.htm.

[120] U.S. Department of State, "U.S.-EU Cooperation on Reform in Eurasia," February 17, 2005, http://www.state.gov/p/eur/rls/fs/42562.htm.

Except in the realm of energy, the EU's influence in Kazakhstan and other Central Asian countries has been limited by two main factors. First, the EU governments have refused to allocate substantial resources for promoting their political reform objectives in Central Asia. Second, the EU has given priority to its relations with other regions—especially the Caucasus and Russia.

Limited resources have constrained the EU's influence in Kazakhstan. For 2006, the European Commission allocated only 66 million euros to help all five Central Asian governments reduce poverty, expand regional cooperation, and support ongoing administrative, institutional, and legal reforms.[121] The small scale of the EU's activities in Central Asia contrast to those it has pursued in the neighboring South Caucasus region. The EU has assigned a Special Representative for the South Caucasus, initiated a European Security and Defense Policy rule of law mission in Georgia, and activated the European Commission's Rapid Reaction Mechanism to help secure democratic gains and avert conflict in that country following its Rose Revolution.[122]

In June 2004, the EU governments decided to let Armenia, Azerbaijan, and Georgia participate in the organization's European Neighborhood Policy (ENP), while continuing to exclude those of Central Asia. Besides Armenia, Azerbaijan, and Georgia, the ENP encompasses the non-member countries of Eastern Europe and even North Africa, but not those of Central Asia. ENP participants receive financial assistance, wider access to EU markets, and other benefits in return for implementing economic and political reforms as specified by their individual action plans.[123] EU officials apparently consider Central Asian states too distant and too unreformed for inclusion in the initiative, but this approach has weakened perhaps the EU's most important source of potential influence in Central Asia—the prospects of greater access

---

[121] Iran News Agency, "EU Aid for Central Asia to Fight Poverty," January 3, 2006.

[122] International Crisis Group, "Conflict Resolution in the South Caucasus: The EU's Role," March 20, 2006, http://www.crisisgroup.org/home/index.cfm?id=4037.

[123] Pal Dunay and Zdzislaw Lachowski, "Euro-Atlantic Security and Institutions," in Alyson J. K. Bailes, ed., *SIPRI Yearbook 2005: Armaments, Disarmament, and International Security* (Oxford: Oxford University Press, 2005), pp. 61-62.

to the prosperous economies of the member governments. The Kazakh government has actively lobbied to enter the ENP.[124]

Another problem for the EU in Kazakhstan is that its members have often acted as if they recognize Russia's superior interests in Central Asia. For the last few years, most EU diplomacy directed at Russia has focused on securing Moscow's agreement to extend its PCA with the EU to the ten new member countries, some of which have acute differences with Moscow regarding treatment of their Russian-speaking minorities and other issues. Disputes over the terms for Russia's entry into the World Trade Organization, the government's human rights policies, and border controls and visa requirements have also preoccupied the EU-Russian dialogue. At their May 2005 summit in Moscow, moreover, Russia and the EU agreed to a *Road Map for the Common Space on External Security* that envisaged enhancing cooperation primarily in their "shared neighborhood"—which they define as "the regions adjacent to the EU and Russian borders" (i.e., not Central Asia).[125] Reflecting EU concerns about sanctioning a de facto spheres-of-influence arrangement, Commissioner Ferrero-Waldner has warned, "Our challenge now is to try to reverse Russia's drift to a bloc mentality."[126] Kazakh officials recognize that EU governments will probably continue to prioritize relations with Russia given the much lower level of economic and other ties between the countries of the EU and Central Asia.

Organization for Security and Cooperation in Europe

On January 30, 1992, Kazakhstan and all the other former Soviet republics joined the Conference on Security and Cooperation in Europe (CSCE). As part of the accession process, they signed the core CSCE accession documents, including the Helsinki Final Act of 1975 and the Charter of Paris

---

[124] Andrew Rettman, "EU Gas Needs Pull Kazakhstan Closer to Brussels," EUobserver.com, May 16, 2006,
http://wennberg.newsvine.com/_news/2006/05/16/198527-eu-gas-needs-pull-kazakhstan-closer-to-brussels.
[125] European Commission, "The EU's Relations with Russia,"
http://ec.europa.eu/comm/external_relations/russia/intro/index.htm.
[126] Cited in Ahto Lobjakas, "Russia: EU Commissioner Criticizes Moscow's 'Assertive' Policy Toward Neighboring States," Radio Free Europe/Radio Liberty, January 26, 2005, http://www.rferl.org/featuresarticle/2005/01/16bf50ce-4f6d-479e-bf52-5f807eebc3b6.html.

for a New Europe. The subsequently renamed Organization for Security and Cooperation in Europe (OSCE) remains Europe's most comprehensive institution in terms of both membership and areas of responsibility. It has 55 member states—including Canada, the United States, and most European and Central Asian countries—and concerns itself with political, economic, and security issues. Since the shocks of 9/11, the OSCE has devoted much greater attention to Central Asia. Current OSCE priorities include curbing illicit trafficking in drugs and small arms, strengthening the security of travel documents and border controls, and countering terrorist financing and other transnational criminal activities.

Although the expansion of NATO and the EU has led to a decrease of the OSCE's influence in most of Europe, this consideration has less influence among Central Asians since their countries' chances of being incorporated into these other two Euro-Atlantic institutions as full members remains remote. In addition, while Russia and the Central Asian states disapprove of the OSCE's stress on improving their respect for human rights and insistence on reforming their other domestic policies, the EU and NATO are making similar demands. The economic and defense benefits of cooperating with the EU and NATO also have declined now that the primary security focus of the Central Asian governments is domestic and regional "terrorism" and "separatism."

The OSCE's leverage over its members derives mainly from its prestige and respect. Its Office for Democratic Institutions and Human Rights (ODIHR) sends well-respected electoral observers to member states. Their assessment regarding a ballot's fairness has a major impact on whether the international community deems the election legitimate. For this reason, Central Asian governments regularly seek its endorsement. The OSCE High Commissioner on National Minorities also has sought, primarily through quiet diplomacy, to secure better treatment of minority ethnic groups in Central Asia and other OSCE members.

Although the OSCE has long sought to resolve regional conflicts—initially, by helping end the 1992-97 civil war in Tajikistan, and subsequently by focusing on the so-called "frozen conflicts" in the former Soviet bloc, including those in Georgia, Moldova, and Azerbaijan—its progress in recent cases has been minimal. ODIHR's seventeen field missions have been more effective at shaping behavior—so much so that they sometimes have run afoul of the incumbent host government. On July 3, 2004, nine of the twelve CIS heads of state endorsed a statement criticizing the OSCE for interfering in members' internal affairs, employing a double standard that unduly focuses on abuses in CIS countries, and for becoming overly preoccupied with human rights issues at the expense of managing new challenges and promoting members' security and economic well-being. The declaration also criticized the ODIHR and the OSCE field operations for spending too much, making unwarranted criticisms of members' domestic political practices, and promoting their own reform agenda.[127] In December 2005, the Chief of the Russian General Staff accused the OSCE of becoming a surveillance agency for overseeing the adherence of democratic principles in CIS states heedless of these governments' right to determine their own destiny.[128] That same month, Russian Foreign Minister Sergei Lavrov said ODIHR had become too independent and required more specific directions to guide its work.[129]

Since 2004 Russian officials have sought to reduce the OSCE's election monitoring missions and other democracy-promotion activities.[130] For several months, the Russian government even refused to approve the OSCE budget until its members agreed to hold talks on its proposals. Since decisions are made by consensus, the other members have had to pay heed to these concerns. Although in the end the OSCE rejected most Russian demands, they did agree to reduce Moscow's share of the OSCE budget.[131] Resource

---

[127] Liz Fuller, "Analysis: Russia Coordinates New Broadside Against OSCE," Radio Free Europe/Radio Liberty, July 12, 2004,
http://www.rferl.org/featuresarticle/2004/7/031A1656-7D0C-4B74-8EA1-5B7B15F2E296.html.
[128] "Russian General Talks NATO, Nuclear, Missile Proliferation," RIA Novosti, December 1, 2005, http://en.rian.ru/russia/20051201/42284792.html.
[129] Valentinas Mite, "2005 in Review: Does the Presence of Western Election Observers Make a Difference?," Radio Free Europe/Radio Liberty, December 22, 2005,
http://www.rferl.org/featuresarticle/2005/12/6a02d87b-fb58-46e4-8e4a-197bfbc3bf9d.html.
[130] Vladimir Socor, "Moscow: Defying OSCE on the Democracy Front," Eurasia Daily Monitor, November 4, 2004,
http://www.jamestown.org/edm/article.php?volume_id=401&issue_id=3130&article_id=2368797.
[131] Roland Eggleston, "OSCE: U.S.-Russia Confrontation Expected at Meeting," Radio Free Europe/Radio Liberty, December 2, 2005,

limitations also constrain the OSCE's influence in Central Asia. The organization allocates far more funds and personnel to its field missions in southeastern Europe than to Central Asia.[132] The OSCE has established a Special Representative for Central Asia, but the incumbent lacks a dedicated staff.

Yet, of all the institutions affecting Kazakhstan, the OSCE could well become the most important. At their November 29-30, 2007, meeting, the foreign ministers of the 55 OSCE member governments designated Kazakhstan as the first Central Asian country—and also the first former Soviet republic—to assume the position of rotating OSCE Chairman. Kazakh Foreign Minister Marat Tazhin, who would become OSCE Chairman-in-Office, called the decision by the 15th annual meeting of the OSCE Ministerial Council to grant Kazakhstan the OSCE chairmanship in 2010 "a testament to the transformation our country has undergone since independence and as a strong vote of confidence by OSCE Member States for the Central Asian region as a whole."[133] Nazarbayev told foreign diplomats in Astana on December 10 that Kazakhstan would seek to strengthen the organization, which he maintained offered a "unique dialogue platform that unites the north Atlantic and Eurasian spaces."

The Kazakh government had waged a multi-year campaign to secure the OSCE Chairmanship. [134] President Nazarbayev had personally lobbied foreign governments to support Kazakhstan's candidacy. During his March 2006 visit to Kazakhstan, Belgian Foreign Minister Karel de Gucht, then OSCE chairman-in-office, characterized Kazakhstan's bid as "both a challenge and an opportunity" since, while Kazakhstan lagged in certain desirable political variables, the country was the "worthiest candidate" in the "very important" region of Central Asia. Like other observers, de Gucht

---

http://www.rferl.org/featuresarticle/2005/12/61147e03-d455-425f-a22d-ce7cd548c430.html.

[132] Solomon Passy, "Transforming the OSCE," *Turkish Policy Quarterly*, vol. 3, no. 3 (Fall 2004), http://www.turkishpolicy.com/default.asp?show=fall2004_Solomon_Passy.

[133] Government of Kazakhstan, "Kazakhstan to Assume Chairmanship of OSCE in 2010," PR Newswire, November 30, 2007, http://www.prnewswire.co.uk/cgi/release?id=214176.

[134] For background on this issue see "Security versus Democracy," *The Economist*, July 26, 2007, http://www.economist.com/displayStory.cfm?story_id=9537446&fsrc=RSS.

believed that it was also important for the OSCE as an institution that "one of the countries that, as we say, is 'east of Vienna' should chair the organization" because it could help reduce the growing tensions that had characterized relations between the OSCE and many CIS countries.[135]

Kazakh officials had originally hoped that their country would assume the OSCE Chairman in 2009. Most European governments—including Russia and Germany—publicly endorsed Kazakhstan's candidacy. But several Western governments—notably Great Britain, the Czech Republic, and the United States—considered 2011 a better date. Their main argument was that Kazakhstan needed to make further progress in upholding democratic principles and human rights at home before taking charge of the main organization tasked with promoting these values throughout Eurasia.[136] In particular, skeptics about awarding Kazakhstan the OSCE chair worried that Kazakhstan's commitment to maintaining good relations with Russia and China as well as Europe and the United States could lead its OSCE representatives to resist censoring Eurasian governments for violating OSCE political and human rights principles.[137] The lack of a consensus regarding Kazakhstan's OSCE aspirations prevented earlier sessions of the OSCE Ministerial Council from reaching a decision on the 2009 chairmanship before the November 2007 session.[138]

The overwhelming victory of the pro-government party in the August 2007 elections for the national legislature reinforced the doubts of those Western governments and analysts concerned about the commitment of the Kazakh government to meeting OSCE political standards. Though noting some improvements since the previous ballot, OSCE election monitors had faulted Kazakhstan's parliamentary elections of August 18, 2007, for failing to meet

---

[135] Mevlut Katik, "Kazakhstan Entertains Grand Economic Development Plan," Eurasia Insight, April 6, 2006,
http://www.eurasianet.org/departments/business/articles/eav040606.shtml.
[136] "German Foreign Minister Calls for Reforms in Central Asia," Deutsche Welle, October 31, 2006, http://www.dw-world.de/dw/article/0,2144,2221637,00.html.
[137] See for example "Security Versus Democracy," *The Economist*, July 26, 2007, http://www.economist.co.uk/displayStory.cfm?story_id=9537446.
[138] Esbergen Tumat, "Setback Likely for Kazaks' OSCE Hopes," Institute for War & Peace Reporting, November 16, 2007,
http://www.iwpr.net/index.php?apc_state=hen&s=0&o=1=EN&p=rca&s=f&o=340703.

international standards for a genuinely free and fair vote. Nazarbayev's Nur Otan party received 88% of the votes and won all available seats in the polls. All the opposition parties fell short of the 7% threshold required to enter parliament through the country's proportional representation system. OSCE monitors complained about overly restrictive legal provisions such as the use of a high threshold for representation in the parliament, rules allowing parties to select after the ballot which of their candidates will become members of the legislature, and excessive restrictions on the Kazakhs' rights to seek public office.[139] Kazakh and OSCE representatives subsequently exchanged views on how to overcome these election problems.[140] In addition, Kazakh leaders reaffirmed their commitment to promote democracy in Eurasia, though primarily indirectly by promoting economic development in their region, which Kazakhs argue would establish the large middle classes that underpin strong democracies.[141]

In the end, Western governments apparently decided that Kazakhstan was too important a country to alienate over the OSCE issue. European governments, for instance, were reluctant to antagonize a country that could provide vital oil supplies to planned Trans-Caspian oil pipelines connecting Central Asia to Europe. According to U.S. officials, moreover, their Kazakh counterparts have pledged to improve their country's civil rights practices by 2010. In explaining Washington's decision to back Kazakhstan's candidacy at the November 2007 OSCE Ministerial, U.S. Under Secretary of State for Political Affairs Nicholas Burns said: "These are very important

---

[139] Organization for Co-Operation and Security in Europe, "Kazakh Elections: Progress and Problems," http://www.osce.org/item/25959.html.

[140] "Kazakhstan, OSCE to Continue Election Cooperation," Radio Free Europe/Radio Liberty, November 8, 2007, http://www.rferl.org/featuresarticle/2007/11/20F6C86F-EBFF-4F62-BA1F-37A2548405B9.html.

[141] Andrew Rettman, "EU Gas Needs Pull Kazakhstan Closer to Brussels," EUobserver.com, May 16, 2006, http://wennberg.newsvine.com/_news/2006/05/16/198527-eu-gas-needs-pull-kazakhstan-closer-to-brussels.

commitments by the Government of Kazakhstan. We intend to see that these commitments are implemented."[142]

The United States and its allies also worried that Russian officials might have exploited their differences with Kazakhstan to bind Astana closer to Moscow. In early November 2007, Russian Deputy Minister of Foreign Affairs Alexander Grushko had warned the OSCE Permanent Council that, "If the Madrid meeting does not unequivocally and unconditionally make a positive decision on Astana's candidacy, then we do not rule out that the OSCE may remain without any chairmanship, and not only in 2009."[143] At the Madrid meeting, Russian Foreign Minister Sergei Lavrov openly attacked Western countries for seeking to link Kazakhstan's appointment to changes in its government's polices: "Unfortunately, during the several years that have preceded today's meeting, there were absolutely unacceptable and unseemly maneuvers concerning this bid aimed at creating conditions on the right of a specific country—an equal member of the OSCE—to chair this organization by making demands on its internal and external policies."[144]

Some human rights and democracy advocates criticized Kazakhstan's designation as OSCE chair as premature. Holly Cartner, Europe and Central Asia director at Human Rights Watch, said that placing Kazakhstan in charge of the OSCE's human rights policies was "a singularly bad idea." [145] Jennifer Windsor, executive director of Freedom House, indicated her organization—which rates Kazakhstan as "not free" and had opposed allowing Kazakhstan to assume the OSCE chairmanship in 2009[146]—would

---

[142] R. Nicholas Burns, "Press Conference at OSCE Ministerial Meeting," U.S. Department of State, November 30, 2007, http://www.state.gov/p/us/rm/2007/96054.htm.

[143] Vladimir Socor, "Russia-Led Bloc Emerges in OSCE," Eurasia Daily Monitor, November 16, 2007, http://www.jamestown.org/edm/article.php?article_id=2372597.

[144] Cited in Bruce Pannier, "Kazakhstan to Assume OSCE Chairmanship in 2010," Radio Free Europe/Radio Liberty, December 1, 2007, http://www.rferl.org/featuresarticle/2007/12/30DF587F-31EC-4350-867B-AFBE80517D2A.html.

[145] Cited in "Kazakhstan Picked to Chair OSCE," BBC News, December 1, 2007, http://news.bbc.co.uk/go/pr/fr/-/2/hi/asia-pacific/7123045.stm.

[146] Freedom House, "Groups Strongly Urge U.S. to Remain Opposed to Kazakhstan's Leadership of OSCE," September 21, 2007, http://www.freedomhouse.org/template.cfm?page=70&release=556.

withhold judgment pending evidence that the Kazakh government would fulfill its promises to make its domestic political system more democratic—such as by changing its election law before 2010—and support the OSCE's human rights objectives internationally.[147]

One of the most important issues for the Kazakhstan presidency could be resolving the dispute between Western governments on the one hand, and Moscow and its allies on the other, over the functions and authority of the OSCE Organization for Democratic Institutions and Human Rights (ODIHR). The governments of Russia and the other former Soviet republics have called for reducing the OSCE's democracy promotion efforts, especially in the area of election monitoring. At Madrid, Lavrov said the OSCE was facing a "moment of truth" since, in his assessment, the organization either had to change its ways or "the whole European security architecture could collapse."[148] In contrast, most Western governments urge the OSCE to continue strong efforts to promote democracy and human rights in the former Soviet Union, where these values are seen as gravely threatened.

At the Madrid meeting, Tazhin pledged to "support ODIHR and its existing mandate." He also committed to strengthen Kazakhstan's own political reform efforts in such areas as media freedoms and electoral processes.[149] Yet, Tazhin also said that Kazakhstan, whose next nationwide elections are scheduled for 2012, plans to work with all OSCE members to achieve a clear understanding on the criteria and standards ODIHR should use in assessing elections throughout the OSCE region, which suggests an openness in principle to revising OHDIR's activities. Russian officials likely will perceive Kazakhstan's chairmanship as an opportunity to advance their OSCE "reforms" in a favorable institutional environment, but the OSCE's consensus decision-making rules would still allow any government to veto

---

[147] Freedom House, "Kazakhstan Pledges to Improve Democratic Performance in Compromise Decision to Assume OSCE Chairmanship in 2010; Freedom House Urges Monitoring of Implementation," December 3, 2007, http://www.freedomhouse.org/template.cfm?page=70&release=594.

[148] "West and Russia Row at OSCE—Moscow Warns of Collapse –Summary," DPA, November 29, 2007, http://www.earthtimes.org/articles/show/150473.html#.

[149] Joanna Lillis, "Kazakhstan: Officials Pledge to Act as OSCE Bridge Connecting North Atlantic, Eurasian States," Eurasia Insight, December 10, 2007, http://www.eurasianet.org/departments/insight/articles/eav121007.shtml.

proposed changes affecting ODIHR. In addition, the appointment of a Central Asian country as OSCE chairman could help strengthen the organization's currently beleaguered position in several of the former Soviet republics.[150] Burns applauded Kazakhstan's designation as "recognition by the rest of us that this organization is more than just about West Europeans and Americans. It's about the people who live in Central Asia, the Caucasus and the Balkans, as well. So, symbolically it's important."[151]

Kazakhstan will soon begin transitioning to a leadership role within the OSCE. In 2009, it will join the OSCE Troika, in preparation to its becoming the OSCE chair in 2010. As one of the leading proponents of economic integration within Eurasia, the Kazakh government likely will use the opportunity to reinforce the OSCE's commitment to ensuring the development of transit and transportation corridors linking the Central Asian countries with one another and with other OSCE members. In addition, Kazakh Foreign Minister Tazhin has expressed a desire to work with Islamic governments to address issues such as Muslim migration and integration in Europe, the rights of Muslim women and young people in Western countries, and international legal and environmental problems.[152]

---

[150] Isabel Gorst and Stefan Wagstyl, "Kazakhstan To Bbe Offered Deal by Watchdog," *Financial Times*, November 27, 2007, http://www.ft.com/cms/s/0/0fa10af0-9c75-11dc-bcd8-0000779fd2ac.html.

[151] Burns, "Press Conference at OSCE Ministerial Meeting."

[152] Ministry of Foreign Affairs of Kazakhstan, "Statement by the Minister of Foreign Affairs of the Republic of Kazakhstan at the 11-th Summit of the Islamic Conference," Dakar, Republic of Senegal, March 13-14, 2008, http://portal.mfa.kz/portal/page/portal/mfa/en/content/ministry/minister/speeches/2008/2008.03.06._VYSTUPLENIE_MINISTRA_ANGL.doc.

Regional Security

Kazakh leaders have adopted a policy of seeking to promote security and stability throughout Central Asia and the Caspian Region as well as contributing to nonproliferation initiatives and international peacekeeping operations throughout the world. In addition to desiring to avert weapons proliferation, terrorism, wars, and other threats to the lives of Kazakh citizens and their neighbors, this approach results from an appreciation that adverse regional security developments would present a major threat to Kazakhstan's growing economic and political potential. Instability in Kazakhstan's neighborhood could scare off investors, disrupt region-wide trade and tourism flows, generate refuges and other unneeded migrants, as well as create other conditions that could adversely affect Kazakhstan.

Countering Regional WMD Threats

Kazakhstan constituted a core republic of the former Soviet Union. Its territory housed important elements of the USSR's military, nuclear, and aerospace industries. In particular, the Soviet military exploited Kazakhstan's favorable geography to conduct numerous weapon tests.[153] The Soviet government used the test sites at Vladimirovka and Saryshaghan to assess aerospace, air defense and ballistic missile systems. They also used facilities at Emba and especially Semipalatinsk for testing the Soviet military's nuclear weapons and related systems. In terms of operational deployments, the Soviet strategic community exploited Kazakhstan's pivotal location at the heart of Eurasia to deploy a robust nuclear force that could reach Europe, Asia, and the Middle East as well as against more distant targets in North America. Kazakhstan also contributed to the Soviet Union's nuclear weapons and nuclear energy programs by mining and processing its extensive stockpiles of natural uranium. At independence, Kazakhstan found itself the unhappy owner of one of the world's largest nuclear arsenals. If the Kazakh government had retained these weapons—1,040 nuclear warheads, 104 intercontinental ballistic missiles, and 40 Tu-95 Bear heavy bombers equipped

---

[153] John Pike, "Federation of American Scientists, "Kazakhstan Special Weapons," http://www.fas.org/nuke/guide/kazakhstan.

with 370 nuclear-armed Kh-55 long-range cruise missiles—it would have possessed the fourth largest nuclear force in the world.[154]

The Soviet Union also researched biological and chemical weapons using production and testing facilities on Kazakh territory. The main facilities for biological weapons included the Vozrozhdeniye Island Open-Air Test Site in the Aral Sea (half of which is located on the territory of Uzbekistan), the Scientific Experimental and Production Base in Stepnogorsk (then the world's largest anthrax production and weaponization facility), the Scientific Research Agricultural Institute in Gvardeyskiy, and the Anti-Plague Scientific Research Institute in Almaty (since renamed the Kazakh Scientific Center for Quarantine and Zoonotic Infections). Diseases tested at these Kazakh facilities include anthrax, plague, smallpox, botulinum toxin, and Q-fever.[155] The Soviets used the Pavlodar complex for researching chemical weapons.[156] Following independence, the Kazakh government worked with the United States and other international bodies to eliminate or secure these materials (e.g., by upgrading safety and security measures). The hoped-for conversion of some of these facilities to civilian use has proven more difficult than expected. For example, the dismantling of the Stepnogorsk facility, located 100 miles north of Astana, was successfully completed. After a joint U.S.-Kazakh program in drug-packaging at Stepnogorsk failed in 1997, however, Congress restricted further funding of civilian conversion projects.[157]

The Kazakh government also acted expeditiously to eliminate its unwanted nuclear weapons inheritance. Astana received considerable foreign assistance in this endeavor, especially from the U.S.-funded Cooperative Threat

---

[154] Dmitry Kosyrev, "Nuclear-free Kazakhstan: An Example to Follow?," RIA Novosti, August 29, 2007, http://en.rian.ru/analysis/20070829/75634106.html.

[155] Nuclear Threat Initiative, "Kazakhstan Biological Overview," March 2008, http://www.nti.org/e_research/profiles/Kazakhstan/Biological/index.html.

[156] Toghzan Kazzenova, "Central Asia: Regional Security and WMD Proliferation Threats," *Disarmament Forum* (2007), http://www.unidir.ch/pdf/articles/pdf-art2684.pdf.

[157] Toghzan Kazzenova, "Central Asia: Regional Security and WMD Proliferation Threats," *Disarmament Forum* (2007), http://www.unidir.ch/pdf/articles/pdf-art2684.pdf.

Reduction (CTR) program. In August 1991, President Nazarbayev signed a decree prohibiting any nuclear weapon tests on the Kazakh territory and closing the Semipalatinsk test range. In December 1994, Kazakhstan signed the Nuclear Nonproliferation Treaty (NPT) as a non-nuclear state. In return for renouncing Astana's nuclear arsenal, Britain, Russia, and the United States offered Kazakhstan formal security guarantees.[158] By the following year, Kazakhstan had removed all nuclear warheads and strategic delivery systems from its territory and destroyed all nuclear missile silos associated with these weapons—becoming the first former Soviet republic to abandon its nuclear arsenal.[159] At the same time, under "Project Sapphire," Kazakh and U.S. officials cooperated to transfer 600 kilograms of highly enriched uranium (HEU) stored under vulnerable conditions at the Ulba Metallurgical Facility in Ust-Kamenogorsk to a more secure storage site in the United States.[160] During the late 1990s, the governments of Kazakhstan and Uzbekistan permitted American scientists and intelligence experts to survey the vast stocks of biological weapons that the Soviets had buried on Vozrozhdeniye Island.[161]

More recently, in cooperation with the U.S. government and the independent Washington-based Nuclear Threat Initiative, the Kazakh government has agreed to downgrade nearly all of Kazakhstan's remaining highly enriched uranium (HEU), which could be used to manufacture nuclear weapons. It also committed to convert the country's nuclear research reactors to use low-

---

[158] Ministry of Foreign Affairs of Kazakhstan, "Kazakhstan i Voprosy Global'noy Bezopastnosti: Razoruzhenie i yadernoe neraspostranenie," http://portal.mfa.kz/portal/page/portal/mfa/ru/content/policy/security/disarmament.

[159] Kazzenova, "Central Asia: Regional Security and WMD Proliferation Threats," and *Kazakhstan's Nuclear Disarmament: A Global Model for a Safer World* (Washington, DC: Embassy of Kazakhstan and Nuclear Threat Initiative, 2006).

[160] John A. Tirpak, "Project Sapphire," Air Force Magazine (August 1995), http://www.afa.org/magazine/Aug1995/0895sapphire.asp. See also Dee Dee Myers, "US-Kazakh Accord Helps Meet New Proliferation Challenges," November 23, 1994, http://www.globalsecurity.org/wmd/library/news/kazakh/941123-368630.htm.

[161] Judith Miller, "Poison Island," *New York Times*, June 2, 1999, http://query.nytimes.com/gst/fullpage.html?res=9507E1D81030F931A35755C0A96F9582 60.

enriched uranium (LEU).[162] At the end of January 2008, Senator Richard
Lugar cited Kazakhs' support for nonproliferation initiatives in arguing that
Kazakhstan should be exempted from the Soviet-era Jackson-Vanik
Amendment to the 1974 Trade Act. The amendment, which applies sanctions
to countries that improperly limit freedom of emigration, has prevented
Kazakhstan from formally obtaining permanent normal trade relations with
the United States. He told listeners that, earlier that month, Kazakhstan had
allowed a team of U.S. scientists to remove Soviet-era samples of bubonic
and pneumatic plague to the U.S. Centers for Disease Control and Prevention
in Fort Collins, Colorado. American and Kazakh scientists are now
undertaking joint research to develop means to prevent and cure these plague
strains.[163]

Furthermore, on September 8, 2006, the foreign ministers of Kazakhstan,
Kyrgyzstan, Tajikistan, Turkmenistan, and Uzbekistan agreed to create a
Central Asian Nuclear-Weapon-Free Zone (CANWFZ). The signing
ceremony at Semipalatinsk in eastern Kazakhstan coincided with the
fifteenth anniversary of the closure of the nuclear testing ground there. In
accordance with Article 3, the signatories pledge not to research, develop,
manufacture, stockpile or otherwise try to acquire a nuclear explosive device.
They also agree not to allow other parties to conduct such activities on their
territories—which cover more than 3.8 million square kilometers—or assist
them to do so elsewhere.

Several distinctive features of the CANWFZ make the accord a landmark
from the perspective of nuclear nonproliferation. First, Kazakhstan is the first
former nuclear weapon state to adhere to a NWFZ. Second, the Treaty
established the world's first NWFZ solely in the Northern Hemisphere,
which contains the preponderance of nuclear weapons states. Its geographic
coverage also resulted in the first multilateral security agreement to embrace
all five Central Asian countries—an important accomplishment because
Turkmenistan has traditionally remained aloof from such initiatives. Third,

---

[162] Joshua Kucera, "Bush: Kazakhstan is a 'Free Nation'," *Eurasia Insight*, September 29,
2006, http://www.eurasianet.org/departments/insight/articles/eav092906.shtml.
[163] Office of Senator Richard G. Lugar, "Lugar Offers Repeal of Jackson-Vanik for
Kazakhstan," Press Release, January 29, 2008,
http://lugar.senate.gov/press/record.cfm?id=291402.

the United Nations, including the General Assembly and members of the UN Secretariat, directly participated in drafting the Semipalatinsk Treaty's provisions. The Central Asian governments made a deliberate effort to ensure that the Treaty conforms to the principles and guidelines on establishing NWFZs adopted by the UN Disarmament Commission in 1999. Fourth, the Semipalatinsk Treaty represents the first NWFZ to contain a provision recognizing the environmental damage associated with nuclear weapons production. Under Article 6, its members pledge to support rehabilitation of areas damaged by past nuclear tests and other Soviet-era nuclear activities on their territories. Fifth, Article 8 of the treaty explicitly requires signatories to adopt the so-called Additional Protocol, which grants the International Atomic Energy Agency (IAEA) enhanced inspection rights at members' civilian nuclear facilities. (Kazakhstan accordingly ratified the Additional Protocol on February 19, 2007.) The Treaty signatories also pledge to meet IAEA-approved international standards for the physical protection of their nuclear facilities and radioactive materials. Finally, the CANWFZ uniquely borders two declared nuclear-weapon states, China and Russia.

On June 11-12, 2007, Astana hosted a major international assembly of the countries participating in the Global Initiative to Combat Nuclear Terrorism (GICNT). Representatives from 38 countries attended, while the European Union and the IAEA sent observers. At the session, the participants reviewed recent progress, addressed implementation problems, and discussed how to further integrate new partners into GICNT projects.[164] In welcoming the June 2007 GICNT meeting in Astana, Foreign Minister Tazhin reaffirmed his country's "determination to actively combat terrorism in all its forms and manifestations. . . . The adoption of effective measures to counter and prevent terrorism is a priority of Kazakhstan's internal and external policies."[165] The attendees agreed to sponsor almost 20 activities during the next two years as

---

[164] U.S. Department of State, "Global Initiative to Combat Nuclear Terrorism: Joint Statement," June 12, 2007, http://www.state.gov/r/pa/prs/ps/2007/jun/86331.htm.
[165] Ministry of Foreign Affairs of Kazakhstan, "Welcoming Remarks by Minister of Foreign Affairs of the Republic of Kazakhstan, Mr. Marat Tazhin, at the Opening of the Third Meeting of the Global Initiative to Combat Nuclear Terrorism," June 11, 2007, http://www.mfa.kz/eng/?news=1&selected=216.

part of their revised work plan.[166] Priorities include limiting the availability of nuclear material to terrorists; improving the capabilities of participating nations to detect, search for, and prevent trafficking in such materials; promoting information sharing and law enforcement cooperation; establishing appropriate legal and regulatory frameworks; minimizing the use of highly enriched uranium and plutonium in civilian facilities and activities; denying safe haven and financial resources to terrorists; and strengthening national response capabilities to minimize the impact of any nuclear terrorist attack.[167] By virtue of its sustained commitment to nuclear nonproliferation, Kazakhstan was selected as the only Central Asian country to serve as a member of the GICNT leadership body, the Implementation and Assessment Group (IAG), which coordinates the GICNT's implementation. The IAG provides assistance to other governments seeking to implement the GICNT Statement of Principles and have organized activities designed to advance these principles. IAG members also help develop the work plan and measures of effectiveness for these activities.[168] In early June 2008, the Kazakh military conducted a large-scale exercise under GICNT auspices that simulated a mock terrorist seizure of a nuclear research facility near Almaty. According to Adil Shayakhmetov, head of the security services' anti-terrorism unit, the scenario allowed the almost 1,000 military and emergency personnel involved to improve their joint communication and operations skills.[169]

At the end of 2007, the Kazakhstan Foreign Ministry hosted an international conference entitled "Kazakhstan's Way To a Nuclear Weapon-Free World," to mark the 16th anniversary of the Semipalatinsk nuclear test site's closure. The symposium's organizers described its purpose as "intended to attract the world's attention to the example of Kazakhstan, which has shown that the most effective and preferable path to ensuring the security of a nation lies

---

[166] John C. Rood, "Keeping Nuclear Arms Out of Wrong Hands," *Miami Herald*, June 16, 2007, http://www.miamiherald.com/851/story/141745.html.

[167] U.S. Department of State, "Global Initiative to Combat Nuclear Terrorism: Joint Statement," June 12, 2007, http://www.state.gov/r/pa/prs/ps/2007/jun/86331.htm.

[168] U.S. Department of State, "Terms of Reference for Implementation and Assessment," November 20, 2006, http://www.state.gov/t/isn/rls/other/76421.htm.

[169] "Kazakhstan Holds Exercise to Hone Response to Nuclear Terrorism Threat," Associated Press, June 6, 2008, http://www.iht.com/articles/ap/2008/06/06/asia/AS-GEN-Kazakhstan-Terror-Exercise.php.

through a nuclear weapon-free choice and a consistently peaceful foreign policy, and not through the creation and development of weapons of mass destruction."[170]

Kazakhstan has joined with Washington, Moscow, and other governments in a multinational effort to apply the CTR process to third-party nonproliferation threats, thereby transforming the traditional donor-recipient model employed by CTR programs into a joint partnership against common WMD challenges. In June 2007, Kazakhstan, Russia, the United States, and other governments discussed how they could best adapt the equipment and techniques developed in their bilateral CTR programs for monitoring radiological movements outside the former Soviet Union.[171]

Kazakh officials share the belief of American, Russian, and other international security experts that the problematic experience the international community has experienced with Iran's nuclear activities requires a restructuring of the nuclear nonproliferation regime. Along with Putin and other world leaders, Nazarbayev has proposed establishing a body under the auspices of the IAEA that would guarantee fuel supplies for civilian nuclear power plants and store or reprocess the resulting spent fuel as a way of addressing a root cause of nuclear proliferation—the desire of countries to develop their own uranium enrichment and plutonium reprocessing facilities in order to have the ability to manufacture and dispose of nuclear fuel.[172] Analysts hope that such centers will discourage individual countries from developing their own nuclear fuel fabrication facilities, which can also be used to produce nuclear weapons if their operators enrich the uranium to sufficiently high levels.

Last year, the Kazakh government acceded to the Convention on the Prohibition of the Development, Production and Stockpiling of Bacteriological (Biological) and Toxin Weapons and on Their Destruction. The "general purpose criterion" used in Article I of the convention does not

---

[170] "Kazakhstan to Host International Conference against Nuclear Weapons," RIA Novosti, August 16, 2007, http://en.rian.ru/analysis/20070816/71788996.html.

[171] John J. Fialka, "Russia, U.S. Step Up Nuclear-Control Drive," *Wall Street Journal*, June 1, 2007.

[172] Anar Khamzayeva, "Denuclearized Central Asia: An Example to Follow," *Central Asia's Affairs*, no. 1 (2007).

ban biological agents or toxins directly, but requires that they be used only for prophylactic, defensive, and other peaceful purposes. The agreement does explicitly prohibit "weapons, equipment or means of delivery designed to use such agents or toxins for hostile purposes or in armed conflict." On April 24, 2008, the parliament of Kazakhstan ratified the International Convention for the Suppression of Acts of Nuclear Terrorism, which obliges State Parties to take steps to avert and punish attempts to use nuclear materials in terrorist acts.[173] Kazakhstan has become a State Party to many other nonproliferation institutions and agreements, including the U.S.-initiated Proliferation Security Initiative. [174] These decisions confirm Kazakhstan's continued commitment to WMD nonproliferation. In the assessment of several Western experts, "Since its independence...Kazakhstan has been a model state, cooperating in the removal of nuclear arms from its territory and fully embracing international nuclear nonproliferation norms."[175]

Enhancing Regional Security

Like the other newly independent countries of the former Soviet Union, Kazakhstan had to design new military institutions based initially on the few resources it managed to inherit from the former Soviet armed forces. The initial focus was on developing military forces suitable for self-defense, especially against the regional terrorist groups that have presented the main transnational military threat to Kazakhstan and other Eurasian governments. Kazakhs have been especially concerned about potential terrorist attacks on the country's valuable (and vulnerable) oil and gas infrastructure, such as the offshore oil drilling platforms along Kazakhstan's Caspian coast. But terrorist operations anywhere in Kazakhstan's neighborhood could cause a deterioration of the region's investment climate as well as other economic

---

[173] "Kazakh Parliament Ratifies UN Nuclear Terrorism Convention," RIA Novosti, April 24, 2008, http://en.rian.ru/world/20080424/105825941.html.

[174] For a partial inventory see Nuclear Threat Initiative, "Kazakhstan," http://www.nti.org/e_research/official_docs/inventory/pdfs/kazak.pdf.

[175] Joseph Cirincione, Jon B. Wolfsthal, and Miriam Rajkumar: *Deadly Arsenals: Nuclear, Biological, and Chemical Threats*, second edition (Washington, D.C.: Carnegie Endowment for International Peace, 2005), p. 370.

damage. [176] More recently, the Kazakh government's basic approach to international security—which posits that Kazakhstan requires a secure environment to develop politically and economically—has led Kazakh officials to seek the capacity to project military power beyond Kazakh territory in support of wider regional security objectives, including peacekeeping and post-conflict reconstruction missions.

In these endeavors, Kazakh authorities have pursued an eclectic approach. Since independence, they have readily sought military training, weapons donations, and other defense assistance from Russia, China, NATO and other foreign sources. For example, under the U.S.-Kazakh Five Year Partnership Plan announced earlier this year, the United States will provide Kazakhstan with Hummer vehicles, communications and engineering equipment, and other military support. [177] More recently, the Kazakh government has used some of its surging budget revenue to increase its own defense spending considerably.

Soon after independence, the terrorist Islamic Movement of Uzbekistan (IMU) emerged as the main threat to the security of the region. The IMU formally came into being in 1998, but precursor organizations had been active in the former Soviet Republics of Central Asia since the USSR's collapse in 1991. The IMU developed extensive connections with al-Qaeda and the Taliban when they ruled Afghanistan. IMU forces fought alongside Taliban forces and their al-Qaeda allies during the subsequent American-led OEF campaign in Afghanistan.

In their August 1999 communiqué, IMU leaders proclaimed their objective of overthrowing the secular regime of Uzbek President Islam Karimov and establishing a Taliban-style Islamic republic. To realize this objective, the organization set off bombs in Uzbekistan and attempted to assassinate Karimov. They also invaded southern Kyrgyzstan, where they seized foreigners as hostages, whom they ransomed for money. IMU guerrillas

---

[176] B. K. Sultanov, "Problemy Sotrudnichestva Stran-Chlenov ShOS v Svere Bezopasnoti," Kazakhstan Institute for Strategic Studies, May 13, 2008, http://www.kisi.kz/site.html?id=5485.

[177] Embassy of Kazakhstan in the USA and Canada, "Kazakhstan's Defense Ministry Hails Military Cooperation with the United States," Kazakhstan's News Bulletin, January 23, 2008, http://www.kazakhembus.com/NB1-012308.html.

sought but failed to establish a base of operations in the Ferghana Valley in order to gather recruits and wage a protracted insurgency against the Uzbek government.[178] Before it could launch its next major offensive, however, the IMU lost its bases, and many of its members, in Afghanistan following the large-scale U.S. military intervention there starting in October 2001.

After a year-long hiatus, the IMU renewed military operations in Kyrgyzstan, especially along the Kyrgyz-Uzbek frontier. Its members allegedly detonated several bombs, including in an alleged attempt to kill National Security Council Secretary Misir Ashirkulov in September 2002. Kyrgyz authorities also feared that IMU operatives had established sleeper cells within their territory, especially the Ferghana Valley, by blending into the local population.[179] In April 2003, Uzbek authorities discovered a possible IMU bomb plot when construction workers found a probable improvised explosive device in the basement of a Tashkent hotel. The explosives were reportedly similar to those used in the 1999 car bombings. The detection occurred a month before Tashkent hosted the annual meeting of the European Bank for Reconstruction and Development in early May 2003.[180]

The present status of the IMU and its offshoots remains unclear, but some of its operatives may have been involved in the bombings that occurred in Uzbekistan in March-April 2004 and the terrorist incidents that reportedly occurred in Tajikistan in 2006.[181] At this time, IMU leader Tahir Yuldashev was still issuing threats against Central Asian leaders: "We will avenge Muslims in Central Asia or in Russia. We insist that all regimes in the region put an end to the practice of persecution of Muslims, the practice of harassment and terror. [Uzbek President] Karimov, [Tajik President]

---

[178] Ahmed Rashid, "Islamic Movement of Uzbekistan's Incursion Assists the Taliban," *Central Asia-Caucasus Analyst*, September 13, 2000,
http://www.cacianalyst.org/newsite/?q=node/268/print.
[179] Arslan Koichiev, "Skirmishes Suggest IMU is Changing Tactics," Europa Insight, August 6, 2001,
http://www.eurasianet.org/departments/insight/articles/eav080601.shtml.
[180] "Terrorism Scare Hits Upcoming Tashkent Conference," Europa Insight, April 15, 2003, http://www.eurasianet.org/departments/insight/articles/eav041503a.shtml.
[181] Gulnoza Saidazimova, "Central Asia: Is Islamic Movement of Uzbekistan Really Back?," Radio Free Europe/Radio Liberty, February 2, 2006,
http://www.rferl.org/featuresarticle/2006/02/81E06ED8-77DA-4BF3-ADE9-5B74EBC07FE0.html.

Rahmonov, and [Kyrgyz President] Bakiyev had better remember that they will be punished for the crimes they are committing."[182] Press reports also repeatedly cite the presence of ethnic Uzbeks, many suspected of being remnants of the IMU, in the ranks of the Islamist fighters active in northwest Pakistan.[183] In May 2008, Dutch, French, and German authorities arrested ten people suspected of involvement in an international network to raise money for the IMU.[184] In any case, Kazakh and other Central Asian security officials remain concerned about a possible revival of Islamist-inspired terrorism in their countries.

Kazakh authorities have stressed that countering the threat from the IMU and other transnational terrorist movements in Eurasia requires a multilateral effort. Terrorists regularly move from country to country, seeking safe havens wherever they can. Although bilateral cooperation with other Central Asian governments has been minimal, Kazakh officials have collaborated with Russia, China, the United States, and other militarily powerful countries to manage such threats. In addition, they have worked within the SCO, NATO, and other international institutions to make counterterrorism an important element of these organizations' security programs. Kazakhstan supports all twelve of the U.N. conventions against international terrorism.[185]

The revival of Kazakhstan's economy since the late 1990s, combined with the post-9/11 influx of foreign militaries into Central Asia and the Caspian region, has more recently enabled the government to pursue its objective of developing a dual-purpose military, one capable of both self-defense and promoting international peace and security. After the September 11, 2001

---

[182] Rober McDermott, "IMU Issues New Threat to Central Asian Leaders," CentralAsia-Southcaucasus.com, September 18, 2006 www.centralasia-southcaucasus.com/index.php?option=com_content&task=view&id=58&Itemid=53.

[183] Ismail Khan, "Foreigners among Rebels Killed Near Afghan Line, Pakistan Says," *New York Times,* October 12, 2007, http://www.nytimes.com/2007/10/12/world/asia/12pakistan.html?ex=1349841600&en=099056ebac38e1a9&ei=5088&partner=rssnyt&emc=rss.

[184] Lisa Bryant, "At Least 10 Detained in EU Countries in Connection with Terror Probe," Voice of America, May 16, 2008, http://voanews.com/english/2008-05-16-voa46.cfm.

[185] Permanent Mission of Kazakhstan to the United Nations, "Kazakhstan Against Terrorism," http://www.kazakhstanun.org/policy_priorities/terrorism/Terrorism.html.

terrorist attacks against the United States, Kazakhstan committed troops to the Central Asian Rapid Reaction Force designed to defend members against a major terrorist incursion such as that led by the IMU in previous years. Kazakhstan also created a 500-strong peace-keeping battalion to contribute to regional and extra-regional security operations.[186] In March 2007, when the Kazakh government approved a new military doctrine, it also announced a 74% increase in defense spending over the previous year. The increase was designed to enhance troop training and readiness as well as fund the acquisition of more advanced military equipment.[187] Kazakh defense firms also plan to sell arms manufactured in Kazakhstan to other Eurasian countries. For example, through a technical cooperation agreement with Israel, they plan to sell Israeli-designed artillery systems to other Central Asian countries.[188]

A more recent priority of Kazakhstan's regional security efforts has been to help defend the natural resources of the Caspian Sea, along with the growing infrastructure developed by foreign and increasingly domestic capital, from terrorists and other threats.[189] The sea contains large reserves of oil and natural gas as well as considerable quantities of sturgeon and other fish. In a March 2006 interview, Kazakh Foreign Minister Kassymzhomart Tokaev argued that, while several security mechanisms deal with Caspian security threats, they all suffer from the fact that "none of them is of a comprehensive nature with universal participation of the Caspian states." Although he acknowledged that the littoral states were unlikely to agree to disarm, Tokaev reaffirmed support for Kazakhstan's 2004 confidence-building initiative to create a "five-sided mechanism of controlling and deterring the armaments on the Caspian, providing a balance of armaments and defining their limits."

---

[186] Rafis Abazov, "Kazakhstan's Security Challenges in a Changing World," in Michael Intriligator, Alexander Nikitin, and Majid Tehranian, eds., *Eurasia: A New Peace Agenda* (Amsterdam: Elsevier, 2005), p. 239.

[187] Embassy of Kazakhstan to the USA and Canada, "Kazakhstan's New Military Doctrine Tackles Security Challenges, Provides Guidance for Further Reforms," Kazakhstan News Bulletin, April 11, 2007.

[188] "Kazakhstan Rising," Silk Road Intelligencer, May 26, 2008, http://silkroadintelligencer.com/2008/05/26/kazakhstan-rising.

[189] Roger N. McDermott, "Kazakhstani Bids for Regional Antiterrorism Agenda," Eurasia Insight, November 20, 2002, http://www.eurasianet.org/departments/insight/articles/eav112002a.shtml.

He added that while Russia's proposal for a joint Caspian Force (the CASFOR) warranted further study, a more effective means of enhancing military collaboration among Caspian countries would be to adopt a "Pact on Stability on the Caspian Sea," which would entail cooperative efforts to counter terrorism, "aggressive separatism," illegal trafficking of weapons and drugs, illegal immigration, as well as other forms of organized crime "and other new threats and challenges."[190]

To contribute to these Trans-Caspian security initiatives as well as defend its other national interests, the Kazakh government has long aspired to develop a navy. When the Soviet Union collapsed, Russia, Azerbaijan, Turkmenistan, and Kazakhstan divided its Caspian flotilla, which was not very large to begin with. Although the United States and Germany have donated ten small ships, it was not until recently that Kazakhstan's growing budget revenue, due largely to world energy prices, has provided the country with the resources to begin procuring modern naval armaments. According to the latest plans, the government aims to acquire several modern warships, military equipment, and a coastal support infrastructure over a two-decade period, with the final of the three modernization stages scheduled for completion in 2025.[191]

Kazakh officials stress that a strong navy would help promote transnational as well as Kazakh security interests, including those of foreign business enterprises and investors.[192] In February 2003, Kazakh First Deputy Foreign Minister Kairat Abuseitov told reporters the country needed a navy that "could fight against new threats, primarily terrorism. Nobody is insured

---

[190] Mevlut Katik, "Kazakhstan Has "Huge Plan" to Expand Energy Links With China," Eurasia Insight, March 13, 2006,
http://www.eurasianet.org/departments/recaps/articles/eav031306.shtml. Russia's CASFOR proposal is discussed in Stephen J. Blank, *Turkmenistan and Central Asia after Niyazov* (Carlisle, PA: Strategic Studies Institute of the U.S. Army War College, 2007), pp. 43, 45.

[191] Embassy of Kazakhstan to the USA and Canada, "Kazakhstan Develops New Navy Concept: Will Pool Resources to Fight Caviar Poachers," March 29, 2007, http://www.kazakhembus.com/032907.html.

[192] "Kazakhstan: Astana Puts New Emphasis on Military," Radio Free Europe/Radio Liberty, June 17, 2003,
http://www.globalsecurity.org/military/library/news/2003/06/mil-030617-rfel-163415.htm.

against the possibility that the Caspian could become, in future, an arena of terrorist acts, a place of drug transit, illegal arms trade and even illegal migration."[193]

Less overtly, a stronger navy could help Kazakhstan moderate Tehran's ambitions regarding the Caspian Sea. [194] Iran continues to differ with Kazakhstan and the other littoral countries regarding how to divide and manage the sea and its valuable subsurface natural resources. The main dispute is whether to treat the Caspian as if it were a sea (despite its being landlocked) or an inland lake (despite its large size and natural resources) according to international law. If the littoral states were to manage the Caspian as if it were a sea, then each country would control the territorial waters along their coasts and corresponding seabeds. The Kazakh government naturally prefers this approach since such a division would leave Kazakhstan with the largest and potentially most lucrative natural sector.[195] If the Caspian were treated legally as a large inland lake, more flexible legal standards would apply. All five littoral states could commonly own the sea and share equally in its collective natural resources, or they could reach some other arrangement.

The first leadership summit of the five countries bordering the Caspian Sea occurred in Ashgabat in 2002, but made little progress in establishing a mutually agreeable legal framework. In May 2003, Kazakhstan, Azerbaijan, and Russia reached a trilateral agreement that divided the northern 64% of the Caspian Sea into three unequal shares, with Kazakhstan receiving the largest portion, some 29%.[196] Iran and Turkmenistan, however, refused to endorse

---

[193] John Daly, "Analysis: Kazakhstan Rules Oceans," United Press International, February 19, 2008,
http://www.upi.com/International_Security/Energy/Analysis/2008/02/19/analysis_k azakhstan_rules_oceans/5032.

[194] John Daly, "Division of the Caspian," United Press International, August 9, 2007, http://www.spacedaily.com/reports/Division_Of_The_Caspian_999.html.

[195] Ministry of Foreign Affairs of Kazakhstan, "Aktual'nye Voprosy Vneshney Politiki Kazakhstana Pravovoy Status Kaspiyskogo Morya,"
http://portal.mfa.kz/portal/page/portal/mfa/ru/content/policy/issues/caspian_sea.

[196] Hooman Peimami, "Iran Intent on Keeping Pace with Caspian Basin Energy Development," Eurasia Insight, August 19, 2003,
http://www.eurasianet.org/departments/business/articles/eav081903.shtml.

this trilateral agreement and restated their claim to larger economic zones than the 2003 formula would provide.

In October 2007, Tehran hosted the second presidential summit of Caspian Sea nations. Nazarbayev joined Azerbaijan's Ilham Aliyev, Iran's Mahmoud Ahmadinejad, Russia's Vladimir Putin, and Turkmenistan's Gurbanguli Berdymukhamedov in adopting a joint declaration affirming their solidarity on important regional security issues. The statement asserted the Caspian should only be used for peaceful purposes, that the five littoral states should resolve their conflicts without force, and that the Caspian governments would not allow anyone to use their territory for launching a military attack against another littoral country.[197] The presidents also insisted that only the littoral states could deploy military forces in or near the sea. They again failed, however, to resolve their differences over how to delineate the littoral states' competing territorial claims.

As of April 2008, Iranian Foreign Minister Manouchehr Mottaki was still insisting on the continued validity of two Soviet-era treaties that describe the Caspian as a "common sea," pending their replacement by a new convention ratified by all five Caspian states.[198] These treaties, signed in 1921 and 1940, assign Tehran and Moscow joint management of the Caspian beyond territorial zones, but do not address undersea mining, only navigation and fishing. The unresolved dispute among the five Caspian states has impeded implementation of plans to exploit undersea energy resources or transport oil and gas through underwater pipelines. Iran has the second-strongest navy in the Caspian and has also used it to enforce its claims over Caspian resources.[199] In 2001, Iran dispatched military ships and aircraft to threaten two Azerbaijani research vessels exploring oilfields in the southern Caspian.[200]

---

[197] "Caspian Sea Leaders Sign Declaration, *Tehran Times*, October 17, 2007, http://www.tehrantimes.com/index_View.asp?code=155078.

[198] Kaveh L Afrasiabi, "Iran Homes in on the Caspian," Asia Times, April 17, 2008, http://www.atimes.com/atimes/Central_Asia/JD17Ag01.html.

[199] Blank, *Turkmenistan and Central Asia*, p. 50.

[200] Andrew Katan, "Iran's Territorial Disputes with its Caspian Sea Neighbors," Power and Interest Report, May 31, 2006, http://www.pinr.com/report.php?ac=view_report&report_id=499&language_id=1.

Another unresolved dispute concerns possible Trans-Caspian energy pipelines. The governments of Russia and Iran argue that all the littoral countries must approve construction of each energy pipeline that would traverse any part of the Caspian. Their stated reason for requiring consensus on regional energy projects is that all five countries could suffer from any environmental damage to the Caspian Sea caused by the pipelines.[201] A desire to block east-west energy conduits that circumvent Russian and Iranian territory by traversing the Caspian might also explain Moscow's and Tehran's demand for veto rights. Energy producers in Kazakhstan and Turkmenistan are eager to diversify their export routes. An obvious means to do so is shipping oil and gas to Europe via pipelines that run along Azerbaijan's sector of the Caspian seabed as well as through Soviet-era pipelines. Although these latter routes are unavoidable given the imperatives of geography and Moscow's preeminent status in Eurasian energy markets, these pipelines fall under the control of Russia's state-controlled energy monopolies, which typically extract monopoly rents for their use.

At the October 2007 summit, Nazarbayev called on the Caspian governments to negotiate a "stability pact" to limit naval weapons and activities in the sea.[202] Putin declined to support Nazarbayev's proposals, however, which could compromise Russian influence over the region. Instead, he reaffirmed Russia's interest in establishing a joint naval group among the Caspian Sea states (the CASFOR) to improve the security of maritime navigation and provide protection for critical energy facilities against terrorist and other threats.[203]

---

[201] Vladimir Isachenkov, "Putin Warns Against Attacks on Iran," Associated Press, October 17, http://www.washingtonpost.com/wp-dyn/content/article/2007/10/16/AR2007101601060.html.

[202] Vladimir Socor, "Caspian Summit Envisions Creation of Regional Institutions," Eurasia Daily Monitor, October 19, 2007, http://www.jamestown.org/edm/article.php?article_id=2372518.

[203] "Caspian Sea Leaders Sign Declaration," *Tehran Times*, October 17, 2007, http://www.tehrantimes.com/index_View.asp?code=155078.

Enhancing Regional Confidence-Building Measures

At the 47th Session of the UN General Assembly in October 1992, President Nazarbayev called for convening a Conference on Interaction and Confidence-Building in Asia (CICA). During the following decade, Kazakh officials and security experts, supported by representatives of other countries, drove the CICA process forward. These efforts included the convening of meetings of Asian governments, scholarly conferences, and other activities intending to promote multilateral approaches towards promoting peace, security and stability in Asia. On September 14, 1999, the foreign ministers of the 15 governments then involved in CICA signed a "Declaration on the Principles Guiding Relations among the CICA States." This initial phase of institution building, which required agreeing on both fundamental principles and administrative procedures, culminated in the first CICA Summit of the Heads of States and Heads of Governments on June 4, 2002.

The 16 governments that attended the first CICA summit signed the "Almaty Act" and "The CICA Declaration about the Elimination of Terrorism and Promotion of Dialogue between Civilizations." [204] The signatories of the Almaty Act commit "to develop the CICA as a forum for dialogue, consultations and adoption of decisions and measures on the basis of consensus on security issues in Asia." [205] The CICA Declaration affirms the belief of the governments involved in CICA that, "We consider CICA as a unique Asian forum which comprises states of different cultures and traditions making it one of the most important mechanisms to promote dialogue among civilizations and cultures." The document also states that, "The CICA Member States intend to comprehensively and actively promote such a dialogue taking into account that Eurasia has not only been a cradle of

---

[204] Jandos Asanov, "Evolution of the CICA," *Today's Zaman*, September 21, 2007, http://www.todayszaman.com/tz-web/detaylar.do?load=detay&link=122679&bolum=109.

[205] Permanent Mission of the Republic of Kazakhstan to the UN office and Other International Organisations in Geneva, "Almaty Act," June 4, 2002, http://www.kazakhembus.com/Almaty_Act.html.

some of the world's largest civilizations but has also served as a bridge between them."[206]

In October 2004, the member governments adopted a "CICA Catalogue of Confidence Building Measures." They subsequently sought to refine the principles and procedures for implementing these measures in the entire range of fields that could contribute to conflict, encompassing military, political, economic, environmental, humanitarian and cultural issues. The measures under discussion included those related to traditional disarmament and arms control; military confidence-building measures; actions to prevent trafficking in narcotics, weapons, and nuclear materials; and activities aimed at countering terrorism and managing transnational refugee flows. In June 2006, the member governments established a CICA Secretariat as a permanent administrative body to assist with this process.[207] To accelerate progress, some of these measures are designed to apply primarily at the sub-regional level, rather than CICA-wide, to issues of most relevance for the relevant countries.

The present full members of CICA include the most important countries affecting Asian security: Afghanistan, Azerbaijan, China, Egypt, India, Iran, Israel, Kazakhstan, Kyrgyzstan, Mongolia, Pakistan, Palestine, Republic of Korea, Russia, Tajikistan, Thailand, Turkey, and Uzbekistan. These countries contain approximately half the world's population and a growing share of the world's gross economic output. The governments of Indonesia, Japan, Malaysia, Ukraine, Vietnam, and the United States have observer status within the CICA, as do the United Nations, the OSCE, and the League of Arab States.[208] The members are assessing how the CICA should interact with the other (less comprehensive) security institutions active in Asia.

---

[206] Permanent Mission of the Republic of Kazakhstan to the UN office and other international organisations in Geneva, "CICA Declaration on Eliminating Terrorism and Promoting Dialogue among Civilizations," June 4, 2002, Almaty, http://missions.itu.int/~kazaks/eng/cica/cica06.htm.

[207] Asanov, "Evolution of the CICA."

[208] Ministry of Foreign Affairs of Kazakhstan, "Kazakhstan i Voprosy globa;'noy bezopastnosti: Soveshchanie po Vzaimodeystviyu," http://portal.mfa.kz/portal/page/portal/mfa/ru/content/policy/security/conference.

Kazakh experts believe that certain characteristics of their country and the Asian security environment made Kazakhstan an ideal leader to expand the role of confidence-building measures in post-Cold War Asia. They note that, as of the early 1990s, the major Asian military powers still had important national differences (China-India, Russia-India, etc) that impeded their security cooperation. In addition, Kazakh analysts argue that Kazakhstan's multi-vector diplomacy, which eschewed both exclusive alignments and isolationist neutrality, made it a suitably disinterested but benign participant in Asian security disputes.[209] Kazakh officials and security experts adduced similar arguments to justify their successful leadership aspirations regarding the OSCE, which like the CICA also addresses political-military, economic; and humanitarian issues within an overarching multilateral framework.

The continued development of the CICA process could help ameliorate the problem identified by international security experts that Asia is not covered by region-wide confidence-building and transparency measures like the Conventional Forces in Europe (CFE) Treaty.[210] In June 2002, the Almaty summit of the CICA provided an opportunity for Kazakh officials to promote engagement and reconciliation between visiting Indian Prime Minister Atal Bihari Vajpayee and Pakistani President Pervez Musharraf.[211] Foreign Minister Marat Tazhin believes that, "CICA has good prospects of becoming an effective mechanism for collective security in Asia."[212] The Kazakh government aims to host another Conference on Confidence and Security Measures in Asia in 2010, a period that will coincide with its OSCE chairmanship.

---

[209] See for example A. G. Kozhikhov, "CICA: Realities and Outlooks," Kazakhstan Institute for Strategic Studies, July 26, 2002, http://www.kisi.kz/site.html?id=516.

[210] Eric Hundman, "CFE Treaty: Prospects for Asia Reinvigoration, Expansion," Center for Defense Information, April 24, 2008, http://www.isn.ethz.ch/news/sw/details.cfm?id=18902.

[211] Marat Yermukanov, "Kazakhstan-India Relations: Partners or Distant Friends?," Eurasia Daily Monitor, November 16, 2004, http://www.jamestown.org/publications_details.php?volume_id=401&issue_id=3142&article_id=2368860.

[212] Marat Tazhin, "Kazakhstan in a Changing World," speech at U.S.-Kazakhstan Business Association dinner, Washington, D.C., May 8, 2007, http://www.kazakhembus.com/050907.html.

Managing Regional Emergencies

The unduly harsh weather and floods suffered by Central Asian countries this past winter reminded many that managing the consequences of natural disasters represents an important regional security issue. Kazakhstan has suffered its share of these problems. More positively, Kazakh authorities are playing a leading role in helping to improve the capabilities of the region to respond to these challenges.

From June 7-12, 2007, the Kazakhstan Ministry of Defense and Ministry of Emergency Situations jointly hosted Regional Cooperation 2007 (RC07). This computer-simulated disaster response exercise involved approximately 230 military and civilian personnel from Kazakhstan, Afghanistan, Kyrgyzstan, Pakistan, Tajikistan, and the United States. It was organized jointly by U.S. Central Command (CENTCOM) and U.S. Joint Forces Command (USJFCOM). The exercise aimed to strengthen the ability of the participating countries to collaborate in preparing for, responding to, and recovering from the effects of a natural or manmade disaster under the framework of a Regional Cooperation Center. Although the scenario involved a natural disaster, RC07 sought to develop national capabilities that can also apply to countering terrorism, narcotics trafficking, illegal migration, and human trafficking. The exercise addressed such goals as effective information sharing, interoperability, and coordinating regional response efforts. As part of the exercise, the Kazakhstan Ministry of Emergency Situations employed its National Crisis Management Center in Astana. The other participating countries staffed national response cells in Bishkek, Kyrgyzstan. Prior to the exercises, representatives from the participating countries held two working meetings and three conferences. Afterwards, they held a post-exercise "lessons learned" seminar to evaluate the results of RC07 and consider next steps.

Since the late 1990s, numerous symposiums, seminars, and computer-assisted command post exercises have been held under the auspices of the Regional Cooperation series. The United States and its NATO allies have sought to organize collective activities on issues related to emergency management with the countries of Central Asia. This type of cooperation is typically less controversial than collaboration involving other military activities such as collective interventions in neighboring countries or domestic anti-terrorist operations. The experience with Uzbekistan has made Western governments wary of enhancing the military instruments available for the region's authoritarian governments to suppress domestic rivals or popular protests. Yet, cooperation on disaster management can, by improving interoperability among participating countries, provide a basis for segueing to more demanding forms of joint military operations in the future. Participation in collective security activities also helps develop military-to-military relations between the armed forces engaged in the region, including with NATO forces hitherto excluded from CSTO and SCO exercises.

Economics and Energy

Thanks to its natural riches and wise economic policies, Kazakhstan has achieved the strongest economy in Central Asia. The gross domestic product (GDP) of Kazakhstan is larger than that of all the other Central Asian countries combined, amounting to an estimated $161 billion in 2007.[213] The Nazarbayev administration has encouraged Kazakhs to engage in regional commerce as well as wider economic intercourse in order to limit Kazakhstan's dependence on any single supplier, customer, investor, or market. In addition, the president has a vision of his country as a nexus of the Eurasian economies.

In 2005, Nazarbayev told the attendees of an international conference entitled "Strategy Kazakhstan-2030," that, "I see Kazakhstan as a junction country in the Central Asian region, an integrator of intra-regional economic ties, a center of gravity of capital and investments, and a location of regional production or the subsidiaries of the world's major companies aimed at the Central Asian market and international services." In time, he added, "Kazakhstan might perform the function of an important link, a transcontinental economic bridge, for interactions between European, Asia-Pacific and the South Asian economic regions."[214]

In his February 2007 annual state of the nation address, Nazarbayev said he wanted Kazakhstan to become a "regional locomotive" of economic

---

[213] "Kazakhstan," *CIA World Fact Book: 2007*,
https://www.cia.gov/library/publications/the-world-factbook/geos/kz.html.
[214] President of Kazakhstan, "Vystuplenie Prezidenta Respubliki Kazakhstan N. Nazarbaeva na mezhdunarodnoy konferentsii 'Strategiya Kazakhstan—2030 v Deystvii," October 11, 2005,
http://www.akorda.kz/www/www_akorda_kz.nsf/sections?OpenForm&id_doc=DE8 C9CA216A02A3F462572340019E7BF&lang=ru&L1=L2&L2=L2-15.

development.[215] In October 2007, Nazarbayev reaffirmed his intent to develop a Eurasian transport corridor that would eventually "connect the Persian Gulf on one end and the Baltic Sea on the other" through "the creation of a high-tech system that includes railroads, highways, power transmission lines, gas, and oil pipelines."[216]

Kazakhstan's extraordinary economic growth during the past decade—after the country recovered from the rupture of the integrated Soviet economy and world oil prices rebounded in the late 1990s—resulted in its becoming the first former Soviet republic to receive an investment-grade credit rating from a major international credit rating agency. The macroeconomic boom the nation has experienced since the late 1990s enabled Kazakhstan to liquidate its debt to the International Monetary Fund (IMF) in 2000. Kazakhstan's economic upturn, though initially driven to a considerable degree by increased oil revenues, has also been sustained through market reforms. During the Soviet period, the country's industrial sector had been closely integrated with enterprises in Russia and the other republics. For example, Kazakhstan's defense companies depended on exchanging supplies and parts with other elements of the Soviet military industrial complex. The country's oil and gas often underwent processing in Russia, while Kazakhstan would import oil from Siberia and gas from Uzbekistan. The rupture of these commercial ties led to the collapse of many Kazakh firms and induced the newly independent Kazakh government to rely primarily on the extraction and export of the country's raw materials, especially hydrocarbons, to sustain the economy.[217]

Though the primary export commodities of Kazakhstan are oil and gas, Kazakhstan has actively sought to expand its range of economic activities through vertical (new products) as well as horizontal (new partners) market

---

[215] Embassy of Kazakhstan to the USA and Canada, "A New Kazakhstan in a New World: President Nazarbayev's Strategic Vision," *Kazakhstan's Echo*, no. 36 (March 2, 2007), http://www.kazakhembus.com/echo36.html.

[216] "Central Asia: Kazakh, Russian Leaders Discuss Transport Corridor," Radio Free Europe/Radio Liberty, October 5, 2007,
http://www.rferl.org/featuresarticle/2007/10/4482ab28-5ab9-4756-8386-48471d684d3f.html.

[217] Pinar Ipek, "The Role of Oil and Gas in Kazakhstan's Foreign Policy: Looking East or West?" *Europe-Asia Studies*, vol. 59, no. 7 (November 2007), pp. 1180-1181.

diversification. Its leaders realize they cannot rely solely on hydrocarbon exports alone for the revenue needed to continue their robust economic growth and relative political stability. Kazakh officials have therefore been using the country's oil and gas revenue to try to finance the development of an economic foundation for expanding into new markets.

An important element in this strategy was the creation in 2001 of the National Fund, under the direct authority of the President of Kazakhstan. The Fund, whose reserves now total billions of dollars, collects revenue by taxing the country's commodity exports. The government then uses the money to finance projects that aim to strengthen the country's socioeconomic infrastructure, especially in the non-energy sectors. More recently, the government has launched a "30 Corporate Leaders" project to promote the development of state-run holding companies and "breakthrough macro-projects" in leading-sector industries—such as petrochemicals, metallurgy, and bio-energy—to make Kazakhstan more internationally competitive in non-energy sectors.[218] In subsequent statements, Nazarbayev has reaffirmed the government's intent to use the country's expanding oil and gas revenue to diversify Kazakhstan's economy and help make the country one of the fifty most developed states in the world.

The recent turbulence in global financial markets, which originated with problems relating to sub-prime mortgages in the United States, has not spared Kazakhstan. In 2007, high borrowing by Kazakh banks led Standard and Poor's (S&P) to downgrade the Kazakh government's sovereign credit rating to BBB-, its lowest investment grade category. According to the Asian Development Bank (ADB), Kazakhstan experienced an 8.5% growth rate in 2007, admirable by world standards but somewhat of a slowdown from its recent pace and a figure that lags behind the growth rates of Georgia, Armenia, and especially Azerbaijan. The ADB concluded that a sharp curtailment in capital flows to the country triggered an abrupt reduction in lending and a major downturn in the non-oil economy, especially real estate.

---

[218] American Chamber of Commerce in Kazakhstan, "Kazakhstan Planning Foreign Trade Increase to $200 Billion," June 19, 2007, http://www.amcham.kz/article.php?article_id=710. See also the speech, entitled "Kazakhstan in a Changing World," by Foreign Minister Tazhin to a Washington, D.C., audience on May 8, 2007, reprinted at http://www.kazakhembus.com/050907.html.

The country also suffered from relatively high inflation (17.4%). The ADB estimates that the country will achieve only 5.0% GDP growth this year and perhaps 6.3% growth in 2009.[219]

Along with Russia, however, Kazakhstan is still the only former Soviet republic whose bonds remain at investment grade (though Russia's rating is higher due to its larger international reserves, lower exposure to domestic property prices, and other factors). In addition, analysts at S&P, the ADB, and other institutions did not see any fundamental problems with the Kazakh economy, especially since the credit crunch could prove self-correcting by reducing bank borrowing and cooling off Kazakhstan's overheated property markets.[220] Despite worries about domestic inflation, large foreign exchange inflows, and the country's current account deficit, the IMF remains optimistic about Kazakhstan's potential to resume its impressive economic performance of recent years, especially if Kazakh leaders continue to pursue prudent macroeconomic, oil revenue, and structural diversification policies.[221]

Energy

Oil is Kazakhstan's main export commodity, accounting for over half the value of its annual exports.[222] In 2007, Kazakhstan produced an estimated 1.45 million barrels per day (bbl/d) of oil; of this total, some 1.2 million bbl/d went to foreign buyers.[223] According to the U.S. Energy Information Administration, Kazakhstan has the largest recoverable oil reserves in the

---

[219] Asian Development Bank, *Asian Development Outlook 2008* (Washington, D.C.), pp. 112-114.

[220] Gulnoza Saidazimova, "Kazakhstan: Global Financial Turmoil Hits Credit Rating," Radio Free Europe/Radio Liberty, October 13, 2007, http://www.rferl.org/featuresarticle/2007/10/C2DCD031-A3E9-4B23-90EC-4491EDF89C85.html.

[221] "IMF Executive Board Concludes 2007 Article IV Consultation with the Republic of Kazakhstan," Public Information Notice (PIN) no. 07/77, July 5, 2007, http://www.imf.org/external/np/sec/pn/2007/pn0777.htm.

[222] "Kazakhstan" *CIA World Fact Book: 2007,* https://www.cia.gov/library/publications/the-world-factbook/geos/kz.html.

[223] Energy Information Administration, "Kazakhstan: Oil," February 2008, http://www.eia.doe.gov/emeu/cabs/Kazakhstan/Oil.html.

Caspian Basin.[224] Estimates of its combined onshore and offshore proven hydrocarbon reserves range from 9 to 40 billion barrels of oil (equivalent). At the low end, this estimate is comparable to Algeria's oil reserves, and at the high end, to those of Libya. At present, the country's most productive oil fields are Tengiz (280,000 bbl/d), Karachaganak (250,000 bbl/d), CNPC-Uzenmunaigas (135,000 bbl/d), Aktobemunaigas (120,000 bbl/d), and Mangistaumunaigas (115,000 bbl/d)). Yet, it is the Kashagan field that has received the most media attention because it contains an estimated 13 billion barrels of recoverable reserves of oil, making it the largest oil discovery in the world during the past 30 years and the largest oil field outside the Middle East.[225]

What also makes these hydrocarbon resources of particular interest to the international community is that Kazakhstan is situated at the heart of the emerging network of energy pipelines traversing Eurasia. The Kazakh government has been a strong supporter of developing multiple energy pipelines for exporting Kazakh oil and, when it becomes available in large quantities a few years hence, natural gas. Its "tout azimuth" approach envisages Kazakh energy flowing westward to Europe through the Caucasus, eastward to China through its Central Asian neighbors, and possibly southward through Iran to South Asian markets.

In an April 6, 2007, television interview, Nazarbayev explained that pragmatic economic considerations—the search for the most cost-effective options—underpinned his government's support for multiple pipelines: "If it is beneficial for us to transport all Kazakhstan's oil and gas through Russia, we will go that way. If transportation via Baku-Ceyhan is 15 dollars cheaper, we will go that way. And if neither is beneficial, we will go to China."[226]

Until now, the overwhelming share of Kazakh oil has been transported northward through Russia. Yet, Kazakh officials are aware of the dangers of

---

[224] Energy Information Administration, "Kazakhstan: Background," February 2008, http://www.eia.doe.gov/emeu/cabs/Kazakhstan/Background.html.
[225] Energy Information Administration, "Kazakhstan: Oil," February 2008, http://www.eia.doe.gov/emeu/cabs/Kazakhstan/Oil.html.
[226] Joanna Lillis, "Energy Profits Provide Kazakhstan with Foreign-Policy Heft," Eurasia Insight, April 18, 2007, http://www.eurasianet.org/departments/insight/articles/eav041807a.shtml.

relying on Russian-controlled transportation routes, which allows Moscow to unilaterally decide how much oil can leave the country and to which destination it can flow. It will still take several years before many of Kazakhstan's oil and gas projects begin producing enough output to sustain these new export routes, especially given that much of the country's existing energy production is locked in long-term preferential agreements with Russian energy companies. Even now, however, Kazakh exporters have increased negotiating leverage with Russia thanks to the expanding export options. On March 11, 2008, Gazprom was forced to agree to start paying considerably higher prices in 2009 for the natural gas it purchases from Kazakhstan, Uzbekistan, and Turkmenistan.[227] In the past, the company had been able to buy Central Asian gas at below-market rates and then resell it on European markets with a hefty markup. Increasing competition from possible European and especially Chinese buyers compelled the Russian energy firm to increase its payments.

The Kazakh government continues to rely heavily on Western energy companies for the advanced technologies needed to develop some of Kazakhstan's most challenging oil fields, though these relations have sometimes been strained. During the 1990s, when energy prices were low and Kazakhstan desperately needed government revenue, the Kazakh government offered generous terms in a successful effort to attract Western capital and technology. Since oil prices rebounded starting in 1999, the governments of Kazakhstan and other energy-producing countries have sought more favorable terms for their national companies. Like their foreign counterparts, Kazakh leaders are depending on increased oil and gas revenue to fund their country's ambitious development plans.

The technical and other problems experienced by the multinational consortium operating the field, the Agip Kazakhstan North Caspian Operating Company (Agip KCO), has made it a particular target of increased pressure from Kazakh authorities. The start-up delays, soaring production costs, and other performance problems at the field climaxed in late July 2007,

---

[227] Brian Whitmore, "Central Asia: Behind The Hype: Russia And China Vie For Region's Energy Resources," Radio Free Europe/Radio Liberty, March 22, 2008, http://www.rferl.org/featuresarticle/2008/3/584864dc-0805-4a5e-b878-edd3e9255760.html.

when the consortium announced it was postponing yet again the scheduled start of production (to 2010 or 2011) and raising the project's estimated costs from $57 billion to $136 billion. In August, the government suspended for three months the license of Italy's Eni SpA, which then led the consortium, alleging that the company had violated Kazakh environmental regulations. On September 26, the lower house of the Kazakh parliament approved legislation authorizing the government unilaterally to alter contracts with firms involved in extracting the country's mineral resources if such changes were necessary to uphold Kazakhstan's economic and security interests.

The redistribution of power between the Western oil firms and the Kazakh government became apparent on January 15, 2008, when Kazakh officials announced that the state-run KazMunaiGaz National Co, Kazakhstan's national oil and gas company, would henceforth assume a lead role in developing the Kashagan oil field. Previously, Italy's Eni SpA, Exxon Mobil Corp., Royal Dutch Shell PLC, and France's Total SA each owned 18.5% of the Kashagan project, while ConocoPhillips held 9.3%, and Japan's Inpex and KazMunaiGas possessed 8.3% each. Under the new deal, KazMunaiGaz has a 16.8% share of the project, while the shares of the other firms in the consortium have proportionally decreased. In addition, Eni now shares the role of main operator with that of the other largest shareholders. The Kazakh government will pay the other members $1.78 billion for these shares, but will recoup about $5 billion from royalties and compensation for lost revenues due to the earlier project delays.[228] Nazarbayev said that the January 14 deal represented a "restoration of justice" because the foreign companies involved had "failed to meet the outlined deadlines, and Kazakhstan has been losing its share of profits."[229]

The Kazakh authorities have already begun developing alternative energy sources to supplement their oil and gas exports as well as provide additional export revenue. A special area of emphasis has been on developing civilian nuclear power. Kazakhstan possesses 19% of the world's reserves of

---

[228] "Kazakhstan to Double Stake in Kashagan Oil Field in $1.8 bln Deal," RIA Novosti, January 14, 2008, http://en.rian.ru/business/20080114/96606642.html.

[229] Embassy of Kazakhstan to the USA and Canada, "Kazakhstan Reaches Consensus with Foreign Oil Companies over Giant Oilfield," Kazakhstan News Bulletin, special issue No 1, January 18, 2008.

uranium—with an estimated 444,000 tons of recoverable uranium deposits, second only to that of Australia[230]—and ranks among the four largest producers of natural uranium. Its national nuclear energy company, KazAtomProm, extracted 5,279 tons of natural uranium in 2006. KazAtomProm aims to raise its level of uranium extraction to 30,000 tons by 2018, which would establish Kazakhstan as the largest global supplier.[231] It also plans to advance from only selling natural uranium to also manufacturing and selling uranium fuel for use in civilian nuclear reactors.[232]

The Kazakh government has been cooperating with other countries to develop its nuclear energy resources as well. For example, the governments of Japan and Kazakhstan signed a memorandum on peaceful nuclear cooperation when Prime Minister Junichiro Koizumi became the first Japanese Prime Minister to visit Central Asia in August 2006.[233] Due to the subsequent purchase of shares in Kazakh uranium mining projects by Sumitomo Corp. and Kansai Electric Power Co., Japan has locked in about one-third of its annual uranium imports from Kazakhstan.[234] In July 2007, Kazatomprom bought a 10% stake in Toshiba's Westinghouse Electric, in order to gain access to its advanced technologies for manufacturing nuclear power plants and their fuel. The company intends to construct a nuclear fuel production center at its Ulby plant in East Kazakhstan to make fuel for Russian and European atomic power plants.[235]

---

[230] "From Car Salesman to Nuclear Tycoon," *New Zealand Herald*, April 26, 2008, http://www.nzherald.co.nz/section/3/story.cfm?c_id=3&objectid=10506242.

[231] Nariman Gizitdinov and Benjamin Rahr, "Kazakhstan to Increase Uranium Output Fivefold, Overtake Canada," Bloomberg, January 10, 2008, http://www.bloomberg.com/apps/news?pid=20601085&sid=aRlO4YTF2cog&refer=europe.

[232] "Kazakhstan Rising," Silk Road Intelligencer, May 26, 2008, http://silkroadintelligencer.com/2008/05/26/kazakhstan-rising.

[233] "Kazakh, Japanese Leaders Sign Up to Nuclear Cooperation," RIA Novosti, August 28, 2006, http://en.rian.ru/world/20060828/53234564.html.

[234] Mari Iwata, "Japan Steals March on Asia Rivals over Uranium Supply," MarketWatch, November 14, 2007, http://www.marketwatch.com/news/story/japan-steals-march-asia-rivals/story.aspx?guid=%7BBC3F3B7D%2D09EB%2D42A0%2D9F0F%2DFE3CAF5E4862%7D.

[235] "From Car Salesman to Nuclear Tycoon," *New Zealand Herald*, April 26, 2008, http://www.nzherald.co.nz/section/3/story.cfm?c_id=3&objectid=10506242.

Russian energy officials and companies have long been interested in gaining access to Kazakhstan's large stocks of uranium to supplement Russia's domestic production, which Russian experts fear may prove insufficient to meet the growing international demand for nuclear energy. In July 2006, Russia and Kazakhstan agreed to launch three joint ventures, with an estimated cost of $10 billion, to conduct uranium mining (at Yuzhnoe Zarechnoe and Budenovsk), uranium enrichment (at Angarsk in eastern Siberia), and develop low- and medium-power nuclear reactors.[236] Kazakhstan thereby became the first foreign country to join Russia's international uranium enrichment center at Angarsk, which will manufacture nuclear fuel for delivery to countries with civilian nuclear power plants that lack their own uranium enrichment capabilities. Russia's nuclear industry is also eager to build new nuclear power plants in Kazakhstan (the Soviet-era plant in Aktau ceased operating in 1999), but popular opposition to their construction remains high among Kazakhs. Many people are aware of the catastrophic health and environmental consequences inflicted on the local population from activities at the former nuclear test site in Semipalatinsk.[237]

Kazakhstan has also been an active participant in the U.S.-led Global Nuclear Energy Partnership (GNEP). The stated dual purpose of the partnership, launched by the Bush administration in February 2006, is to develop new technologies and new fuel-lending arrangements to allow for the expanded use of nuclear energy globally without encouraging further nuclear weapons proliferation. In implementing the program, the Department of Energy has pursued four broad objectives: decrease U.S. reliance on foreign energy sources without impeding U.S. economic growth; employ improved technologies to recover more energy and reduce waste when recycling spent nuclear fuel; encourage the use of energy sources that emit the least atmospheric greenhouse gasses; and reduce the threat of nuclear proliferation.

---

[236] Sergei Blagov, "Nazarbayev Reassures Russia on Energy Cooperation," Eurasia Insight, March 20, 2007,
http://www.eurasianet.org/departments/insight/articles/eav032007a.shtml.
[237] Gulnoza Saidazimova, "Kazakhstan: Government Pushing Nuclear Power Despite Public Fears," Eurasia Insight, February 25, 2006,
http://www.eurasianet.org/departments/civilsociety/articles/pp022506.shtml. For a graphic description of these environmental problems see Walton Burns, "Not Another Disaster Tourist," *Financial Times*, January 24, 2008.

When Nazarbayev met with Bush in Washington at the end of September 2006, the two presidents signed a joint statement that referred to an "energy partnership" that would "facilitate the participation of US companies in developing reserves in Kazakhstan, including nuclear energy." [238] On September 16, 2007, Kazakhstan formally became a GNEP partner by signing the GNEP Statement of Principles. India, Pakistan, and other Eurasian countries might become future GNEP partners.

Labor Mobility

The Russian Federation is the most important destination country for labor migrants from the other CIS countries, including those from Central Asia. Russian authorities periodically harden their approach to foreign laborers by tightening restrictions on the issuance of work permits and employee visas, as well as giving Russian citizens priority in highly visible small retail businesses, where the previously large number of foreigners aroused popular animosity. Yet, they desire to attract more Slavic immigrants to bolster the declining number of ethnic Russian workers in the Russian population. In June 2006, for instance, the Russian government launched a "State Program to Aid the Voluntary Repatriation of Compatriots." The program's impact has proved minimal thus far, but Russia's higher standard of living regularly pulls millions of non-Slavic migrants from Central Asia into the Russian labor market, especially in the booming construction industry. Only a small percentage of these immigrants have obtained official permission to work in Russia, where even documented workers of Central Asian ethnicity encounter discrimination and abuse.[239] Their remittances make an essential contribution to the GNPs of their countries of origin, remove potentially dissatisfied social elements from these states, and give Central Asian governments another reason to stay on Moscow's good side.[240]

---

[238] Office of the White House Press Secretary, "Joint Statement Between the United States of America and the Republic of Kazakhstan," September 29, 2006, http://www.whitehouse.gov/news/releases/2006/09/20060929-1.html.

[239] Erica Marat, "Russia Decreases Immigration Quota Threefold in 2008," *Central Asia-Caucasus Institute Analyst*, January 9, 2008, http://www.cacianalyst.org/?q=node/477.

[240] For more on the implications of this development see Fiona Hill, "Beyond the Colored Revolutions," Brooking s Institution, September 30, 2005, pp. 9-10, http://www.brookings.edu/views/papers/hillf/20050930.pdf.

Joint Kazakh-Russian initiatives have helped curb the flow of illegal migrants across their lengthy joint frontier. In 2007, Vladimir Pronichev, deputy director of Russia's Federal Security Service, stated that these endeavors had improved border security substantially in recent years.[241] Another factor curbing Kazakh migration into Russia has been the continuing improvement in Kazakhstan's economy, which has enhanced living standards of many potential emigrants and expatriates. At present, some one million ethnic Kazakhs live in Russia, but they are generally long-term residents engaged in legal employment.

In recent years, Kazakhstan has emerged in its own right as an important center of attraction for labor migrants from the other Central Asian countries. The country's improving socioeconomic conditions, political stability, and harmonious ethnic relations have pulled laborers from the surrounding regions. Conversely, negative factors in nearby Central Asian countries—including excess labor resources, low workers' compensation, unemployment as well as underemployment—push workers into Kazakhstan.[242] Nazarbayev considered the migration issue sufficiently important to select it as the single subject of priority discussion for the CIS in 2007, the year Kazakhstan held the CIS presidency.[243] In October of that year, the member governments created a special body to supervise migration among their countries.[244]

As of July 2007, the largest number of legal immigrants to Kazakhstan arrived from Uzbekistan, Russia and China: 49.5%, 18.9% and 11.4%, respectively, of the 28,100 total number of immigrants. In addition, the government has an annual quota for government-supported resettlement of Oralmans (Kazakhs returning to the country from abroad) to their historic homeland. In 2008, the

---

[241] "Central Asia: Kazakh, Russian Leaders Discuss Transport Corridor," Radio Free Europe/Radio Liberty, October 5, 2007,
http://www.rferl.org/featuresarticle/2007/10/4482ab28-5ab9-4756-8386-48471d684d3f.html.

[242] Yelena Sadovskaya, "Labor Migration and Remittances in Central Asian Countries: New Challenges and Solutions," *Central Asia's Affairs*, no. 3 (2006).

[243] "CIS Leaders Pledge Further Integration," RIA Novosti, June 10, 2007,
http://en.rian.ru/world/20070610/67047803.html.

[244] "CIS Leaders Agree to Form Body Controlling Migration—Putin," RIA Novosti, October 6, 2007, http://en.rian.ru/world/20071006/82769544.html

quota was set at 15,000 families. Nazarbayev has asked that the figure be raised in 2009 to 20,000 families.[245] Kazakhstan's citizens emigrate mainly to Russia and Germany: 86.5% and 5.9%, respectively, of the total number of emigrants (16,700 people).[246] One noteworthy fact is that so many ethnic Russians have been moving to Kazakhstan from Uzbekistan that, in 2003 and 2004, more ethnic Russians entered Kazakhstan than departed the country, a major reversal of the migrant flows seen one decade earlier.[247]

These official figures probably vastly underestimate the number of labor migrants entering Kazakhstan. Since the government has a visa-free entry regime with all other CIS countries except Turkmenistan, migrants most often enter the country legally, but some then undertake work in "unregulated status" (i.e., outside of legally recognized labor contracts).[248] Various sources estimate unregulated labor migration into Kazakhstan as ranging from 300,000 to 1 million people annually in recent years. Many of these illegal immigrants come from other Central Asian countries, particularly Kyrgyzstan and Uzbekistan. Workers can normally earn much higher salaries in Kazakhstan than in their home countries, and in a currency that is easier to convert.[249] The large number of illegal workers in Kazakhstan relative to the size of its population has led some experts to urge the Kazakh government to adopt measures to encourage foreigners to obtain Kazakh citizenship and develop legal businesses in Kazakhstan by, for example, simplifying procedures for obtaining work permits and citizenship.[250] Kazakh authorities are also considering allowing seasonal migrant laborers from

[245] Embassy of Kazakhstan to the USA and Canada, "President Nazarbayev Delivers Annual State-of-the-Nation Address, Announces Kazakhstan's 'Road to Europe'," News Bulletin, Febraury 8, 2008, http://www.kazakhembus.com/NBSpecialIssue_3_020808.html.

[246] Yuri Shokamanov, "Statistical Overview on Economy and Society," *Kazakhstan International Business Magazine*, no. 3 (2007).

[247] Sebastien Peyrouse, "The Russian Minority in Central Asia: Migration, Politics, and Language," Occasional Paper no. 297 (Washington, D.C.: Woodrow Wilson International Center for Scholars, 2007), p. 5.

[248] Yelena Sadovskaya, "Labor Migration and Remittances in Central Asian Countries: New Challenges and Solutions," *Central Asia's Affairs*, no. 3 (2006).

[249] Economist Intelligence Unit, "Country Profile 2007: Kazakhstan."

[250] Sadovskaya, "Labor Migration and Remittances in Central Asian Countries."

Kyrgyzstan to work legally in Kazakhstan for up to 90 days under special regulations.[251]

Transnational Trade and Commerce

During the Soviet period, the central government ministries in Moscow controlled Kazakhstan's foreign economic activity. This situation allowed Soviet planners to dispose of the territory's rich natural resources unilaterally, directing many Kazakh products to other Soviet republics or to the USSR's fellow socialist countries within the Council of Mutual Economic Assistance. When Western countries purchased Kazakh exports, Moscow-based planners used the hard-currency revenue for whatever schemes the Soviet government supported at the time.

The disruption of economic ties that followed the breakup of the USSR triggered a collapse in the trade among the former Soviet republics. This development proved especially traumatic for Kazakhstan. In 1992, 92% of Kazakhstan's exports and 85% of its imports involved these other republics.[252] At first, this disruption of Soviet-era commerce induced Kazakh government and business leaders to widen the scope of their economic intercourse to encompass a larger number of countries. As the economies of many of the former Soviet republics have rebounded, Kazakhstan's trade flows with its former Soviet neighbors have resumed and, in many cases, exceeded Soviet-era levels.

Nevertheless, most analysts believe commerce throughout Eurasia remains considerably below desirable levels, with bilateral and multilateral relationships characterized by widespread "undertrading" due to poor policy choices and the absence of effective international institutions at the regional or global level (Kazakhstan and many other former CIS states have not yet joined the World Trade Organization). According to the 2005 U.N.

---

[251] Bruce Pannier, "Central Asia: Kyrgyz President Returns from Astana with Wheat-Export Deal," Radio Free Europe/Radio Liberty, April 18, 2008, http://www.rferl.org/featuresarticle/2008/04/a6fc862a-649e-4cc3-acf4-57dc77effa9c.html.

[252] Markhamat Khasanova, "Kazakhstan: Foreign Trade Policy" in Boris Rumer and Stanislav Zhukov, eds., *Central Asia: The Challenges of Independence* (Armonk, New York: Sharpe, 1998), pp. 169-170.

Development Report, greater cooperation among the core Central Asian republics of Kazakhstan, Kyrgyzstan, Tajikistan, Turkmenistan, and Uzbekistan could yield many political and economic gains, including 50%-100% increases in their citizens" average incomes over the next decade.[253] At the time of the report, only 2-2.5% of Kazakhstan's trade went to the four other core Central Asian countries of Kyrgyzstan ($2.51 billion in bilateral goods turnover in 2005), Tajikistan ($1.11 billion), Turkmenistan ($540 million), and Uzbekistan $3.85 billion).[254]

Nazarbayev has lamented this failure to achieve deeper economic ties, which threaten to deprive Kazakhstan of its natural status as Eurasia's commercial linchpin. He warned that, "the destiny of all Central Asian peoples depends on this most important factor—whether we can become a transportation route of global significance or will be pushed off to the side of the road again."[255] In February 2005, the president argued that a failure of the Central Asian states to improve their economic integration would invariably leave them too weak to resist falling under the control of yet another extra-regional power: "We have a choice between remaining an eternal supplier of raw materials for the world economy and waiting patiently for the arrival of the next imperial master or pursuing genuine economic integration of the Central Asian region. I propose the latter."[256]

Nazarbayev has emphasized that, thanks to Kazakhstan's strong economic development, successful imposition of market reforms, and commitment to regional prosperity, the country can become a driver in regional economic integration mechanisms among Eurasian states. Such a process, in the view of Kazakh leaders, would in turn promote Kazakhstan's own development by

---

[253] United Nations Development Programme, *Bringing Down Barriers: Regional Cooperation for Human Development and Human Security* (New York, 2005), http://europeandcis.undp.org/archive/?wspc=CAHDR2005.

[254] Sanat Kushkumbayev, "Kazakhstan," in S. Frederick Starr, ed., *The New Silk Roads: Transport and Trade in Greater Central Asia* (Washington, D.C.: Central Asia-Caucasus Institute, 2007), pp. 278-279.

[255] Cited in Yerzhan Kh. Kazykhanov, "On Kazakhstan," *American Foreign Policy Interests*, vol. 28, no.3 (July 2006), p. 191.

[256] Embassy of Kazakhstan to the USA and Canada, "President Nazarbayev Calls for New Stage of Accelerated Economic, Political Reforms, Drastic Upgrade in Life Quality," *Kazakhstan's Echo*, February 23, 2005, http://www.kazakhembus.com/echo13.html.

making Kazakhstan a more attractive market for foreign investors as well as by increasing the number of possible consumers of Kazakh goods.

Kazakhstan has pursued this objective through the Central Asia Regional Economic Cooperation (CAREC) Program. Its membership encompasses Afghanistan, Azerbaijan, China, Kazakhstan, Kyrgyzstan, Mongolia, Tajikistan and Uzbekistan, as well as six multilateral institutions (Asian Development Bank, European Bank for Reconstruction and Development, International Monetary Fund, Islamic Development Bank, United Nations Development Program and the World Bank). The institution focuses on economic cooperation among its participants in the areas of transport, trade and energy.

On November 2-3, 2007, CAREC held its 6th annual Ministerial Conference in Dushanbe. At the meeting, the ministers approved a long-debated multi-billion dollar Transport and Trade Facilitation Strategy.[257] The plan foresees substantial infrastructure investments to improve the flow of goods along six main transnational corridors—including both road and rail links—connecting countries within the region as well as with the rest of Eurasia:

- from northwestern Kazakhstan to Xinjiang, to facilitate traffic from Europe to East Asia;

- from Baku across the Caspian through Turkmenistan, Uzbekistan and the Ferghana Valley in Tajikistan and Kyrgyzstan into Xinjiang, roughly following the old Silk Road;

- from Siberia to Iran through eastern Kazakhstan, splitting into two parts – one through Uzbekistan and Turkmenistan, the other through Kyrgyzstan, Tajikistan and Afghanistan;

- from Siberia to China through Mongolia;

- from Pakistan to China through Afghanistan and Tajikistan, to make it easier to ship Chinese goods to South Asia; and

---

[257] Asian Development Bank, "CAREC Transport and Trade Facilitation Strategy," http://www.adb.org/Documents/Events/2007/6th-Ministerial-Conference-CAREC/Transport-Trade-Strategy.pdf.

- from western Siberia to the Middle East and South Asia; through western Kazakhstan and Uzbekistan and either Afghanistan and Iran or Tajikistan, Afghanistan and Pakistan.

The summit statement declares that, in addition to deepening their economic integration over the next decade, the CAREC members would like to cooperate more in managing other regional challenges such as environmental problems, communicable diseases, and consequences of natural disasters.[258] The Ministers also supported increased cooperation with other regional organizations, a sensible recommendation given that the CIS, Eurasec, the SCO, and most recently the CSTO have affirmed an interest in promoting economic integration among their members. The CAREC nations have already begun to implement some of these measures, though the continued absence of Russia from the process may complicate its implementation in the long run.[259] (Turkmenistan has given indications that it may soon join.)

Kazakhstan has sought to realize its potential as a land-based transportation hub connecting Europe and Asia through participation in other regional economic integration initiatives. These include the Euro-Asian Transport Links Project, the International Transport Consortium, the Common Transport Policy, and the North-South Meridian Transport Corridor agreement (a Russian-Indian-Iranian project that Kazakhstan joined in 2003). Astana has also pursued this objective within Eurasec, the OSCE, the SCO, and other multilateral institutions. Inside Kazakhstan, various complementary public and private efforts have constructed new railway lines (Ays-Kyzylorda-Aktobe-Uralsk; Arys-Lugovaya; Chu-Almaty-Aktogai-Semipalatinsk) to integrate its disparate regions with each other as well as these emerging international transportation lines.[260]

On the negative side, developments during the last few months have called into question Kazakhstan's potential to remain a leading grain supplier to

---

[258] Raphael Minder, "Plan Agreed on $19bn New Silk Road," *Financial Times*, November 5, 2007, http://www.ft.com/cms/s/0/8974eef0-8b40-11dc-95f7-0000779fd2ac.html?nclick_check=1.

[259] Joshua Kucera, "Central Asia: A Vision For a Regional Transport Network Takes Shape," Eurasia Insight, January 14, 2008, http://www.eurasianet.org/departments/insight/articles/eav011407.shtml.

[260] Kushkumbayev, "Kazakhstan," p. 290.

neighboring countries. In recent years, Kazakhstan has been the only Central Asia country to export grain, including to Kyrgyzstan, Tajikistan, Turkmenistan, and Uzbekistan.[261] The harsh winter, combined with the rising food prices in the country, led the authorities in April 2008 to curtail gain and bread exports until September.[262] Although the measure will likely prove temporary, it will reinforce the reluctance of other countries to rely on Kazakhstan grain supplies in the future.

Kazakh Foreign Investment

Kazakhstan still seeks large-scale foreign direct investment for its own needs, most notably to finance improvements in the country's energy and transportation infrastructure as well as to access the most advanced global technologies. At the same time, many more Kazakhs are acquiring the means to invest in other countries, especially by buying shares of foreign companies. In terms of purchasing power parity, Kazakh citizens' per capita GDP is almost twice as high as that of citizens of Kyrgyzstan, Uzbekistan, and Turkmenistan, and about four times greater than the citizens of Tajikistan.[263] As of last year, Kazakh entrepreneurs had invested more than $18 billion in foreign countries.[264]

In his February 2007 annual state of the nation address, Nazarabyev said he wanted to work with neighboring countries to create a more favorable business environment for Kazakh companies, especially by removing protectionist, bureaucratic, and other unnatural barriers.[265] Longstanding

---

[261] Bruce Pannier, "Central Asia: Kazakhstan's Neighbors Await Decision on Grain Exports," Radio Free Europe/Radio Liberty, April 9, 2008, http://www.rferl.org/featuresarticle/2008/04/9AA08A9D-12EF-4076-812A-8F77326996D3.html.

[262] Ellen Rosen, "The Bread Basket Takes a Hit," *New York Times*, April 27, 2008, http://www.nytimes.com/2008/04/27/nyregion/nyregionspecial2/27Rflour.html?pagewanted=1.

[263] Daly, *Kazakhstan's Emerging Middle Class*, p. 73.

[264] Marat Tazhin, "Kazakhstan in a Changing World," speech at U.S.-Kazakhstan Business Association dinner, Washington, D.C., May 8, 2007, http://www.kazakhembus.com/050907.html.

[265] Embassy of Kazakhstan to the USA and Canada, "A New Kazakhstan in a New World: President Nazarbayev's Strategic Vision," *Kazakhstan's Echo*, no. 36 (March 2, 2007), http://www.kazakhembus.com/echo36.html.

factors discouraging foreign investment in Central Asia include the region's limited transportation connections with markets in Europe, America, and Asia as well as an undeveloped and unstable legal foundation that increases foreign investors' uncertainties about the expected return on their capital.

The Astana government encourages Kazakh investors to assist in the development of other Central Asian countries because increasing prosperity could lead their national businesses and consumers to purchase more Kazakh products, decrease the flow of illegal migrants into Kazakhstan, and potentially reduce a source of domestic discontent and political instability. But Kazakh officials also support investment flows to more distant countries, such as those of the South Caucasus, where improvements in transportation and related infrastructure could facilitate the transit of Kazakh goods through these countries and on to European and other international markets. This latter process also helps reduce Kazakhstan's dependence on Soviet-era transportation, communication, and other networks that bind the country's economic activities perhaps uncomfortably closely to Russia.

Regional Commercial Services

Given its pivotal location and region-wide business enterprises, it is only natural that Kazakhstan is emerging as an important linchpin of regional commercial networks. In the communications sector, the state-owned KazTelecom has become a leading Internet service provider throughout Central Asia.[266] Each year, Kazakhstan hosts a Eurasian Media Forum, which helps leading global news and information outlets understand developments within Central Asia and the Caspian region. Hundreds of editors, reporters, policy experts, and business leaders from dozens of countries regularly attend. According to the organizers of this April's session, the forum is "aimed at defining the strategic role of Eurasia in world affairs, exploring a new approach to international relations, promoting equality of access to reliable

---

[266] "Central Asia: OSCE Appeals to Kazakhstan to Restore RFE/RL Website," Radio Free Europe/Radio Liberty, May 22, 2008, http://www.rferl.org/featuresarticle/2008/05/9D3C6B1B-6A99-490C-AE52-16513B333F13.html.

public information throughout the area and encouraging the highest standards of journalism."[267]

In the area of financial services, President Nazarbayev has set the goal of turning Kazakhstan "into the financial centre of the Central Asian region" of 2020.[268] Starting in 1995, the Kazakh government launched a sustained effort to reform the country's banking system in order to meet international commercial standards. Along with the overall growth of the economy, these measures (increasing transparency, adopting internationally recognized accounting methods, etc.) have led to a substantial growth in the country's financial sector. At present, Kazakh banks offer financing and other services to business projects throughout Eurasia. For example, TuranAlem, Kazakhstan's second-largest bank by assets, aims to develop its presence in Armenia, Georgia, and Russia to become the biggest private bank in the CIS by 2010, surpassing Russia's Alfa-Bank.[269]

Kazakh banks are continuing to extend their range of operations as well as their range of services. For instance, Kazakh banks have begun providing Islamic financial products to their clients and are considering offering more in the future. In July 2007, the deputy head of the state agency that regulates Kazakhstan's financial market, Gani Uzbekov, said that discussions with various Muslim companies and countries had led him to hope that Kazakhstan "stands a good chance of becoming a regional center of Islamic banking."[270]

The government took a major step towards realizing its financial objectives by creating the Regional Financial Center of Almaty (RFCA) in February 2006. The RFCA, which officially began operations in October 2007, aspires to become a financial center for greater Central Asia, providing commercial services to clients east of Dubai and west of Hong Kong. The center is

---

[267] "Eurasian Media Forum," http://www.eamedia.org/.

[268] Speech at Otan Party Congress, reproduced in Kazinform, *The Times of Central Asia*, September 11, 2005.

[269] "Kazakh TuranAlem Aims to Become Leading CIS Bank," Reuters, September 27, 2006, http://www.turkishdailynews.com.tr/article.php?enewsid=55124.

[270] Jean-Christophe Peuch, "Central Asia: Governments, Banks Gradually Open Up to Islamic Banking," Radio Free Europe/Radio Liberty, July 13, 2007, http://www.rferl.org/featuresarticle/2007/07/7B16FE17-3F7B-4AB9-A081-4CACDB00FFB1.html.

managed by the Agency for RFCA development, a government body that directly reports to the country's president. The RFCA has introduced special legal and tax regimes to encourage foreign and domestic businesses to establish a presence there.[271]

The Kazakh government has also sought to strengthen the role of independent directors in national companies throughout Eurasia. Recent legislation, for instance, requires that at least one-third of the board members in a joint stock company should be independent. From November 27-28, 2007, Almaty hosted the first Summit of CIS Independent Directors. According to the media, the summit participants discussed "a number of current issues of the development of the institute of independent directors in the Commonwealth of Independent States, share their experience of introduction of the best Western practices in terms of independent directors operation, and hear success stories from Russian and Ukrainian companies."[272]

Kazakhstan's landlocked location has made developing air connections with foreign countries essential for promoting tourism, trade, and other transnational ties. During the Soviet period, travelers could not fly directly from an international location into Kazakhstan. They had to fly first to Moscow or Leningrad (St. Petersburg) and then take a connecting flight to Kazakhstan. Shortly after independence, Kazakhstan Airlines began to operate as the country's national carrier. In 2001, it was superseded as Kazakhstan's flag carrier by Air Astana, a joint venture with 51% owned by the Kazakh government (through Samruk State Holding) and 49% by BAE Systems.

Air Astana has a fleet of modern Western commercial aircraft, employs almost 2,000 employees, and serves 21 international routes as well as 25 domestic locations from its hubs in Almaty, Astana and Atyrau. In August 2005, the industry journal *Airline Business* rated the carrier fourth among the world's 200 leading airlines in terms of the rate of growth of passenger

---

[271] Regional Financial Centre of Almaty City, Dobro Pozhalovat'"
http://www.rfca.kz/.
[272] Embassy of Kazakhstan in the USA and Canada, "First Summit of CIS Independent Directors to be held in Almaty, 27-28 November 2007," Kazakhstan News Bulletin, November 14, 2007, http://www.kazakhembus.com/NB16-111407.html.

volume and total number of kilometers traveled by passengers in 2004.[273] Its revenue rose by over 100% in the first half of 2007.[274] According to its Strategic Business Plan, the airline's fleet will expand from 18 aircraft at present to 63 aircraft in 2022.[275]

In addition, a number of foreign airlines fly to Almaty several times a week from locations in Europe, Asia, and the former USSR.[276] Due to its central location, Almaty International Airport (ALA) is the natural hub for air travel within Central Asia. Besides Air Astana, passenger airlines serving ALA include Altyn Air, Asiana Airways, Atyrau Aue Joly, British Airways, Carat, China Southern Airlines, Imair, Iran Air, Irbis, KLM Royal Dutch Airlines, Kokshetau-Avia, Krasair, Lufthansa German Airlines, Pulkovo Aviation, Semeyavia, Skat, Tochikiston Air, Transaero Airlines, Turkish Airlines, Turkmenistan Airlines, UM Air, Uzbekistan Airways, and Zhezkagan Air. United Parcel Service, Aeroflot Cargo, and Cargolux use ALA to transfer air cargo to, from and around Central Asia.[277]

Culture and Tourism

Kazakh leaders have identified the promotion of tourist, academic, and other cultural ties with foreign countries as important national goals. Not only do such efforts showcase Kazakhstan's achievements in this area, but they also reinforce national pride and, by enhancing mutual understanding, contribute to the development of commercial, scientific, and other links between Kazakhstan and foreign partners.[278] Given Kazakhstan's status as an ethnically and culturally diverse nation, cultural and humanitarian

[273] Air Astana, "About Air Astana," http://www.airastana.com/kaz/gb/history.

[274] Cargonews Asia, "Kazakhstan Carrier Posts Record First Half Growth," Kazakhstan News Bulletin, January 7, 2007, http://www.kazakhembus.com/2NB080807.html.

[275] Embassy of Kazakhstan in the USA and Canada, "The Breakthrough of Kazakh Aviation," Kazakhstan's News Bulletin, January 14, 2008, http://www.kazakhembus.com/NB1-011408.html.

[276] Reuel R. Hanks, *Central Asia: A Global Studies Handbook* (Santa Barbara: ABC-CLIO, 2005), p. 201.

[277] Almaty International Airport, "Almaty International Airport Meets New Aircrafts," September 4, 2007.

[278] G. G. Rakhmatulina, "Economic Integration in the Framework of the EEC and SCO—The Most Important Priority of the Foreign Policy of Kazakhstan," Kazakhstan Institute of Strategic Studies, June 2007, http://www.kisi.kz/site.html?id=1509.

cooperation also helps counter what the former Secretary of the Kazakh Security Council, Marat Tazhin, called "the whole gloomy prognosis on the future of Eurasia," which Tazhin observed "is postulated on the inevitability of the conflict of cultures and civilizations."[279] The population of Kazakhstan includes over a hundred different ethnic groups. Many of these enjoy cultural ties with co-ethnics in other Eurasian countries.

The government's commitment to developing Kazakhstan's tourism potential became evident earlier this year when the Ministry of Tourism and Sports announced it would spend $2.5 billion to develop 24 priority infrastructure projects.[280] Some of this construction relates to preparing Kazakhstan to host the 7th Asian Winter Games in Almaty in 2011. In addition, at Nazarbayev's initiative, the Kazakh government has organized widely attended meetings of the leaders of the world and traditional religions. The first Congress of World and Traditional Religions occurred in Astana in September 2003 and the second in September 2006. Kazakhstan will host the third congress in 2009. In addition to affirming Kazakhstan's commitment to cultural and sectarian diversity, hosting these congresses boosts the country's international profile.[281]

Kazakhstan encourages tourism and cultural exchanges with other former Soviet republics by maintaining a visa-free tourist regime within the CIS. The government has also negotiated special arrangements with neighboring states. For example, Kazakhstan and Kyrgyzstan signed an agreement in 2007 that involves the mutual recognition of tourist visas in adjacent regions of the two countries for nationals of third countries—permitting, for example, Western tourists to visit the Lake Issyk Kul region of Kyrgyzstan without a visa.[282] Kazakh authorities have also relaxed the visa requirements for short-

---

[279] Yuri Kozlov, Interview with Secretary of Kazakhstan's Security Council Marat Tazhin, *Nazavisimaya Gazeta*, March 16, 2000, p. 5.
[280] Embassy of Kazakhstan in the USA and Canada, "Kazkhstan to Spend $2.5 bl on Tourism Infrastructure Projects," Kazakhstan News Bulletin, January 23, 2008, http://www.kazakhembus.com/NB1-012308.html.
[281] Ministry of Foreign Affairs of Kazakhstan, "Aktual'nye Voprosy Vneshney Politiki Kazakhstana S'ezd Liderov Mirovyx I Traditsionnyx Religii," http://portal.mfa.kz/portal/page/portal/mfa/ru/content/policy/issues/congress.
[282] Embassy of Kazakhstan to USA and Canada, "Nazarbayev Visits Bishkek, Pledges Economic Investment," Kazakhstan News Bulletin, April 26, 2007, http://www.kazakhembus.com/042607.html.

term (under 90 days) tourists and business visitors from Western countries. Kazakhstan's popularity as a tourist destination increased substantially following the extraordinary success of the film, *Borat: Cultural Learnings of America for Make Benefit Glorious Nation of Kazakhstan*, and the skillful way in which the Kazakh tourist industry has transformed what could have been a cultural disaster into a tourism bonanza.[283] Although not its primary purpose, the Kazakh government's policy of sustaining Russian, still widely used in the other Soviet republics as well, as the language of interethnic communication among Kazakhs, as well as the policy of promoting knowledge of English as the language of international commerce has also facilitated cultural exchange and tourism with non-Kazakh speakers.

For various reasons, the number of people traveling to Kazakhstan as tourists from other Eurasian countries, and vice-versa, is small. According to government figures, the most popular outbound destinations for Kazakhstan's 3.0 million tourists were Russia (1,654,616 tourists), China (84,963), Turkey (60,802), Germany (50,965), United Arab Emirates (22,894), the Netherlands (16,352), Austria (10,811), and the United Kingdom (6,563). In terms of the 3.3 million foreign tourists who visited Kazakhstan in 2005, the Russian Foundation again provided about half the total (1,696,691 tourists), followed by tourists from Germany (72,529), China (76,806), Turkey (42,064), the United Kingdom (16,530), the United States (19,513), and South Korea (9,311).[284] Although Western tourists still come to Kazakhstan far less than visitors from Russia, they probably spend more per capita, especially when they combine their private excursion with a business trip, helping to sustain the boom in luxury hotels seen in Astana and a few other cities in the last few years.

Kyrgyzstan's scenic Lake Issyk Kul district is probably the most popular foreign destination in Central Asia for Kazakh tourists. But this case well illustrates a major factor decreasing tourist flows within Central Asia: inadequate transportation networks. Although Issyk Kul is located only 50

---

[283] Dan Mangan, "Kazakh Tourism's 'Borat Boom'," *New York Post*, December 4, 2006, http://www.nypost.com/seven/12042006/news/nationalnews/kazakh_tourisms_borat_boom_nationalnews_dan_mangan.htm.
[284] Embassy of Kazakhstan to the United Kingdom, "The Market for Tourism, Hospitality and Recreational Services in Kazakhstan," http://www.kazakhstanembassy.org.uk/cgi-bin/index/266.

miles from Almaty, the city's 1.5 million residents (and potential tourists) must travel 300 miles along a circuitous mountain road to reach the vacation spot.[285]

Kazakhstan has some of the leading academic institutions in Central Asia. The Lev N. Gumilev Eurasianist University in Astana has the explicit mission of teaching and researching subjects relating to Eurasia.[286] It sponsors conferences on pan-Eurasia topics that engage scholars from neighboring countries. Kazakhstan's educational institutions, as well as the Kazakh government, also support academic exchanges programs with foreign countries. These enable Kazakh students and scholars to study at foreign institutions as well as support Kazakh institutions seeking to host foreign visitors on short- or long-range exchange programs. The well-known Bolashak (Future) international scholarship program presently permits some 3,000 Kazakh students to win competitive fellowships to study abroad, though they typically enroll in American and European universities to take courses in engineering, science, and technical subjects. While the improving quality of Kazakhstan's own higher education institutions, including those run on a fee-paying basis, probably decreases interest among young Kazakhs in studying in other Central Asian or Caspian institutions, it does make study in Kazakhstan more attractive to potential students from other Eurasian countries.

---

[285] Embassy of Kazakhstan to USA and Canada, "Kazakhstan is Kyrgyzstan's Largest Investor, Plans More Provided Political Stability Is There," Kazakhstan News Bulletin, March 9, 2007, http://www.kazakhembus.com/030907.html.
[286] Marlene Laruelle, *Russia's Central Asia Policy and the Role of Russian Nationalism* (Washington, D.C.: Central Asia-Caucasus Institute, April 2008), pp. 55-56.

Key Bilateral Relationships

This section presents a third perspective on Kazakhstan's role in Eurasia's evolving international system. Whereas the first section examines the most important international institutions shaping regional politics, and the next two chapters employ a functional approach to the main security and economic factors affecting Kazakhstan's neighborhood, this chapter examines each of Kazakhstan's most important bilateral ties in Eurasia as a discrete relationship. The intent is to consider how some of the broader issues discussed previously manifest themselves with each country.

Major Powers

China

For centuries, Kazakh leaders perceived China as their main security threat, inducing them to ally with Russia as a great power balancer.[287] During the Cold War, Kazakhstan served as a forward base for potential Soviet military operations against China. After the USSR's collapse, the initial focus of Astana and Beijing, after establishing diplomatic relations in 1992, was to delineate their new 1,782-km common border. They progressively resolved their frontier differences in their joint communiqué of November 23, 1999, their bilateral protocol on border demarcation on May 10, 2002, and their comprehensive border agreement of December 20, 2006. The two governments also signed a bilateral accord to govern the use and protection of their cross-border rivers on September 12, 2001.[288]

---

[287] Shireen T. Hunter, *Central Asia Since Independence* (Washington, DC: Praeger, 1996), pp. 124-125.

[288] Embassy of Kazakhstan in China, "Relations between China and Kazakhstan," http://www.kazembchina.org/create/bike/home.jsp?tablename=itemcontent&iiid=738 6256821857348225&tableFlag=itemtable.

Excluding Russia, Kazakhstan has now become China's most important strategic and economic partner in Central Asia. In 2002, the Kazakh and Chinese governments signed a "Good Neighbor Treaty of Friendship and Cooperation," an "Agreement on Cooperation Against Terrorism, Separatism, and Extremism" and an "Agreement Between the Chinese Government and the Kazakhstani Government on Preventing Dangerous Military Activities."[289] In May 2004, the two countries established a China-Kazakhstan Cooperation Committee, which has served as a major governmental mechanism for developing their bilateral relationship. It includes ten specialized sub-committees consisting of policy makers and technical experts from both governments. For example, the Economic and Trade Cooperation Sub-Committee seeks both to increase the overall volume of trade between the two countries and rebalance the exchange to counter Kazakhstan's growing trade deficit. The bilateral Cooperation Committee also supervises the work of the Cross-Border Rivers Joint Committee, an important group given the tensions that have arisen over water rights and water management between both countries. The Kazakh and Chinese presidents typically meet several times a year in bilateral and multilateral gatherings; other senior government officials often meet more frequently.[290]

A major Chinese concern in relations with Kazakhstan is securing Astana's support for Beijing's efforts to curb "separatism" among China's Uighur population. About 180,000 Uighurs reside in eastern Kazakhstan. In addition, some one million ethnic Kazakhs live in China, especially in Xinjiang.[291] The Chinese government has long been concerned about Muslim-inspired ethnic separatism in the Xinjiang Uighur Autonomous Region, an area constituting one-sixth the land area of China that contains the world's fourth largest concentration of Turkic peoples (after Turkey, Iran, and Uzbekistan), effectively requiring analysts "to view China not as a neighbor of Central

---

[289] Eugene Rumer, Dmitri Trenin, and Huasheng Zhao, *Central Asia: Views from Washington, Moscow and Beijing*, (London: M.E. Sharpe, 2007), pp. 170-172.
[290] Embassy of Kazakhstan in China, "Relations between China and Kazakhstan," http://www.kazembchina.org/create/bike/home.jsp?tablename=itemcontent&iiid=738 6256821857348225&tableFlag=itemtable.
[291] Cummings, *Kazakhstan: Centre-Periphery* Relations, p. 35; and Nichol, "Kazakhstan: Current Developments and U.S. Interests," p. 3..

Asia but as a part of Central Asia".[292] Of the region's twenty million inhabitants, approximately half are non-Han Chinese Muslims with ethnic and religious links to neighboring Turkic populations in Central Asia, especially Kazakhstan and Kyrgyzstan. Xinjiang adjoins Afghanistan, Pakistan, and several Central Asian countries. Many of its local Muslims, like the Buddhists of Tibet, oppose the continuing influx of Han Chinese into their traditional homeland, which enjoyed de facto independence before 1949, when Beijing incorporated Xinjiang into China. Although their economic standards of living have improved under Chinese rule, many perceive that Beijing discriminates against them.

Some Uighurs have responded to the Chinese presence by joining anti-Beijing groups, most prominently the East Turkestan Islamic Movement. The United Nations, the U.S. government, and other bodies list the movement as a terrorist group. Some of its members have employed violence against Chinese civilians in their campaign to secure Xinjiang's independence. Chinese officials accuse the organization of collaborating with al-Qaeda and, more recently, the Dalai Lama.[293]

The Chinese government has employed primarily diplomatic initiatives and direct security assistance to bolster Central Asian governments against domestic threats as well as induce them to crack down on East Turkestan activists. Chinese pressure forced the dissolution of the independent associations of Uighurs that had existed in Kazakhstan as well as the closure of the Institute of Uighur Studies that had been based at the Institute of Oriental Studies in Almaty.[294] By 2004, Beijing had signed bilateral counter-terrorism agreements with all four of its Central Asian neighbors. They include provisions for joint law enforcement operations, bilateral police

---

[292] Graham E. Fuller and S. Frederick Starr, *The Xinjiang Problem* (Washington, D.C.: Central Asia-Caucasus Institute, 2004), p. 10; italics deleted.
[293] Chris Buckley, "Chinese Anger and Terror Warnings Cloud Olympics," Reuters, April 12, 2008,
http://uk.reuters.com/article/topNews/idUKPEK20364920080411?feedType=RSS&fee dName=topNews.
[294] Sebastien Peyrouse, *The Economic Aspects of Chinese-Central Asia Rapprochement* (Washington, D.C.: Central Asia-Caucasus Institute & Silk Road Studies Program, 2007), p. 12.

training, and enhanced intelligence sharing.[295] To bolster ties with these governments as well as enhance their counterterrorist capabilities, Beijing has also supplied Central Asian governments with defense equipment, military training, and intelligence information regarding terrorist threats. The National Security Committee of Kazakhstan and the Public Security Ministry of China regularly conduct joint anti-terrorist exercises in border regions. Kazakh and Chinese law enforcement agencies also collaborate against trafficking in narcotics and weapons. China's defense academies now enroll Kazakh military personnel in their classes.[296]

Kazakhs and other Central Asians often sympathize with the Uighurs' separatist aspirations, especially since Uighur activists may have been inspired by the Central Asians' own successful drives for independence and share the same Muslim faith as do many Central Asians. Nevertheless, Kazakhstan and other Central Asian governments, while allowing Uighurs to practice limited degrees of political activity, do not permit Uighurs to engage in unauthorized activities in China and have deported Uighurs accused of terrorism by the Chinese.[297]

In line with Chinese preferences, Central Asian governments also regularly profess solidarity with Beijing's counterterrorist concerns. For example, when Chinese President Hu Jintao visited Astana in June 2004, the two governments issued a joint declaration that stated: "The two sides are determined to continue to take effective measures and work together in cracking down on all forms of terrorism, including the terrorist force of the 'Eastern Turkestan Islamic Movement' in order to safeguard the peace and stability in the two countries and this part of the world." In addition, the communiqué affirmed that, "The two sides maintain that the crackdown on

---

[295] "Chinese Parliament Okays Anti-Terrorism Pact with Neighbours," Press Trust of India, October 28, 2004. For a review of how Kazakhstan has tried to meet Beijing's concerns regarding Xingjian (and Taiwan), see Marat Yermukanov, "Chinese Conundrum of Kazakhstan's Multi-Vector Policy," *Central Asia-Caucasus Analyst*, July 13, 2005, http://www.cacianalyst.org/view_article.php?articleid=3463.

[296] "China-Kazakhstan Relations Grow Stronger," *China Daily*, October 15, 2007.

[297] Kathleen Moore, "Central Asia: China's Mounting Influence, Part 4—Facing Militant Threats," Radio Free Europe/Radio Liberty, November 18, 2004, http://www.rferl.org/featuresarticle/2004/11/d541f15b-c660-4310-8afd-33c787f5ecae.html.

the terrorist force of the 'East Turkestan Islamic Movement' is an important part of the international fight against terrorism."[298]

Joint Kazakh-Chinese declarations also normally include a clause affirming the mainland's position regarding Taiwan—that Beijing is the only legitimate government of China and that Taiwan is an inseparable part of Chinese territory. The communiqué issued when Hu visited Astana in August 2007, for instance, states that, "On the Taiwan issue, the Kazakh government reiterated its steadfastness in upholding the one-China policy and throws its support behind China for all efforts it has made to realize national reunification, recognizing that the Taiwan issue is China's internal affair." [299] When Taiwan held a referendum on March 22, 2008 on Taiwan's joining the United Nations as a separate country, the Kazakh Ministry of Foreign Affairs declared Astana's opposition to Taiwan's independence aspirations and any attempt to create "two Chinas."[300]

During the past year, as various international groups have called on foreign government leaders to boycott the Beijing Olympics, or at least the opening ceremonies, to signal disproval of China's policies regarding Darfur, Tibet, or other issues, the Chinese government has sought to solicit their endorsement of Beijing's management of the Olympics. The governments of Central Asia, including Kazakhstan, have normally obliged. After Kazakh Prime Minister Karim Masimov met with Chinese Premier Wen Jiabao in April 2008, they issued a communiqué declaring that, "Kazakhstan supports China's efforts in the preparations of the Beijing Olympics and will enhance coordination with China on strengthening the Olympic security work to ensure the successful and smooth holding of the Beijing Olympics."[301]

---

[298] "Chinese, Kazakh Leaders Issue Joint Declaration," BBC Monitoring, June 4, 2003.
[299] "China, Kazakhstan Sign Joint Communiqué on Promoting Relations, Trade," Xinhua, August 18, 2007, http://news.xinhuanet.com/english/2007-08/18/content_6561247.htm.

[300] Ministry of Foreign Affairs of Kazakhstan, "Zayavlenie MID Respubliki Kazakhstan po Vstupleniyu Tayvanya v OON," March 25, 2008, http://portal.mfa.kz/portal/page/portal/mfa/ru/content/press/statement/2008.
[301] "Kazakhstan Supports China on Beijing Olympics, Taiwan Issues: Joint Communiqué," Xinhua, April 12, 2008, http://english.cri.cn/2946/2008/04/12/48@345120.htm.

The long border and overlapping ethnic groups between the two countries has also encouraged cultural and commercial ties between Kazakhstan and China. As one Chinese scholar observed, "Kazakhstan represents a type of connecting bridge between the states of Central Asia and China on the Eurasian continent. That is why once Chinese-Kazakhstan free economic zone will be created; it must become such an element that will push forward the creation of free trade zone of the SCO."[302] Although it took years to overcome the legacy of the Sino-Soviet confrontation, when trade between Kazakhstan and China was minimal due to the defense and security barriers along the Sino-Soviet border, Kazakhstan has become by far China's largest economic partner in Central Asia. Of the $8.7 billion in total trade between China and Central Asia in 2005, approximately $7 billion involved Kazakhstan, making Kazakhstan the second-largest trading partner of China among the CIS members.[303] (Precise figures are difficult to establish since the Kazak and Chinese governments report widely divergent totals, which results from underreporting and other distortions due to efforts to minimize customs and other payments.) In late 2007, the Kazak Ministry of Transportation offered for consideration the possible construction of a railway that would connect China with the Caspian port of Aktau, which could allow Chinese goods to travel overland from the Caspian to European markets.[304]

Chinese officials have been especially eager to enhance commerce between their country's relatively impoverished northwestern regions and their Central Asian neighbors. This consideration applies particularly to restless Xinjiang since over half the province's income derives from trade with Central Asian countries, with Kazakhstan being Xinjiang's largest foreign trading partner.[305] Trade across China's other borders with Central Asia also

---

[302] Lu Gang, "Creation of a Free Trade Zone in the Framework of the SCO: Importance in Advancing Chinese-Kazakhstan Cooperation," Kazakhstan Institute of Strategic Studies, September 26, 2006, http://www.kisi.kz/site.html?id=1434.

[303] Rumer, Trenin, and Zhao, *Central Asia: Views from Washington, Moscow and Beijing*, p. 171.

[304] Sergei Blagov, "Russia Urges Formation of Central Asian Energy Club," Eurasia Insight, November 7, 2007, http://www.eurasianet.org/departments/insight/articles/eav110707a.shtml.

[305] Zhao Huaheng, "China, Russia, and the United States: Prospects for Cooperation in Central Asia," *CEF Quarterly: The Journal of the China-Eurasia Forum* (February 2005), p.

has been increasing since Beijing began opening China's western border after 1985, albeit starting from very low levels. The Chinese government has granted hundreds of millions of dollars in credits to the Central Asian countries for the purchase of Chinese goods. In 2006, according to Kazakh figures, official bilateral trade between Kazakhstan and China amounted to $8.36 billion, a 22.8% increase over the previous year.[306] In addition, the underground shuttle trade between Kazakhs and Chinese merchants, which evades taxation, amounts to several more billion dollars.[307] The two governments now aim to increase their bilateral trade volume to $15 billion by 2015.[308] If current trends continue, the volume of Kazakhstan's trade with China will exceed that with Russia for the first time in centuries. Increased commerce could help promote the economic development of Xinjiang, Tibet, and other regions that have lagged behind China's vibrant eastern cities. Although trade with Central Asia represents less than one percent of China's overall foreign trade, it will likely continue to play a more important role for western China due to their geographic and other links with the region.

The Chinese government has also sought to increase its economic ties with Kazakhstan and other countries in Greater Central Asia because they see this region as an important source of raw materials, especially oil and natural gas. Chinese policy makers are uneasy about relying so heavily on vulnerable Persian Gulf energy sources. Gulf oil shipments traverse sea lanes susceptible to interception by the U.S. or other navies. In addition, the Chinese government recognizes that terrorism, military conflicts, and other sources of instability in the Middle East could abruptly disrupt Gulf energy exports. Since Chinese efforts to import much additional oil and gas from Russia have

---

24,
http://www.silkroadstudies.org/new/docs/CEF/CEF_Quarterly_Winter_2005.doc.pdf; and Peyrouse, p. 16..
[306] Embassy of Kazakhstan to the USA and Canada, "Chinese President Visits Kazakhstan, Signs Important Agreements," Kazkahstan's News Bulletin, August 20, 2007, http://www.kazakhembus.com/NB4-200807.html.
[307] S. Frederick Starr, "Introduction," in S. Frederick Starr, ed., *The New Silk Roads: Transport and Trade in Greater Central Asia* (Washington, D.C.: Central Asia-Caucasus Institute, 2007), p. 14.
[308] "China, Kazakhstan to Strengthen Extensive Co-op in Economic, Energy, Environment, Cultural Sectors," Xinhua, April 12, 2008, http://news.xinhuanet.com/english/2008-04/12/content_7966399.htm.

proven problematic, Beijing has strongly pushed for the development of land-based oil and gas pipelines that would direct Central Asian energy resources eastwards towards China. The new inland routes would provide more secure energy supplies to China than existing seaborne links. These burgeoning energy ties have also made avoiding political instability in these countries a concern of Chinese policy makers.

Beijing's cultivation of energy ties with Kazakhstan has been making steady progress. While retaining a strong presence in Pakistan, Chinese firms have been increasing their investments in new South and Central Asian markets, especially in India and Kazakhstan. The Chinese government has been helping finance the development of roads, ports, and energy pipelines linking South and Central Asia to China because significantly increasing Chinese economic intercourse with these regions will require major improvements in the capacity and security of east-west transportation links. Over the past decade, two countries have been establishing the core infrastructure required by their expanding economic ties—creating border posts, energy pipelines, and roads and railways that have converted the informal shuttle trade that arose in the 1980s to a large-scale, professional economic relationship.[309]

Yet, much additional progress is needed in this area to achieve the higher levels of bilateral commerce sought in both Astana and Beijing. When Kazakh Prime Minister Karim Masimov met with Chinese Premier Wen Jiabao on April 9, 2008, he stressed Kazakhstan's commitment to enhancing bilateral commerce through infrastructure development, specifically citing the need to improve Kazakhstan's ports, customs and banking systems, railways, highways and other commercial networks involving China.[310] In addition to the underdeveloped economic infrastructure connecting the two sides, other impediments to expanded commercial exchanges include unsupportive visa policies, special regulations on Chinese consumer products, corrupt commercial practices in both countries, and Kazakhstan's non-membership in the WTO. (Ironically, one factor working against Kazakhstan's rapid entry into the WTO has been Kazakhs' concerns about

---

[309] Peyrouse, *Economic Aspects of Chinese-Central Asia Rapprochement*, pp. 10ff.
[310] Ministry of Foreign Affairs of China, "Premier Wen Jiabao Holds Talks with Kazakh Prime Minister Masimov," April 9, 2008, http://www.chinaconsulatesf.org/eng/xw/t423831.htm.

having their national industries devastated by Chinese competition in the absence of protective barriers—as happened with neighboring Kyrgyzstan).

China has imported Kazakh oil via railroad for a decade. In addition, hydropower plants in China supply about 20 percent of Kazakhstan's electricity consumption.[311] Western firms were initially able to block the efforts by Chinese energy companies to join Kazakhstan's largest oil and gas projects.[312] But energy cooperation has accelerated in recent years after the Kazakh government fully committed to directing a share of its energy exports eastward to China. In July 2005, Chinese President Hu Jintao signed a declaration of strategic partnership with Nazarbayev that, among other things, provided for expedited development of the 1,300-km Atasu-Alashankou pipeline to transport at least ten million tons of oil annually from Kazakhstan's Caspian coast to China's Xinjiang province.[313] This 50-50 joint venture between the Chinese National Petroleum Corporation (CNCP) and KazMunaiGaz began operating on a limited basis in December 2005, marking the first eastward flow of Central Asian oil and China's first use of a pipeline to import oil. In August 2007, the CNPC signed an agreement with KazMunaiGaz to extend the Atasu-Alashankou pipeline 700km westward, linking China directly to Kazakhstan's Caspian fields.[314] The CNCP has also acquired a substantial stake in a new natural gas field in western Kazakhstan. Chinese oil firms operate four oil fields in the country, and in 2005 purchased Petrokazakhstan, a leading Kazakh energy firm. Sinopec, CNPC, and other Chinese energy firms produce about 13 million tons of oil annually in Kazakhstan.[315] Beijing views Kazakhstan's cooperation with China on energy

---

[311] Ian Pryde, "Another Big Player for a Neighbor," Eurasia Insight, March 23, 2006, http://www.eurasianet.org/departments/business/articles/pp032306.shtml
[312] "New Rebuff for China on Kazakh Oil," *New York Times*, May 17, 2003, http://query.nytimes.com/gst/fullpage.html?res=9B05E0DD143EF934A25756C0A9659C8B63.
[313] "Courting Kazakhstan," Eurasia Security Watch, July 7, 2005, http://www.afpc.org/esw/esw93.shtml.
[314] XFN-ASIA, "China, Kazakhstan Agree on Sino-Kazakh Oil Pipeline Extension to Caspian Sea," Kazakhstan's News Bulletin, August 20, 2007, http://www.kazakhembus.com/NB4-200807.html.
[315] Zheng Lifei, "China, Kazakhstan Build on a Solid Foundation," *China Daily*, October 15, 2007, http://french.10thnpc.org.cn/english/international/228117.htm.

imports as an important contribution toward realizing its goal of becoming less dependent on Middle East oil supplies.[316]

Although many Kazakhs welcome China's increasing involvement in their economy, especially as a supplier of cheap consumer goods and a potential market for Kazakh products, they also fear Chinese long-term ambitions in their country. A widespread worry is that demographic imbalances—Kazakhstan has the lowest population density in Central Asia—could entice Chinese immigration that would eventually lead to China's de facto annexations of Kazakh territory. A related anxiety is that China's growing wealth will result in Chinese ownership of important sectors of Kazakhstan's economy.[317] These concerns became most evident in 1999, when the media criticized the decision by the national legislature to ratify what many Kazakhs deemed as excessively generous concessions to Beijing regarding where to demarcate the China-Kazakhstan border. Popular concerns about "peaceful Sinification" of Kazakhstan's under-populated regions compelled Kazakh authorities to re-impose visa requirements on Chinese nationals seeking to enter Kazakhstan. More recently, Kazakhs have complained about China's excessive consumption and unilateral management of transborder water resources.[318] Concerns also have arisen in Kazakhstan about the growing imbalance in Sino-Kazakh trade—with Kazakhs urging the Chinese to buy (and help develop) Kazakhstan's non-resource sectors.

The continuing attractiveness of Russian culture and the Russian language has also limited Chinese influence in Kazakhstan. Although some 3,000 Kazakh students are studying in Chinese universities and colleges, the number of Chinese speakers in Kazakhstan is miniscule compared to the many Kazakhs who are fluent in Russian.[319] It was only on May 29, 2008, that

---

[316] "China-Kazakhstan Pipeline Starts to Pump Oil," *China Daily*, December 15, 2005, http://www.chinadaily.com.cn/english/doc/2005-12/15/content_503709.htm.
[317] "The Economic Crusaders," Asiamoney, September 7, 2006, http://www.asiamoney.com/default.asp?Page=7&PUBID=185&ISS=22460&SID=64955 2&SM=ALL&SearchStr=The%20Economic%20Crusaders.
[318] Sebastien Peyrouse, "Flowing Downstream: The Sino-Kazakh Water Dispute," *China Brief*, May 16, 2007, http://www.jamestown.org/china_brief/article.php?articleid=2373402
[319] Zheng Lifei, "China, Kazakhstan Build on a Solid Foundation," *China Daily*, October 15, 2007, http://french.10thnpc.org.cn/english/international/228117.htm.

the first direct passenger train, which will make one run every week, began operating between Astana and Urumqi Railway Station. The 1,898-km route takes 37 hours to travel.[320] Even so, as Nazarbayev himself observed about China in his March 2006 annual address to the Kazakh parliament and nation, "There is no alternative to mutually advantageous ties with that dynamically developing country."

Russia

At independence, two factors made Kazakhstan's relationship with Russia unique among the Central Asian states. First, the country had the largest percentage of ethnic Russians among the former Soviet republics. Second, Kazakhstan was the only Central Asian country that shared a lengthy frontier with the new Russian Federation.

Many observers believed that the disintegration of the Soviet Union could be followed by the division of Kazakhstan along ethnic lines, with the Slavic-dominated provinces of northern Kazakhstan seeking to join the Russian Federation, with which they enjoyed deep economic as well as ethnic ties. Some Russian nationalists—most notably Aleksandr Solzhenitsyn in his 1990 publication, *Rebuilding Russia*—explicitly argued in favor of Russia incorporating northern Kazakhstan, with its large ethnic Russian population and relatively prosperous economy, into the Russian Federation. The initial electoral strength of Russian nationalist Vladimir Zhirinovsky (whom Kazakh authorities eventually banned from visiting their territory) in post-Soviet Russia stimulated some support among Kazakhstan's ethnic Russians to join the Russian Federation. They had experienced declining living standards, deteriorating education opportunities, restrictions on their political activities, and limits on employment in certain key government and business sectors. Some of these trends began in the late Soviet period, while others affected all Kazakh citizens regardless of nationality due to the deteriorating economic conditions after independence. The end result, however, was to generate considerable ethnic Russian dissatisfaction with their status in newly independent Kazakhstan and a sharp increase in their emigration from

---

[320] "New Passenger Rail between China and Kazakhstan Opens," People's Daily Online, May 30, 2008, http://english.people.com.cn/90001/90776/90882/6421620.html.

the country. As a result, Kazakhstan's population decreased considerably between 1989 and 1999, leading to shortages of skilled personnel in some economic sectors.[321]

Several factors prevented an even larger movement of ethnic Russians from Kazakhstan to Russia. The political and economic chaos that characterized Yeltsin's Russia did not make that country an especially attractive new home. Within Kazakhstan, the government strove to assuage the anxieties of ethnic Russians and other national minorities even while advancing the social, economic, and political status of ethnic Kazakhs. In addition, the Russian governments under both Yeltsin and Putin rendered little practical assistance to ethnic Russians in Kazakhstan seeking to move to Russia.[322] Despite a desire to sustain the size of Russia's ethnic Slav population and concerns that Central Asian governments discriminated against their Russian co-nationals in seeking to advance the status of the republics' titular nationalities, Russian leaders have actively discouraged ethnic Russian separatism or irredentism in Kazakhstan or the other Central Asian states. The May 1992 bilateral treaty of friendship, cooperation, and mutual aid helped stabilize the situation by confirming Kazakhstan's territorial integrity while still allowing for extensive ties between border communities across their shared frontiers.[323] Many Kazakh citizens, including non-Russian ethnics, desired to maintain close economic, cultural, and other ties with Russia. Conversely, the departure of many of the most alienated ethnic Russians served as a safety valve by removing potential regime opponents and weakening Russian independent groups in Kazakhstan. The end result of all these factors was a de-politization of most of the four million ethnic Russians who chose to remain in Kazakhstan.[324]

---

[321] Kazakhstan's ethnic problems during the 1990s are reviewed in Martha B. Olcott, *Kazakhstan: Unfulfilled Promise* (Washington, D.C.: Carnegie Endowment for International Peace, 2002), pp. 51-86.

[322] Nonna Chernyakove and Russell Working, "Hurry Up and Wait," *Moscow Times*, November 30, 2001.

[323] Cummings, *Kazakhstan: Centre-Periphery Relations*, pp. 34-35.

[324] For a detailed discussion of these factors see Sebastien Peyrouse, "Nationhood and the Minority Question in Central Asia: The Russians in Kazakhstan," *Eurasia-Asia Studies*, vol. 59, no. 3 (May 2007), pp. 481-501; and Sebastien Peyrouse, "The Russian Minority in Central Asia: Migration, Politics, and Language," Occasional Paper no. 297 (Washington, D.C.: Woodrow Wilson International Center for Scholars, 2007).

Under Vladimir Putin, who became Russia's prime minister in late 1999 and president in early 2000, the Russian government has continued Yeltsin's policy of supporting Kazakhstan's preservation as an independent state. Yet, Putin has made restoring Moscow's influence in Central Asia more of a priority than his predecessor. In his April 2005 state-of-the-nation address, Putin described the collapse of the USSR as the "greatest geopolitical catastrophe" of the 20th century.[325] Under Putin, Russian officials strove to ensure that Russian firms participate in developing the region's energy resources and that Central Asian oil and gas exporters continue to use Russian pipelines.[326] With Russian government assistance, state-controlled companies such as Gazprom, Lukoil, Rosneft, and Unified Energy System of Russia have substantially expanded their presence in Kazakhstan's energy sector since 2003.[327] Russian negotiators have sought to secure a durable presence in the Central Asian energy market by securing preferential long-term sale agreements for Russian energy companies. Thanks to the legacy of the integrated Soviet economy, Central Asia's landlocked states continue to rely heavily on transportation, communications, supply-chains, and other networks that either traverse Russia or fall under Russian control. Russian officials have also waged a low-keyed but effective campaign to limit American, Chinese, and other foreign economic competition in Kazakhstan and the neighboring Central Asian countries.

From Moscow's perspective, Kazakhstan's foreign and domestic policies have proven much less problematic for Russia than that of many other former Soviet republics. Since independence, Russia has remained Kazakhstan's most important economic partner, especially for Kazakh energy exports, which are still heavily dependent on Russian-controlled pipelines first constructed during the Soviet period (such as the Central Asia-Centre pipeline, which carries all of Kazakhstan's gas exports).[328] In March 2000, then Secretary of the Kazakh Security Council, Marat Tazhin, nicely characterized the attitude

---

[325] "Putin Deplores Collapse of USSR," BBC News, April 25, 2005,
http://news.bbc.co.uk/2/hi/europe/4480745.stm.
[326] Martha B. Olcott, *Kazakhstan: Unfulfilled Promise* (Washington, D.C.: Carnegie Endowment for International Peace, 2002), p. 323.
[327] Marlene Laruelle, *Russia's Central Asia Policy and the Role of Russian Nationalism* (Washington, D.C.: Central Asia-Caucasus Institute, April 2008), pp. 22-24.
[328] *Ibid.*, p. 24.

of many Kazakh leaders when he stated in an interview with the Russian newspaper *Nezavisimaya Gazeta*, "I am a supporter of simple truths: one does not choose one's neighbors; they are from God."[329]

The Russian-Kazakh frontier represents the world's longest continuous land borders at over 7,000 kilometers. During the Soviet period, ethnic Russians and ethnic Kazakhs sprawled across either side of the then largely meaningless administrative borders separating the two republics, which were highly integrated as economic entities. The transformation of these administrative boundaries into national frontiers almost overnight in 1991 created real problems for the communities on either side. In addition, the issue of border security arose as the Russian authorities were torn between wanting to allow ethnic Russians in Kazakhstan easy access to their relatives that happened to have found themselves north of the boundary after 1991 while also desiring to prevent the entry of terrorists, illegal migrants, and other undesirable aliens across the virtually unmonitored frontier.[330] The Kazakh and Russian governments also found it difficult to monitor cross-frontier trade or collect customs duties on even legitimate commerce given the length of the border and its many possible crossing points. Further problems arose concerning dual taxation, the lack of uniform railroad freight tariffs, the exploitation of transborder mineral deposits, and the environmental protection of trans-border rivers.[331]

On the whole, the parties have managed this problematic situation well. On January 17, 2005, Nazarbayev and Putin signed a comprehensive border delimitation agreement that, while still not satisfying all Russian and Kazakh nationalists, nevertheless has settled the issue at the governmental level.[332]

---

[329] Yuri Kozlov, Interview with Secretary of Kazakhstan's Security Council Marat Tazhin, *Nazavisimaya Gazeta*, March 16, 2000, p. 5.

[330] Marat Yermukanov, "Kazakh Foreign Ministry Refutes Arguments About Territorial Concessions," Eurasia Daily Monitor, August 10, 2005, http://www.jamestown.org/publications_details.php?volume_id=407&issue_id=3432&article_id=2370131; and Dmitri Trenin, "Southern Watch: Russia's Policy in Central Asia," *Journal of International Affairs*, vol. 56, no. 2 (Spring 2003), p. 126.

[331] Iu. V. Levashov, "Prospects for the Development of Transborder Cooperation Between the Russian Federation and the Republic of Kazakhstan," *Problems of Economic Transition*, vol. 47, no. 12 (April 2005), pp. 56-57.

[332] Marat Yermukanov, "Russian-Kazakh Border Agreement Sparks Nationalist Reaction," Eurasia Daily Monitor January 27, 2005,

The two governments have established a bilateral commission to manage the more than 70 rivers and 20 lakes that traverse their common boundary.[333] Each year, the heads of the frontier regions of the Russian Federation and Kazakhstan meet to discuss mutual concerns. From Kazakhstan's perspective, the main issue now is the failure of the Russian border authorities to match Kazakhstan's efforts to develop an integrated commercial and transportation infrastructure to facilitate cross-boundary commercial exchanges—an issue Nazarbayev raised during the October 2007 Russian-Kazakh border regions summit with Putin.[334]

More generally, Kazakh officials have sought not to antagonize Moscow as they have cultivated ties with other countries. They normally take care to emphasize the positive dimensions of the mixed cooperative-competitive energy relationship between Kazakhstan and Russia. Although both countries sell oil to European and Chinese consumers, Nazarbayev insists that he sees Kazakhstan and Russia as energy partners, not competitors. Even though Kazakh officials have continued to express interest in these undersea pipelines, and have relied heavily on Western energy firms to provide the technologies to exploit Kazakhstan's vast but difficult-to-access offshore oil resources, they have regularly assured Russian energy firms active participation in any multinational consortium operating in Kazakhstan.

In practice, overlapping energy dependencies require Kazakh-Russian collaboration in this as in other areas. Astana still needs access to Russian energy pipelines to reach many consumers in Europe, while Moscow relies on imports of Central Asian gas—some of which passes through Kazakhstan—to meet its domestic demand and free up Russian energy supplies for export to Europe. For the past decade, Russia has profited immensely by being able to buy Central Asian energy supplies below market prices while selling oil and

---

http://www.Jamestown.Org/Publications_Details.Php?Volume_Id=407&Issue_Id=3212&Article_Id=2369163.

[333] Ministry of Foreign Affairs of Kazakhstan, "Aktual'nye Voprosy Vneshney Politiki Kazakhstana: Voprosy Transgranichnyx Rek," February 23, 2006, http://portal.mfa.kz/portal/page/portal/mfa/ru/content/policy/issues/rivers/01.

[334] Andrey Kolesnikov, "Pogranichnoe Stoyanie," *Kommersant*, October 5, 2007, http://www.kommersant.ru/doc.aspx?DocsID=811630.

gas to foreign customers at much higher rates, yielding Russian energy players a hefty mark-up.

The new Russian President, Dmitry Medvedev, appears just as interested in his predecessor in sustaining Russian influence in Kazakhstan. "Astana did not become the first foreign capital that I have visited as president of Russia by chance," Medvedev, who assumed office on May 7, observed after completing discussions with Nazarbayev on May 22 in the Kazakh capital. Rather, his choice was deliberate because "Russia values the genuinely friendly and mutually-advantageous relations with Kazakhstan, our strategic partner."[335] Medvedev also added that the high degree of economic integration between the two countries means that Russians and Kazakhs "converse in a single economic language."[336] Nazarbayev reciprocated by describing their ties as tighter than that between any other two countries: "I think that nowhere in the world can we see such close and fraternal relations as those between Kazakhstan and Russia, as those between us and Russia and the CIS."[337]

Medvedev seems keener than Putin to strengthen the institutional role of the CIS, which coincides with Nazarbayev's priorities. "It is our duty to pay close attention to cooperation with countries of the Commonwealth of Independent States," Medvedev observed during a joint news conference with Nazarbayev. "The time has come for ties to be intensified."[338] The Russian president also endorsed the Kazakh government's proposal to make energy cooperation the priority issue of the CIS agenda in 2009.[339]

---

[335] Cited in Joanna Lillis. "Russia-Kazakhstan: Medvedev Tries To Pick Up Where Putin Left Off," *Eurasia Insight*, May 23, 2008, http://www.eurasianet.org/departments/insight/articles/eav052308.shtml.

[336] "Medvedev nazval svoy visit 'dobrym prodolzheniem' kursa Putina I Nazarbayeva," Ferghana.ru, May 22, 2008, http://www.ferghana.ru/news.php?id=9232&mode=snews.

[337] Ministry of Foreign Affairs of The Russian Federation, "Beginning of Russian-Kazakhstani Talks in Expanded Format," May 22, 2008, http://www.mid.ru/brp_4.nsf/e78a48070f128a7b43256999005bcbb3/0b95f9340bf2587fc325745200217fbf?OpenDocument.

[338] Nikolaus von Twickel, "Medvedev Plugging CIS on First Trip," *Moscow Times*, May 23, 2008, http://www.themoscowtimes.com/article/600/42/367645.htm.

[339] "Kazakh, Russian FMs Discussed Agenda of 1ˢᵗ Medvedev's Visit to Kazakhstan," Kazinform, May 6, 2008, http://www.inform.kz/showarticle.php?lang=eng&id=164075.

Although Medvedev's background as a former chairman of Gazprom may have contributed to his interest in making energy a core element of CIS as well as Russian diplomacy, one reason both sides readily agreed to have the CIS focus on energy issues is that Kazakh and Russian negotiators still have not finalized the details of their plan to more than double the capacity of the Caspian Pipeline Consortium (CPC). In April 2006, the two countries signed an accord to increase the volume of Kazakh crude oil transported through the CPC, which extends from the Tengiz field in western Kazakhstan to the Russian port of Novorossiysk, to 67 million tons annually by 2012.[340] Russia's state pipeline monopoly Transneft has a 24% stake in the CPC—which was commissioned in 2001 as a joint project of Gazprom, Lukoil, and Yukos—while Kazakhstan owns a 19% share.[341] Russian negotiators have been demanding a greater share of the CPC's profits in return for agreeing to the expansion.[342]

In May 2007, the Kazakh, Russian and Turkmen governments also agreed to construct a major new natural gas pipeline whose route would wind around the Caspian Sea from Turkmenistan through Kazakhstan to Russia. Although the planned Caspian gas pipeline is scheduled to enter into service in 2011, the details of this arrangement remain under negotiation. Kazakhstan is supposed to contribute half of the volume while Turkmenistan will supply the remainder.[343]

These oil and gas pipelines are seen as the main competitors for those backed by Western governments that would circumvent Russia by crossing under the Caspian Sea. The Russian government has objected to the development of such underwater pipelines until the littoral states resolve the Caspian Sea's

---

[340] Sergei Blagov, "Russia Registers Significant Victory In Caspian Basin Energy Contest," Eurasia Insight, May 4, 2006, http://www.eurasianet.org/departments/insight/articles/eav050208.shtml.

[341] "Russia, Kazakhstan Agree to Double Pipeline Capacity by 2012," RIA Novosti, May 7, 2008, http://en.rian.ru/business/20080507/106846493.html.

[342] Joanna Lillis. "Russia-Kazakhstan: Medvedev Tries To Pick Up Where Putin Left Off," Eurasia Insight, May 23, 2008, http://www.eurasianet.org/departments/insight/articles/eav052308.shtml.

[343] "Russian, Kazakh Leaders Sign Accords," *Calgary Herald*, May 23, 2008, http://www.canada.com/calgaryherald/news/calgarybusiness/story.html?id=a8b68a8f -1ccb-4f8d-88e8-b5150b458d92&k=89570.

legal status. Moscow has also raised concerns that undersea pipelines could cause environmental damage. This deadlock has thus far ensured that Kazakhstan and Turkmenistan send most of their oil and gas northward overland to Russia.

The Russian and Kazakh governments also continue to disagree regarding Nazarbayev's proposal to build a canal linking the Caspian and Black Seas, a connection that could potentially provide currently landlocked Kazakhstan a more direct outlet to the world's oceans. Nazarbayev has called for the creation of a "Eurasia Canal" that would traverse Russia's mountainous North Caucasus, whereas Russian officials have advocated simply upgrading the existing Volga-Don waterway. Before Medvedev's election, Nazarbayev had argued that, "The Central Asian and Caspian regions are rich in energy resources ... but these reserves have to be delivered to world markets ... [the new canal] would be a powerful corridor providing an outlet for the whole of Central Asia to the sea via Russia."[344] Nazarbayev implicitly threatened to circumvent Russian opposition on this and other transport issues if Moscow proved too unyielding: "We never intend to bypass anyone, still less Russia, if the opportunities are provided."[345]

Even pending the canal's construction, commercial relations between Russia and Kazakhstan continue to expand. Russian-Kazakh bilateral trade amounted to $16.3 billion in 2007, a 27% increase over 2006.[346] Some 3,500 Kazakh-Russian joint ventures were operating in Kazakhstan in 2006, while Kazakh investors were active in the Russian Federation, if on a smaller scale.[347] According to Kazakh government data, during the first three months

---

[344] John C.K. Daly, "Analysis: Russia, Kazakhs Eye Rival Canals," United Press International, February 7, 2008, http://www.upi.com/International_Security/Energy/Analysis/2008/02/07/analysis_r ussia_kazakhs_eye_rival_canals/5702.

[345] Lillis. "Russia-Kazakhstan: Medvedev Tries To Pick Up." http://www.eurasianet.org/departments/insight/articles/eav052308.shtml.

[346] Oleg Sidorov, "Abroad Debut of Dmitriy Medvedev," Gazeta.kz, May 22, 2006, http://www.gazeta.kz/eng/art.asp?aid=110776.

[347] Embassy of Kazakhstan to the USA and Canada, "Kazakhstan and Russia Stress String Ties," Kazakhstan News Bulletin, March 21, 2007, http://www.kazakhembus.com/032107.html. For instance, Kazakh investors were helping to build the Ritz-Carlton Moscow Hotel.

of 2008, bilateral trade rose to \$4.13 billion, a 26% increase over the January-March 2008 period. [348] Nevertheless, Moscow's recent efforts to induce Lufthansa to relocate its transshipment facilities from Kazakhstan to Siberia underscore that Russian and Kazakh economic interests do not always coincide.

In any case, the two governments also signed accords aimed at promoting cooperation in high-technology sectors that could dominate the world economy in coming decades. Medvedev explained that, "Of course energy is a very important sphere, but the 21st century cannot be without innovative development." [349] To encourage bilateral cooperation in nanotechnology, Russia's state-owned Development Bank agreed to loan \$300 million to the Kazakh Development Bank. [350] Medvedev also said that the two governments sought to "transition to deeper nuclear energy integration." [351] He confirmed that Russia and Kazakhstan would establish a joint venture to build nuclear-power plants in Kazakhstan. [352]

Resolving Kazakh-Russian disagreements relating to their joint operation of the Baikonur space launch facility was another important high-technology item on the summit agenda. During the Soviet period, this facility contributed to the Soviet government's military as well as civilian space programs. After Kazakhstan declared independence, debate raged about ownership of the facility. Russian officials believed Moscow should retain control of the installation since most of the operations, mandates, and funds

---

[348] Sergei Blagov, "Medvedev Kicks off Kazakhstan Courtship," Eurasia Insight, May 15, 2008, http://www.eurasianet.org/departments/insight/articles/eav051508.shtml.

[349] Embassy of Kazakhstan to the USA and Canada, "Russia Approves Baikonur Deal with Kazakhstan," Kazakhstan News Bulletin, June 22, 2005, http://www.kazakhembus.com/062205.html; and "Russian, Kazakh Leaders Sign Accords," *Calgary Herald*, May 23, 2008, http://www.canada.com/calgaryherald/news/calgarybusiness/story.html?id=a8b68a8f -1ccb-4f8d-88e8-b5150b458d92&k=89570.

[350] Nikolaus von Twickel, "Medvedev Plugging CIS on First Trip," *Moscow Times*, May 23, 2008, http://www.themoscowtimes.com/article/600/42/367645.htm.

[351] "Kazakhstan Set for Long-Term Cooperation Deal with Russia," RIA Novosti, May 22, 2008, http://en.rian.ru/world/20080522/108135208.html.

[352] Twickel, "Medvedev Plugging CIS on First Trip."

came from the Kremlin. Kazakhstan's new government argued that the cosmodrome's location on its territory warranted greater Kazakh control. In 1994, the two governments ratified an agreement that recognized Kazakhstan's ownership of the site but allowed Russia to continue to use the location under a 20-year lease. A January 2004 accord, which entered into force in 2005, extended the leasing arrangement through 2050, with Russia paying $115 million annually to use the facility. [353] The document also established a joint venture with both countries providing $223 million to construct a Baiterek complex to launch Angara carrier rockets, capable of delivering 26 metric tons of payload into low-Earth orbits.[354] Although some Kazakhs oppose the facility's continued use as an environmental hazard, others consider Kazakhstan's major role in space as an important driver of scientific and technological development, as well economic growth. The Kazakh space industry launched its first satellite in 2006 and aims to launch a second this year. Kazakh officials want to have one of their astronauts visit the International Space Station.[355]

The debate over Baikonur sharpened in 2007, when a Russian rocket crashed on Kazakh territory shortly after launch. Kazakh authorities claim that the mishap produced approximately $60 million in damage. The Russian government subsequently offered only $2.5 million in compensation.[356] On April 12, 2008, Anatoly Perminov, the head of the Russian Federal Space Agency (Roscosmos) told journalists that Russia intended to use the Baikonur center until 2050.[357] The joint declaration at the May 2008 summit pledged that the parties would employ Baikonur in a way that benefited Kazakhstan, Russia, and other countries. Kazakhstan also agreed to support development

---

[353] "Russia's Medvedev Travels to Kazakhstan," Associated Press, May 22, 2008, http://www.iht.com/articles/ap/2008/05/22/news/Kazakhstan-Russia.php.

[354] "Kazakh President Signs Law Re Baiterek Rocket Center," SPX, October 24, 2005, http://www.space-travel.com/reports/Kazakh_President_Signs_Law_Re_Baiterek_Rocket_Center.html.

[355] Joanna Lillis. "Russia-Kazakhstan: Medvedev Tries To Pick Up."

[356] *Ibid.*

[357] "Russia to Use Baikonur Space Center until 2050—Roscosmos," RIA Novosti, April 12, 2008, http://en.rian.ru/science/20080412/104910818.html.

of the Russian-controlled Glonass navigation system, a competitor to the U.S. Global Positioning System that also has military applications.

The two governments continue to deepen their defense cooperation. Before Medvedev arrived in Astana, Kazakh Defense Minister Daniyal Akhmetov reaffirmed Astana's interest in purchasing additional Russian weapons systems and in sending Kazakh personnel for training in Russian military academies.[358] A Kremlin source stated that the Kazakh government had inquired about purchasing Russian air defense systems.[359] Other media sources reported that Kazakhstan will buy new warships solely from Russia. According to Interfax, the Kazakh Defense Ministry plans to order smaller ships from the Kazakhstan-Russian "Zenith" joint venture wharf in Uralsk, Western Kazakhstan, but will arrange for more sophisticated warships to be constructed by Russian shipyards.[360]

Russian Defense Minister Anatoly Serdyukov accompanied the Russian delegation to Astana. Following the presidential consultations, Medvedev and Nazarbayev released a statement that, while not detailing any specific new weapons purchases, declared that, "Russia and Kazakhstan will maintain close cooperation aimed at securing a solid joint defense within the common military strategic space under the Collective Security Treaty."[361] Russia sells weapons to Kazakhstan and its other close allies at subsidized prices. This policy simultaneously helps fortify Russian allies against internal and external threats while also keeping these countries dependent on Russian-made weapons and susceptible to the Kremlin's influence.

United States

Both Republican and Democratic administrations have sought to maintain good economic, political, and security relations with Kazakhstan since it

---

[358] "Russia and Kazakhstan Defence Ministers Announce Military Cooperation Programme," February 13, 2008, BBC Monitoring.

[359] "Medvedev to Discuss Space Center, Arms Deals During Kazakh Visit," RIA Novosti, May 22, 2008 , http://en.rian.ru/russia/20080522/108063754.html.

[360] Sergei Blagov, "Medvedev Kicks off Kazakhstan Courtship," Eurasia Insight, May 15, 2008, http://www.eurasianet.org/departments/insight/articles/eav051508.shtml.

[361] "Medvedev in Kazakhstan, Leaders Agree to Expand Ties," RTTNews, May 22, 2008, http://www.rttnews.com/Content/GeneralNews.aspx?Node=B1&Id=613291.

gained independence from the Soviet Union. Many Washington policy makers believe Kazakhstan's growing role in its extended neighborhood has advanced significant American interests. Through its increasing economic engagement in Eurasia—which has involved both direct investment and trade as well as support for improving regional commercial and transportation infrastructure—Kazakhstan has helped transform Central Asia and the Caspian region into an "arc of opportunity" rather than an "arc of crisis." Hundreds of American companies directly benefit from their large foreign direct investment in Kazakhstan, which presently amounts to over \$15 billion. In addition, a strong Kazakhstan helps check excessive Chinese and Russian influence in Central Asia. Kazakh authorities have supported the development of energy pipelines that do not rely exclusively on Moscow and have endorsed a continued U.S. and NATO military presence in the region even after the situation in Afghanistan stabilizes. Of course, the inherent volatility of the region and bilateral differences over democracy promotion means that relations could change at any time. At present, however, the general impression in Washington is that Kazakhstan has become the most important U.S. partner in Central Asia.

Since the Cold War had precluded the development of substantial direct ties between the United States and Kazakhstan, the initial focus of bilateral relations was establishing mutual diplomatic representation. On December 25, 1991, the United States became the first government to recognize Kazakhstan's independence.[362] The State Department opened a new embassy in the then capital of Almaty in January 1992.

Since then, U.S. policies have consistently aimed to facilitate Kazakhstan's transition to a stable, democratic country with a prosperous free market and harmonious relations with its neighbors and the larger international community.[363] "For Kazakhstan, the political support of the USA during the first years of independence was very important," President Nazarbayev later

---

[362] U.S. Department of State, "Background Note: Kazakhstan," February 2007, http://www.state.gov/r/pa/ei/bgn/5487.htm.
[363] Office of the White House Press Secretary, "Joint Declaration on Relations Between the United States and Kazakhstan by President Bush and Kazakhstan President Nursultan Nazarbayev," May 19, 1992, http://findarticles.com/p/articles/mi_m1584/is_n21_v3/ai_12511837/pg_1?tag=artBody;co l1.

remarked. "This support made entry to the world association and the world economy much easier–it helped to choose the more effective and far-sighted political reference points."[364]

Under President Bill Clinton, the U.S. government had two main priorities regarding Kazakhstan.[365] Both objectives were important for the preceding and subsequent Bush administrations as well. The first goal was to eliminate or better secure the nuclear arsenal and other weapons of mass destruction Kazakhstan inherited following the demise of the Soviet Union.[366] American officials worked with the Kazakh government and other groups to destroy or transfer to Russia the nuclear weapons and strategic delivery systems (long-range bombers and missiles) located on Kazakhstan's territory in the early 1990s. U.S.-Kazakh nonproliferation initiatives have also included dismantling the Stepnogorsk anthrax production facility and enhancing joint cooperative efforts against bioterrorist threats.[367] More recently, the two countries have begun collaborating to dispose of spent nuclear fuel from the closed BN-350 reactor in Aktau.[368] The two governments have also assumed leading roles in the Global Initiative to Combat Nuclear Terrorism, the Proliferation Security Initiative, and other multilateral nonproliferation efforts.[369] Kazakhstan received approximately $240 million under the U.S.-

---

[364] "Kazakhstan Emerges as a Major World Player," *Washington Times* Advertising Supplement, December 20, 1999,
http://www.internationalspecialreports.com/ciscentralasia/99/kazakhstan/3.html.
[365] For a more comprehensive listing of joint U.S.-Kazakh goals and objectives during the 1990s see Office of the White House Press Secretary, "Joint Statement on U.S.-Kazakhstan Relations," November 18,1997,
http://www.nti.org/e_research/profiles/Kazakhstan/6184.html.
[366] Martha Brill Olcott, "Towards a New Stage in US-Kazah Relations," Kazakhstan and the USA Conference Remarks, August 23 2006,
http://www.carnegieendowment.org/publications/index.cfm?fa=view&id=18700&prog=zru.
[367] U.S. Department of Defense, "United States Extends Strategic Partnership with Kazakhstan," December 13, 2007,
http://www.defenselink.mil/Releases/Release.aspx?ReleaseID=11560.
[368] National Nuclear Center of the Republic of Kazakhstan, "Mezhdunardnoe Sotrudnichestvo," http://www.nnc.kz/ru/cooperation.html.
[369] Nuclear Threat Initiative, "Kazakhstan,"
http://www.nti.org/e_research/official_docs/inventory/pdfs/kazak.pdf.

funded Cooperative Threat Reduction Program to eliminate its weapons of mass destruction.[370]

President Clinton's second priority was to increase the volume of Kazakh energy product entering world markets, especially along routes that did not traverse Russian territory. The administration encouraged U.S. companies such as Chevron and Exxon-Mobil to invest in Kazakhstan's energy sector, resulting in Americans becoming a leading source of private investment capital in Kazakhstan.[371] In 2006, U.S. capital accounted for 27% of all foreign direct investment in Kazakhstan.[372] Due to geography and other factors, bilateral trade is of lesser importance in their economic relations. Neither country is a leading trade partner of the other.[373]

After the 9/11 terrorist attacks, the United States expanded its security cooperation with Kazakhstan and other Central Asian countries. American policies aimed primarily to secure support for NATO military operations in Afghanistan and to bolster regional governments' national capacity to counter transnational terrorist threats, especially those that could involve unconventional weapons. Although the United States does not have a permanent military base in Kazakhstan, whose location is less useful for providing logistical support for OEF than some of Afghanistan's other neighbors, the Kazakh government has granted American warplanes permission to fly over Kazakhstan's territory and to make emergency landings at Almaty national airport.[374] Furthermore, American officials appreciate the support Kazakh diplomats have given to U.S. efforts to retain access to the Manas Air Base in Kyrgyzstan and to dissuade the SCO from veering in an overtly anti-American direction.

[370] Department of State, "Background Note: Kazakhstan."
[371] Gulnoza Saidazimova, "Central Asia: Could Regional Dynamics Spell Closer U.S.-Kazakh Ties?," Radio Free Europe, June 08, 2008,
http://www.rferl.org/content/article/1069000.html.
[372] Department of State, "Background Note: Kazakhstan."
[373] For example, Kazakhstan is currently the 75th largest export market for U.S. goods 2005; Office of the United States Trade Representative, "Kazakhstan,"
http://www.ustr.gov/assets/Document_Library/Reports_Publications/2008/2008_NTE_Report/asset_upload_file942_14631.pdf.
[374] Jim Nichol, "Kazakhstan: Current Developments and U.S. Interests," May 4, 2004, (Washington, D.C.: Congressional Research Service, May 4, 2004, p. 4, http://www.ndu.edu/library/docs/crs/crs_971058f_04may04.pdf.

The Bush administration has also welcomed the small but symbolically important Kazakh military contribution to the war in Iraq. The Kazakh government has kept around 30 engineers in Iraq to assist with de-mining and water purification despite widespread public opposition to Kazakhstan's involvement in the conflict. [375] By expanding the number of countries nominally part of the "coalition of the willing" in Iraq, the troop deployment—one of the few from a primarily Muslim country (Azerbaijan and Albania being the others) and the only ground force commitment made by a Central Asian government—helped legitimize the American military presence.

More generally, American officials argue that Kazakhstan's growing role in regional affairs will help promote a range of U.S. security goals in Eurasia. In May 2007, for instance, U.S. Deputy Assistant Secretary of Defense for Eurasia Policy James MacDougall maintained that, "Kazakhstan as a strong and stable country in the Central Asia region has the ability to play a leadership role and a stabilizing role to ensure in part that the Central Asia region geographically doesn't become more susceptible than it may already be to terrorism and to terrorist elements."[376]

One bilateral relationship promoting the two countries' regional military, economic, and energy security objectives has been joint U.S.-Kazakh efforts to strengthen the security of Kazakhstan's land and maritime borders. The U.S. Department of State, the U.S. Coast Guard, and the U.S. Department of Defense and other U.S. agencies provide the Kazakh government with training and equipment to increase its border control capabilities. Prominent joint efforts include the Caspian Guard initiative and the U.S. Export Control and Related Border Security Assistance Program.[377]

Although some estimates of the probable recoverable energy resources in the Caspian have declined during the Bush administration, American officials

---

[375] Olga Oliker, "Kazakhstan's Security Interests and their Implications for the U.S.-Kazakh Relationship," *China and Eurasia Forum Quarterly*, vol. 5, no. 2 (2007), p. 68, http://www.silkroadstudies.org/new/docs/CEF/Quarterly/May_2007/Oliker.pdf.
[376] Cited in Saidazimova, "Central Asia: Regional Dynamics."
[377]GlobalSecurity.org, "Caspian Guard," http://www.globalsecurity.org/military/ops/caspian-guard.htm; and U.S. Diplomatic Mission to Kazakhstan, "U.S. and Kazakhstan Team up to Improve Border Security," May 17, 2007, http://kazakhstan.usembassy.gov/pr-05-17-en.html.

have continued previous U.S. efforts to ensure that Kazakhstan exports at least some of its energy production westward through the South Caucasus. Vice President Richard Cheney and other senior U.S. government representatives have made recurring visits to Kazakhstan to promote U.S. energy objectives in Eurasia. In particular, American policy makers launched a sustained diplomatic campaign to secure Kazakh participation in the Baku-Tbilisi-Ceyhan oil pipeline. More recently, U.S. officials have sought to direct some of the country's expected natural gas exports through undersea Trans-Caucasus pipelines. Conversely, Washington has sought to minimize the flow of Kazakh energy products to Iran pending changes in that country's foreign policies.

American officials have also attempted to enhance regional economic integration in areas other than energy. In June 2004, the United States signed a Trade and Investment Framework Agreement (TIFA) with Kazakhstan and the other Central Asian countries.[378] The TIFA process aims to overcome impediments to intra-regional trade, economic development, and foreign direct investment through ongoing dialogue and other initiatives. Representatives from the governments of Afghanistan, India, and Pakistan also typically participate since U.S officials seek to deepen economic ties between Central and South Asian countries to exploit their complementary economies, as well as to create a larger potential market to entice foreign investors. The State Department has designated a Special Ambassador for Trade in Greater Central Asia and, in February 2006, reorganized its geographic bureaus in order to place South and Central Asian issues within a single office.[379] A current U.S. government priority is assisting Kazakhstan's entry into the World Trade Organization under mutually acceptable conditions.

The TIFA process also presumes a close connection between economic and security issues in Eurasia. American officials hope that by promoting the

---

[378] The text of the agreement is available at
http://www.ustr.gov/assets/Trade_Agreements/TIFA/asset_upload_file683_7722.pdf.
[379] The Bureau of South Asian Affairs merged with the Office of Central Asian Affairs to create a newly renamed Bureau for South and Central Asian Affairs. The Office for Central Asian Affairs had been part of the Bureau for European Affairs, a legacy of the Cold War, when the Central Asian republics were part of the USSR

region's socioeconomic development, they will reduce the appeal of extremist ideologies and transnational criminal activities, especially terrorism and narcotics trafficking. Ensuring Afghanistan's continued economic development is seen as an essential component of this process given the resurgence of the Taliban insurgency and the drug production networks in that country. During a December 2001 visit to Washington, Nazarbayev and Bush issued a joint statement expressing their mutual belief "that the expansion of trade and economic ties among the states of Central Asia, and deepening of regional integration in important areas, such as the environment, water resources, and transportation systems are a basis for regional security."[380]

The current Bush administration has launched numerous programs designed to improve conditions for private business—Kazakh as well as foreign—in Kazakhstan. Educational, training, and other programs seek to expand employment opportunities for Kazakhs. Particular priority has been placed on elevating Kazakh commercial and financial standards. The U.S. Chamber of Commerce has established a Public-Private Economic Partnership Initiative between the two countries that aims to expand opportunities for private enterprises in Kazakhstan.[381] While American business activity in Kazakhstan still consists primarily of firms engaged in the oil, gas, and other extractive industries, a number of American companies—including small and medium-sized businesses—have extended their activities to other sectors in recent years.[382]

U.S. officials have also backed Nazarbayev's vision of Kazakhstan as a "locomotive" for increasing regional commerce. In an October 2005 speech in Astana, Secretary of State Condoleezza Rice argued that the country could enhance regional stability through its growing commercial role in Eurasia:

---

[380] Office of the White House Press Secretary, "Joint Statement by President George W. Bush and President Nursultan Nazarbayev on the New Kazakhstan-American Relationship," December 21, 2001,
http://www.whitehouse.gov/news/releases/2001/12/20011221-10.html.
[381] American Chamber of Commerce in Kazakhstan, "U.S.-Kazakhstan Public Private Economic Partnership Initiative Inaugural Forum," June 24, 2008,
http://www.amcham.kz/event.php?event_id=181.
[382] Evan A. Feigenbaum, "The U.S.-Kazakhstan Relationship," Press Roundtable, Astana, Kazakhstan, U.S. Department of State. November 20, 2007,
http://www.state.gov/p/sca/rls/rm/2007/95676.htm.

As this nation's economy continues to develop, Kazakhstan should view its role as an engine for growth within Central Asia. Both Kyrgyzstan and Tajikistan would benefit immensely from Kazakhstani investment and energy to stimulate growth and create jobs. And Afghanistan needs the full partnership of this entire region to overcome the destitution that tyrants, and extremists, and warlords, and civil war have compounded over several decades. A secure and prosperous Afghanistan, which anchors Central Asia and links it to South Asia, is essential to the future of economic success.[383]

At present, a large number of U.S. government agencies are engaged with Kazakhstan. Formal U.S. government assistance programs to Kazakhstan in Fiscal Year 2007 amounts to $26.80 million. This figure includes $9.55 million for peace and security programs; $5.72 million for democracy and governance programs; $2.93 million for human resource programs ("Investing in People" projects); and $7.73 million to promote economic growth. The bulk of these funds were appropriated under the Freedom Support Act.[384]

Two factors have most limited U.S. influence in Kazakhstan. First, although the United States is a global superpower, it is a distant one from the perspective of Kazakh officials, who are constantly engaged in managing relations with Russia, China, and other neighboring countries. Although Kazak leaders desire a sustained major U.S. role in Eurasia to provide geopolitical balance as well as economic, military, and other resources, many in Kazakhstan and elsewhere remain uncertain about the durability of the major American presence in Central Asia, which is a relatively new historical phenomenon.

Second, America's strong commitment to promoting human rights and democratic principles in Eurasia has irritated some Kazakh officials. Bilateral tensions over the pace of political and economic reforms as well as allegations of corrupt practices by Kazakh officials and their American partners have persisted since the country's independence.[385] Differences became especially

---

[383] Embassy of Kazakhstan to the USA and Canada, "Rice Calls Central Asia 'Arc of Opportunity' and Kazakhstan 'Engine for Growth' for Region Stretching to Afghanistan," Kazakhstan News Bulletin, February 3, 2006, http://www.kazakhembus.com/020306.html.
[384] U.S. Department of State, "Foreign Operations Appropriated Assistance: Kazakhstan," April 16, 2008, http://www.state.gov/p/eur/rls/fs/103634.htm.
[385] See for example Nikola Krastev, "Kazakhstan: Country Again Features In U.S. Efforts To Combat Corruption, Radio Free Europe/Radio Liberty, May 23, 2005,

acute when these considerations initially led U.S. officials to resist Kazakhstan's receiving the rotating chair of the OSCE. American political culture, with its emphasis on civil liberties, and the U.S. political system, which provides democracy advocates with considerable influence within Congress and the media, ensures that promoting democracy and human rights will remain a constant feature of U.S. policies towards Kazakhstan and other countries. American representatives are now working with Kazakh officials to implement the political and other reform commitments endorsed by the Kazakh government as it prepares to assume the OSCE chair in 2010.[386]

Regional Powers

India

President Nazarbayev's visit to India in 2002 led Kazakh leaders to consider more clearly that country's role as another component of Eurasia's post-Cold War international system. In April 2003, Kazakhstan joined the Indian-Iranian-Russian initiative to develop a large-scale North-South transportation corridor that would extend from northern Russia to the Persian Gulf.[387] In March 2006, Foreign Minister Tokaev indicated that, while his government welcomed the increasing presence of Chinese energy companies in Kazakhstan and other Eurasian markets, "We also would like to see other countries [coming into the region]. For example, we are negotiating with India. The general balance of interests must be thoroughly sustained."[388] While the presence of Indian energy companies in Kazakhstan remains limited, in October 2007, President Nazarbayev reaffirmed interest in sending

---

http://www.rferl.org/content/article/1058968.htm; and Ron Stodghill, "Trial Puts Spotlight on U.S.-Kazakh Relations," *International Herald Tribune*, November 7, 2006, http://www.iht.com/articles/2006/11/07/business/kazoil.php; Agence-France Presse, "Rice Calls For More Democracy in Central Asia," October 13, 2005, http://www.sras.org/news2.phtml?m=458#4.

[386] "U.S. Envoy To OSCE Says Kazakhstan Lagging In Reforms," Radio Free Europe/Radio Liberty, June 26, 2008, http://www.rferl.org/content/U.S._Envoy_OSCE_Says_Kazakhstan_Lagging_Reforms/1145556.html.

[387] Kushkumbayev, "Kazakhstan," p. 288.

[388] Mevlut Katik, "Kazakhstan Has 'Huge Plan' to Expand Energy Links with China," Eurasia Insight, March 13, 2006, http://www.eurasianet.org/departments/recaps/articles/eav031306.shtml.

Kazakh oil and gas southward through Iranian territory to Persian Gulf ports, where tankers could transport the supplies to India and other countries.[389] The previous month, Kairat Akhmetalim, Counselor in the Embassy of Kazakhstan in New Delhi, said that his government "would like a great economic power like India to become a member" of the SCO, where it is presently only an observer.[390]

Although India does not share a land border with Kazakhstan or any other Central Asian country, the two regions of Central and South Asia have extensive historical ties. For centuries, Central Asian leaders such as Tamerlane and the Moghuls ruled much of northwest India. The March 2008 decision of New Delhi's Jamia Millia Islamia University to open India's first Centre for Kazakh Language and Studies should help further these cultural ties. The center will come under the jurisdiction of the Department of Persian Studies and its Nelson Mandela Centre for Peace and Conflict Resolution.[391]

Contemporary Indian policy towards Central Asia, as during the British Raj, often treats the region as India's "extended strategic neighborhood."[392] Given New Delhi's concerns about geopolitical encirclement, Pakistani and Chinese activities in Central Asia have traditionally received much attention. Since the USSR's disintegration, Indian security policy towards Central Asia has sought to prevent Kazakhstan and other Central Asian states from joining any "Islamic camp" that could adopt anti-Hindu policies. New Delhi's nightmare would be the emergence of a bloc of hostile Islamic governments in Central Asia, Afghanistan, and Pakistan, linked closely with China, which would seek to contain India, support terrorism in Kashmir, and perhaps stir

---

[389] "Central Asia: Kazakh, Russian Leaders Discuss Transport Corridor," Radio Free Europe/Radio Liberty, October 5, 2007,
http://www.rferl.org/featuresarticle/2007/10/4482ab28-5ab9-4756-8386-48471d684d3f.html.
[390] "India-SCO-Entry," IRNA, September 3, 2007,
http://www2.irna.ir/en/news/view/menu-236/0709032581170740.htm.
[391] "Jamia Launches India's First Centre for Kazakh Language and Studies," ANI, March.29, 2008, http://www.keralanext.com/news/?id=1203420.
[392] "Pakistan, India Both Eye Central Asia," *Daily Times*,
http://www.dailytimes.com.pk/default.asp?page=story_12-8-2005_pg7_57.

up trouble among India's other Muslim minorities.[393] The growth of terrorism and Islamic radicalism has become a more recent concern. In June 2005, Defense Minister Pranab Mukherjee said that India had a vital stake in the outcome of the struggle between extremist and moderate interpretations of Islam in the region.[394]

India's limited military capabilities and inability to access Central Asia easily by a land route constrain Indians' ability to affect security developments in the region. As a result, Indian strategists have largely welcomed the increased American presence in Central Asia since 9/11 as well as Russia's persistent influence in Central Asia. Both security and economic concerns have led Indian governments to work with the United States and other countries to stabilize Afghanistan. New Delhi never recognized the radical Sunni Taliban, with its ties to Pakistan and anti-Hindu terrorists in Kashmir, as the official government of Afghanistan. The Indian government instead supported the Northern Alliance throughout the Afghan civil war.[395] Since 2001, Indian officials have strongly backed the anti-Taliban regime in Kabul, extending hundreds of millions of dollars in reconstruction aid. Both the Afghan and Indian governments have been pressuring Pakistan to relax border controls that hinder Indian-Afghan trade, as well as India's commercial ties with Central Asia.

Besides geopolitical concerns, Indian policy makers have been motivated by a desire to obtain access to additional energy supplies to supplement India's traditional reliance on Persian Gulf oil, which presently accounts for approximately two-thirds of its domestic needs. The country's booming economy will require it to import increasing volumes of oil and natural gas in

---

[393] Stephen Blank, "India's Continuing Drive into Central Asia," *Central Asia-Caucasus Institute Analyst*, January 14, 2004, http://www.cacaianalyst.org/view_article.php?articleid=3459.

[394] Robert McMahon, "Central Asia: Defense Minister Touts India's Potential Moderating Influence in Region," Radio Free Europe/Radio Liberty, June 28, 2005, http://www.rferl.org/featuresarticle/2005/06/908899c2-7a6a-4de2-8ca7-a2a5391a12dc.html.

[395] Hooman Peimani, "The Afghan and Central Asian Factor in Indian-Pakistani Rivalry," *Central Asia-Caucasus Institute Analyst*, April 10, 2002, http://www.cacaianalyst.org/view_article.php?articleid=3459.

future years.[396] The director general of the Tata Energy Research Institute, R. K. Pachauri, pointed out the implications of this trend for Indian foreign policy: "We now realize we have to get a large part of our energy from our extended neighborhood, and that means we have to engineer and structure new relationships."[397] Like China, Indian policy makers express concern about their excessive dependence on Persian Gulf oil supplies. Former Foreign Minister K. Natwar Singh advocated making energy cooperation a SCO priority, including by convening regular meetings of energy ministers under its auspices.[398] On a bilateral basis, Indian firms, including the state-owned Oil and Natural Gas Corporation (ONGC), have invested in Kazakhstan's Alibekmola and Kurmangazi oil fields. They also are considering various hydroelectric projects in several Central Asian countries.[399]

A major purpose of President Nazarbayev's trip to India in 2002 was to deepen economic ties between the two countries. Nazarbayev was especially eager to entice greater Indian technological and pharmaceutical investment in Kazakhstan, including through joint ventures with Kazakh firms.[400] Economic ties between Kazakhstan and India substantially expanded after Nazarbayev's visit, though they lag behind the levels desired by both sides. Kazakh-Indian trade increased from $60 million in 2002 to almost $200 million in 2007. Kazakhstan's main export items to India consist of salt, lime, brimstone, cement, raw leather, and ferrous metals. India mainly sells coffee, tea, spices, tobacco, organic chemical compounds, pharmaceuticals, plastics,

---

[396] Detailed projections can be found at Energy Information Administration, U.S. Department of Energy, "Country Analysis Briefs: India," January 2007, http://www.eia.doe.gov/cabs/India/Full.html.

[397] Cited in Somini Sengupta, "India's Quest for Energy is Reshaping its Diplomacy," *International Herald Tribune*, June 6, 2005, http://www.iht.com/articles/2005/06/05/news/energy.php.

[398] Press Trust of India, "India Pitches for Full Membership of the Shanghai Cooperation Org," Asia Pulse, October 27, 2005, http://goliath.ecnext.com/coms2/gi_0199-4843981/INDIA-PITCHES-FOR-FULL-MEMBERSHIP.html.

[399] Blank, "India's Continuing Quest." http://www.cacaianalyst.org/view_article.php?articleid=3459.

[400] United Nations Development Programme, *Bringing Down Barriers: Regional Cooperation for Human Development and Human Security* (New York, 2005), p. 73, http://europeandcis.undp.org/archive/?wspc=CAHDR2005

rubber, electrical machines, equipments and mechanical devices.[401] In 2006, Indian investment in Kazakhstan increased to $16 million, while Kazakh investors purchased shares in India's oil exploration firm, Kaspain Shelf.[402] The two governments have recently been considering how Indians might cultivate idle lands in Kazakhstan, perhaps through an arrangement in which Indians would grow crops in leased plots, and then ship the food to India.[403]

A major impediment to expanding commercial ties between Kazakhstan and India is the lack of a direct land route between them. The conflict with Pakistan over Kashmir and other issues has compounded this natural barrier with manmade complications. Lacking inexpensive direct transit routes, most Indian exporters to Afghanistan, Kazakhstan, and the rest of Central Asia have had to ship goods via Iran's port of Bandar Abbas and a lengthy overland road system.[404] In order to bring Eurasian oil and gas to Indian industries and consumers, and to increase Indian commerce with Central Asia more generally, Indian officials have promoted the development of the region's transportation and commercial infrastructures. The Indian government is helping Iran develop its new Persian Gulf port of Chabahar as well as supporting construction of a highway connecting Chabahar through Afghanistan into Tajikistan.[405]

The previous Indian government under Prime Minister Manmohan Singh conducted a strong campaign to obtain access to Kazakhstan's oil resources.

---

[401] Ministry of Foreign Affairs of Kazakhstan, "Sotrudnichestvo Respubliki Kazakhstan s Respublikoy Indiya," July 12, 2006,
http://portal.mfa.kz/portal/page/portal/mfa/ru/content/policy/cooperation/asia_afri ca/17.

[402] John C.K. Daly, "Analysis: India Eyes Kazakh Energy," United Press International, April 11, 2008,
http://www.upi.com/International_Security/Energy/Analysis/2008/04/11/analysis_in dia_eyes_kazakh_energy/4684.

[403] Vishnu Makhijani, "India to Boost Energy Ties with Kazakhstan, Turkmenistan,"

April 10, 2008, IANS, http://www.thaindian.com/newsportal/business/india-to-boost-energy-ties-with-kazakhstan-turkmenistan_10036545.html.

[404] S. Frederick Starr, "Introduction," in S. Frederick Starr, ed., *The New Silk Roads: Transport and Trade in Greater Central Asia* (Washington, D.C.: Central Asia-Caucasus Institute, 2007), p. 18.

[405] Sudha Ramachandran, "India Revels in New Diplomatic Offensive," Asia Times, November 22, 2003, http://www.atimes.com/atimes/South_Asia/EK22Df05.html.

With government encouragement, Indian firms sought a formal role in the international consortium involved in the Tengiz and Kashagan oil fields and the Kurmangazy and Darkhan exploration blocs. They also expressed interest in working elsewhere in the Caspian Sea region. Indian Energy Minister Mari Shankar Aiyar also proposed that India's Gail Ltd., join the consortium helping to construct Kazakhstan's three energy pipelines with China. Gail and other Indian companies sought to invest in the natural gas processing and petrochemical plants in Atyrau and Akhtau and improve the recovery infrastructure at older oil fields in Kazakhstan.[406] Indian and Kazakh officials established a Joint Working Group to develop a comprehensive plan for involving India in Kazakhstan's diverse oil and gas projects.[407]

Thus far, however, India has largely lost out to China in its quest for Kazakhstan's energy resources.[408] In 2005, after an intense bidding war, CNPC outbid ONCG for PetroKazakhstan, previously a private, Canadian-owned energy company. This $4 billion purchase of Kazakhstan's second-largest foreign oil producer represented the most expensive acquisition by a Chinese company.[409] Another obstacle has been Indian investors' unease about the continuing changes in Kazakhstan's legislation regarding foreign investment in the country's energy sector.[410]

Continued instability in Afghanistan and Pakistan's Baluchistan province, uncertainties about the capacity of Turkmenistan's Dauletabad field to supply sufficient natural gas, and Indians' reluctance to become excessively dependent on Pakistan for their vital energy supplies have thus far impeded construction of a Trans-Afghan pipeline from Turkmenistan to India through

---

[406] Blank, "India's Continuing Quest."

[407] Stephen Blank, "India's Energy Offensive in Central Asia," *Central Asia-Caucasus Institute Analyst*, March 9, 2005, http://www.cacaianalyst.org/view_article.php?articleid=3459.

[408] Chietigj Bajpaee, "India, China Locked in Energy Game," Asia Times, May 17, 2005, http://www.atimes.com/atimes/Asian_Economy/GC17Dko1.html.

[409] Christopher Pala, "China Pays Dearly for Kazakhstan Oil," *New York Times*, March 17, 2006, http://www.nytimes.com/2006/03/17/business/worldbusiness/17kazakh.html.

[410] "India Eyes Kazakh Oil," neweurasia.org, April 15, 2008, http://kazakhstan.neweurasia.net/2008/04/15/india-eyes-kazakh-oil.

Afghanistan and Pakistan.[411] The envisaged Trans-Afghan Pipeline (TAP) enjoys the strong backing of the Asian Development Bank and Washington, which sees the project as a way to promote Indian-Pakistan reconciliation, provide the pro-U.S. regime in Afghanistan with transit revenues, and build additional energy pipelines not under Russian or Iranian control. In April 2008, the Indian government, previously an observer, formally joined the now renamed Turkmenistan-Afghanistan-Pakistan-India (TAPI) gas pipeline.[412]

Although energy experts remain dubious about the project's realization, events in April 2008 may finally precipitate the long-sought upturn in Kazakh-Indian energy relations. In Astana, President Nazarbayev told visiting Indian Vice-President Hamid Ansari that India could play its part in Kazakhstan's plan to double oil output to 100 million tons over the next 10 years. The two leaders agreed to make their cooperation more concrete by developing detailed plans for Indian participation in Kazakh energy projects. An Indian official told the media after the meeting that, "Both agreed that given our closeness, there was a need to get into project-specific cooperation."[413] Kazakh representatives, besides indicating that Nazarbayev expected to visit India in the near future, expressed most interest in gaining access to Indian energy technologies.[414] The Indian Oil Corporation (IOC) subsequently announced that it had begun evaluating whether to establish a refinery and other petrochemical facilities in Kazakhstan and Turkmenistan, which Ansari had visited immediately before arriving in Astana. KMG

---

[411] Svante E. Cornell and Mamuka Tsereteli, "After the Baku-Tbilisi-Ceyhan Pipeline: Looking Ahead," *Central Asia-Caucasus Institute Analyst*, June 15, 2005, http://www.cacianalyst.org/view_article.php?articleid=3374.

[412] "India Joins Mega Gas Pipeline Project," *Economic Times*, April 25, 2008,

http://economictimes.indiatimes.com/News/News_By_Industry/Energy/India_joins_mega_gas_pipeline_project/articleshow/2980537.cms.

[413] "Kazakh Offers India Greater Role in Oil, Gas Exploration,"*Indian Express*, April 9, 2008, http://www.indianexpress.com/story/294364.html.

[414] "Kazakh Offers India Greater Role in Oil, Gas Exploration,"*Indian Express*, April 9, 2008, http://www.indianexpress.com/story/294364.html.

would be the local partner in Kazakhstan, and might also work with the IOC in developing its new petrochemical complex at Ceyhan in Turkey.[415]

A senior Indian Foreign Affairs Ministry official related that, during the April 2008 Kazakh-Indian summit, the two sides "agreed on enlarging exchange of visits and expanding cooperation in areas of mutual complementarities," which he identified as food and textile production, education, and information technology as well as energy.[416] An Inter-Governmental Commission, chaired by both governments' energy ministers, is seeking to expand cooperation in these and other sectors, including outer space exploration and possible Indian purchases of Kazakh uranium. Both governments are also providing mutual support for Kazakhstan's efforts to join the WTO and India's efforts to secure a permanent seat on the UN Security Council.[417]

One factor working in India's favor is the long-term perspective of its leaders. Although Ansari admitted to "certain obstacles" in realizing his vision for a "more vibrant relationship" with Kazakhstan and Turkmenistan in the energy sector, he observed that, "We are not looking at one or two years but thinking in terms of decades."[418]

Iran

If it were not for the Iranian government's self-induced political alienation, its territory would have long served as a natural transit route between Kazakhstan and other Central Asian countries and the world's oceans. Even

---

[415] Anupama Airy, "IOC Plans Refinery, Petrochem Units in Central Asia," *Financial Express*, April 11, 2008, http://www.financialexpress.com/news/IOC-plans-refinery-petrochem-units-in-Central-Asia/295763.

[416] John C.K. Daly, "Analysis: India Eyes Kazakh energy," United Press International, April 11, 2008, http://www.upi.com/International_Security/Energy/Analysis/2008/04/11/analysis_india_eyes_kazakh_energy/4684.

[417] John C.K. Daly, "Analysis: India Eyes Kazakh Energy," United Press International, April 11, 2008, http://www.upi.com/International_Security/Energy/Analysis/2008/04/11/analysis_india_eyes_kazakh_energy/4684.

[418] Vishnu Makhijani, "India to Boost Energy Ties with Kazakhstan, Turkmenistan," April 10, 2008, IANS, http://www.thaindian.com/newsportal/business/india-to-boost-energy-ties-with-kazakhstan-turkmenistan_10036545.html..

now, Nazarbayev has reaffirmed interest in sending Kazakh oil and gas southward through Iranian territory to Persian Gulf ports, where tankers could transport the supplies to India and other countries.[419] At present, Kazakhstan only ships a small flow of oil to Iran under a swap arrangement. Every year, somewhat more than one million barrels are transported from Aktau, a Caspian port in southwest Kazakhstan, to other Persian Gulf countries. The improvements in Aktau's port facilities have positioned Kazakhstan well to benefit from any change in Iran's semi-pariah status.[420]

When he attended the Second Caspian Summit in Tehran in October 2007, Nazarbayev promoted construction of a railroad that would run along a 650-km Usen-Gyzylgaia-Bereket-Etrek-Gorgan route. The line would link Kazakhstan directly to the Persian Gulf. Nazarbayev and other Kazakh officials also endorsed deepening mutual investment. They invited Iranian financing of infrastructure, manufacturing, telecommunications, and transportation projects in Kazakhstan, while urging opportunities for Kazakh participation in the privatization of Iranian state enterprises.[421]

In 2006, commodity turnover between Iran and Kazakhstan amounted to \$2 billion dollars. The total for 2007 approached \$3 billion and could rise much further if Iran carries out its plan to build a massive trade and port facility at Bandar-e Anzali on its north Caspian shore. Iranian officials are trying to entice Kazakh investors by offering to allow Kazakh (and Turkmen) goods duty-free transit. Construction of the half-billion dollar project is scheduled to begin in early 2009.[422] Russian and Indian representatives are seeking to

---

[419] "Central Asia: Kazakh, Russian Leaders Discuss Transport Corridor," Radio Free Europe/Radio Liberty, October 5, 2007, http://www.rferl.org/featuresarticle/2007/10/4482ab28-5ab9-4756-8386-48471d684d3f.html.

[420] "American Threat Looms over Kazakh-Iranian Talks," *Central Asia-Caucasus Institute Analyst*, October 20, 2004, http://www.cacianalyst.org/?q=node/2534.

[421] Embassy of Kazakhstan to USA and Canada, "President Nursultan Nazarbayev arrives in Iran to take part in the Second Caspian States Summit," Kazakhstan News Bulletin, January 5, 2007, http://prosites-kazakhembus.homestead.com/NB12-101707.html.

[422] John C.K. Daly, "Iran Develops Caspian Port," United Press International, May 21, 2008, http://www.upi.com/International_Security/Energy/Analysis/2008/05/21/analysis_iran_develops_bandar-e_anzali/4876.

construct a road and railroad connection between Russia and the Persian Gulf that would traverse Kazakhstan and Iran as well as Turkmenistan.[423] The resulting reduction in the costs of transporting cargo to Iran from its northern neighbors would make many Kazakh goods more competitive. At present, for instance, it is cheaper for Iranians to import grain from distant Australia by sea than to bring it overland from neighboring Kazakhstan.[424]

One issue that has not had a major negative effect on Kazakh-Iranian relations has been Kazakhstan's close ties with Israel, a reflection of Astana's multi-vector foreign policy as well as Kazakhs' desire to promote understanding among diverse religions and civilizations. Kazakh officials have used their good relations with both countries to help Iran's isolated Jewish community develop contacts with Jews in Israel and other countries. Nazarbayev also sought to use his contacts with then Iranian President Mohammad Khatami to secure the release of Israeli military personnel captured in Lebanon by pro-Iranian groups.[425]

Yet, Kazakh-Iranian relations are not trouble-free. Iranian and Russian officials have colluded to impede the construction of Trans-Caspian oil and gas pipelines linking Kazakhstan to Azerbaijan without transiting Iranian or Russian territory. Besides the absence of an agreed legal framework to govern underwater mining and shipments, the two governments have cited alleged environmental concerns to hinder Kazakhstan's expanding energy ties with European countries. Kazakh officials also do not appear especially eager to help the current Iranian government realize its ambitions to join the SCO. Tehran's entry could compromise Kazakh leaders' position that the organization is not directed against any bloc or country.

In addition, being too associated with Iran at a time when the latter's nuclear intentions remain dubious could detract from Kazakhstan's exemplary nonproliferation record. According to media accounts, in June 2006, Nazarbayev wrote a letter to Iranian President Mahmoud Ahmadinejad in

---

[423] Frederick Starr, "Introduction," in S. Frederick Starr, ed., *The New Silk Roads: Transport and Trade in Greater Central Asia* (Washington, D.C.: Central Asia-Caucasus Institute, 2007), p. 22.

[424] Kushkumbayev, "Kazakhstan," p. 290.

[425] Lev Krichevsky, "In Kazakhstan, Strong Hand Maintains an Ethnic Peace," Jewish Telegraphic Agency, April 11, 2002, http://www.ncsj.org/AuxPages/110402JTAd.shtml.

which he reaffirmed Kazakhstan's oppositions to the proliferation of nuclear weapons and stressed that the entire international community had an interest in resolving the Iranian nuclear crisis.[426] Kazakh leaders do not object to an Iranian civil nuclear energy program, as permitted under the Nuclear Non-Proliferation Treaty, but oppose any Iranian effort to acquire nuclear weapons.

Pakistan

Pakistani policy-makers see both opportunities and dangers in Central Asia. Pakistani officials originally welcomed the decline of Moscow's control over Afghanistan and Central Asia, and anticipated gaining strategic depth and geopolitical maneuvering room vis-à-vis India by expanding their influence in the region.[427] Some Pakistanis even hoped that, out of Islamic solidarity, the new Central Asian regimes would support Pakistan's policies in its competition with India (e.g., over Kashmir). More recently, India's increased presence in the region has aroused concerns about strategic and economic encirclement.

During the 1990s, suspicions surrounding Pakistanis' ties with Islamic terrorism impeded efforts to strengthen ties with the secular elites of Kazakhstan and the other Central Asian countries. In Afghanistan, Pakistan provided essential support to the Mujahedeen guerrillas battling against Soviet occupation forces and their local allies. Once in power, the Taliban, with the assistance of influential parts of the Pakistani security apparatus, provided support for the Islamic Movement of Uzbekistan and other Sunni extremist groups seeking to establish Islamic republics in Central Asia. In 1999, IMU operatives narrowly failed to assassinate Uzbekistan President Islam Karimov but did manage to infiltrate—and disrupt life in—several Central Asian states, especially Tajikistan and Kyrgyzstan.

---

[426] Marat Yermukanov, "Kazakhstan Seeks Iran's Reconciliation with the West," *Eurasia Daily Monitor*, June 16, 2006, http://www.jamestown.org/edm/article.php?article_id=2371193.

[427] Stephen Blank, "Indo-Pakistani Negotiations: What's In Them For Central Asia?," *Central Asia-Caucasus Institute Analyst*, February 11, 2004, http://www.cacianalyst.org/?q=node/1854.

Since the Pakistani government formally broke with the Taliban and other terrorist groups operating in Central Asian following the 9/11 attacks, the region's leaders have gradually become more receptive to working with Islamabad. Thanks to strong Chinese backing, Pakistan finally received formal observer status in the SCO at the organization's July 2005 summit. Pakistani Prime Minister Shaukat Aziz said the SCO would "provide a platform to Pakistan to present its views and interface with countries who are very important in the region and they transcend from European coast to Asian continent."[428]

Economic considerations have underpinned Pakistan's reintegration into the region. Pakistani leaders regularly highlight the country's pivotal location at the crossroads of South Asia, the Middle East, and Central Asia. In presenting his case for Pakistan's becoming a full SCO member at the June 2006 summit, President Pervez Musharraf said: "Both in geo-political and geo-economic terms, Pakistan is most suitably positioned to promote the interests of the SCO. Pakistan provides the natural link between the SCO states to connect the Eurasian heartland with the Arabian Sea and South Asia. We also offer important overland routes for mutually beneficial trade and energy transactions."[429]

Central Asians appreciate Islamabad's efforts to make Pakistani ports available for regional commerce. Musharraf said Pakistan wants to serve as "a trade and energy corridor" between China and Central Asia.[430] The deepwater port of Gwadar, located along the Arabian Sea in southwest Baluchistan, provides the shortest route to the sea for many landlocked parts of Central Asia. With appropriate supporting infrastructure, especially improved road and rail networks linking Gwadar with the rest of Pakistan and its neighbors, goods can proceed from there by ship to China, India, the Middle East, and

---

[428] "Prime Minister Leaves for Moscow to Attend SCO Meeting," *Balochistan Times*, October 26, 2005.

[429] "President Musharraf"s Address at SCO Summit," June 16, 2006, http://www.presidentofpakistan.gov.pk/FilesSpeeches%5CForeignVisits%5C615200610 3647PMAddress_SCO_Summit.pdf.

[430] Press Trust of India, "Pak Offers China Use of Port," http://www.thestatesman.net/page.news.php?clid=8&theme=&usrsess=1&id=107651.

other global markets.[431] The port of Karachi is also well-situated to offer Central Asia trade wider access to world markets.[432] Air services between Almaty and Pakistan provide an additional link for high-priority commerce and passenger travel.

In December 2002, Turkmenistan, Afghanistan and Pakistan agreed to construct a pipeline that would transport natural gas from Turkmenistan to Pakistan through Afghanistan. Although the project subsequently stalled, the recent decision of the Indian government to support the Trans-Afghan pipeline has revived its prospects. The three countries are also considering constructing railways that would link Turkmenistan and Pakistan through Afghanistan, though transiting through Afghanistan remains too insecure for now for any large-scale rail or road traffic.[433] Pakistani authorities are working with China to improve the Karakoram Highway that links the two countries via a tortuous route through Kyrgyzstan and Kazakhstan. At present, high transportation costs and other barriers limit Pakistan's trade with Central Asian countries to low figures, but realization of these infrastructure projects could increase this level substantially.

Pakistan and Kazakhstan both belong to the Economic Cooperation Organization—which also includes Afghanistan, Azerbaijan, Iran, Kyrgyzstan, Tajikistan, Turkey, Turkmenistan, and Uzbekistan—but this organization has not proven an effective framework for regional economic cooperation, as Aziz himself noted. In May 2004, Pakistan and Kazakhstan also signed, along with China and Kyrgyzstan, a Quadrilateral Agreement that aims to promote regional trade through Pakistan's Karakoram Highway and onward road connections. Perhaps most useful has been the Joint Economic Commissions that Islamabad has established with each Central

---

[431] Besides the need to develop a suitable infrastructure, the anti-Islamabad (and occasionally anti-Chinese) insurgency in Baluchistan presents another threat to Gwadar's role as a possible gateway for Central Asia; see Zahid Hussain, "'It's War Now': A Major Rebellion Puts President Pervez Musharaf's Tribal Policies to the Test," *Newsweek* (international edition), January 16, 2006.

[432] Asma Shakir Khwaja, "The Changing Dynamics of Pakistan's Relations with Central Asia," Central Asia-Caucasus Institute Analyst, February 23, 2005, http://www.cacianalyst.org/?q=node/2824.

[433] *Ibid.*

Asian government to enhance trade and other commercial ties.[434] Besides transiting oil and gas through their territory, Pakistanis agreed in 2006 to purchase hydropower power from Kyrgyzstan and Tajikistan for their own consumption.[435]

Turkey

During the Cold War, political differences between Ankara and Moscow made it hard for Turks to take advantage of their considerable cultural, historical, ethnic, religious, and linguistic ties with Central Asians. After the Soviet Union's demise, some Turks believed these connections would—along with Turkey's proximity to Central Asia and the status Turkey enjoyed as a NATO member—enable Turkey to establish a leading presence in the post-Soviet republics. At times, Prime Minister Suleyman Demirel and President Turgut Ozal spoke of establishing a commonwealth of Turkic peoples or an association of independent Turkic states. Americans and Europeans encouraged Turkish engagement and eagerly sought to market Turkey as a model for Central Asia's newly independent states. In the early 1990s, Turkish officials provided substantial technical assistance to the region, and offered thousands of scholarships Central Asian students to study in Turkey.

It soon became apparent, however, that Turkey lacked the resources to compete at the same level as Russia or China. In addition, Turks realized that Western governments, despite their declarations of support, were unwilling to provide substantial backing to help realize Turkey's ambitions in Central Asia. Finally, although Central Asian leaders' would stress their affinity with the Turks whenever expedient, they did not especially welcome a major political role for Turkey in their region. As a result, cultural issues increasing dominated the agenda of the annual "Turkic summits." Turkish governments

---

[434] Asma Shakir Khwaja, "The Changing Dynamics of Pakistan's Relations with Central Asia," *Central Asia-Caucasus Institute Analyst*, February 23, 2005, http://www.cacianalyst.org/?q=node/2824.

[435] Rizwan Zeb, "Pakistan's Bid for SCO Membership: Prospects and Pitfalls," *Central Asia-Caucasus Institute Analyst*, July 26, 2006, http://www.cacianalyst.org/?q=node/4085.

refocused their political attention to managing their complex relations with the European Union, Washington, and Iraq.[436]

At present, the most important dimension of Turkey's ties with Kazakhstan and the other countries of Central Asia lies in the realm of energy and economics. Turkey currently imports most of its oil and gas from Russia. In addition to the long-standing deliveries of gas through a convoluted pipeline that traverses Moldova, Ukraine, Romania, and Bulgaria, the two countries began using a new direct $3-billion "Blue Stream" natural gas pipeline on a limited basis in February 2003. It became fully operational in November 2005. Since January 2002, Turkey has also has imported natural gas from northern Iran through a much-delayed Tebriz-Ankara pipeline, but deliveries have been interrupted by disagreements over the quality and price of the gas.[437]

To diversify its sources of energy imports further, Turkish officials have been seeking to develop options to transship, and possibly purchase for domestic use, natural gas from Kazakhstan as well as Azerbaijan and Turkmenistan— especially by constructing additional pipelines that bypass Russia. Central Asian governments, hoping to reduce their own dependence on Russian-controlled pipelines, have supported this endeavor. The slow-down in the Turkish economy in the early 2000s, which resulted in Turkey contracting for more imported natural gas than it needed, dampened Turkish interest temporarily in purchasing Kazakh gas for domestic consumption. The recent surge in world energy prices, however, has reinforced Turkish interest in serving as a "natural energy bridge" between the supplier countries to Turkey's east and international energy markets to Turkey's north, west, and south.[438]

Environmental considerations are another factor prompting the Turkish government to seek to import energy from Kazakhstan primarily via

---

[436] Daniel Pipes, "The Event of Our Era: Former Soviet Muslim Republics Change the Middle East," in Michael Mandelbaum, ed., *Central Asia and the World: Kazakhstan, Uzbekistan, Tajikistan, Kyrgyzstan, and Turkmenistan* (New York: Council on Foreign Relations Press, 1994), pp. 49-52, 71-73.

[437] Energy Information Administration, U.S. Department of Energy, "Country Analysis Briefs: Iran" (March 2005), at http://www.eia.doe.gov/emeu/cabs/iran.html.

[438] Energy Information Administration, U.S. Department of Energy, "Country Analysis Briefs: Turkey" (July 2005), at http://www.eia.doe.gov/emeu/cabs/turkey.html.

pipelines. For years, Turkish officials have expressed alarm about accidents resulting from the increasing oil and gas tanker traffic through the already congested Bosporus Straits, which connect the Black and Mediterranean Seas and flow along Istanbul, Turkey's largest city. For this reason, they have encouraged Central Asia exporters to make greater use of Turkey's southwestern port of Ceyhan, which already adjoins the Mediterranean. In June 2006, Kazakhstan agreed to transport from the Kashagan fields through the Baku-Tbilisi-Ceyhan Pipeline Project (BTC). The BTC and other possible pipelines have the potential to relieve some of this pressure, as well as yield the Turkish treasury billions of dollars in transit revenue. Nevertheless, much Central Asian oil will continue to transship the Black Sea from the Russian port of Novorossiysk to world markets.[439]

Turkish small businesses and merchants have developed a substantial presence in Kazakhstan and other Central Asia countries, especially in such sectors as banking, construction, telecommunications, trade, textiles, and food processing.[440] Turkish investment in Kazakhstan is about $1.1 billion, which involves almost 1,700 joint ventures.[441] Both Turkish and Kazakh-Turkish construction firms have a major presence in Kazakhstan. They have been most visible in constructing the new international airport and parliament building in Astana and in developing Almaty's Financial District. The Turkuaz group of 11 Turkish companies involved in Central Asia established its head office in Almaty in 1998. Of its 22 offices in Central Asia, 18 of them are in Kazakhstan. The Turkuaz Foundation provides financial and other

---

[439] For more details on these pipelines see two recent reports by the Energy Information Administration of the U.S. Department of Energy: "Country Analysis Briefs: Caspian Sea" (September 2005), http://www.eia.doe.gov/emeu/cabs/Caspian/Full.html, and "Country Analysis Briefs: Turkey" (July 2005),
http://www.eia.doe.gov/emeu/cabs/turkey.html.
[440] Reuel R. Hanks, *Central Asia: A Global Studies Handbook* (Santa Barbara: ABC-CLIO, 2005), pp. 195-196; Heinz Kramer, *A Changing Turkey: The Challenge to Europe and the United States* (Washington, DC: Brookings Institution Press, 2000), pp. 111-113; and Martha Brill Olcott, "Central Asia," in *Asian Aftershocks: Strategic Asia 2002-03* (Seattle, Washington: National Bureau of Asian Research, 2002), pp. 244-245.
[441] President of the Republic of Kazakhstan, "In the Akorda Palace, President Nursultan Nazarbayev Meets with President of the Republic of Turkey Abdullah Gul Who Arrived in Kazakhstan on State Visit," December 13, 2007,
http://www.akorda.kz/www/www_akorda_kz.nsf/4db47a8e8f1a638d4625723300323d1c/4e04df8d83959c4d462573b00058de8b?OpenDocument&Highlight=0,turkey.

support for social and cultural activities in Kazakhstan and other Central Asian countries.[442]

The Turkish government provides the Kazakh military with some defense equipment and training.[443] In addition, the two governments cooperate on counterterrorism issues. The levels of these security interactions remain low, however, compared to Kazakhstan's more extensive cooperation with NATO and Russia. Another factor limiting Turkey's influence in Kazakhstan is the longstanding practice of Turkish firms of hiring Kazakhs primarily as cheap laborers while employing Turkish émigré nationals as managers and skilled laborers. [444] Whatever the original logic of such a policy, Kazakhstan's strengthening socioeconomic conditions—which includes an improving educational system and growing commercial sophistication—makes this approach both obsolete and counterproductive.

Kazakh investment in Turkey amounts to some 350 million dollars. [445] These projects range from holiday homes in southern Turkey to Kazakh purchases of securities through Turkish investment funds to the plans of KazMunaiGas to construct an oil refinery on Turkey's Black Sea coast. Turkish President Abdullah Gul has urged Kazakh businesses to help construct the Kars-Tbilisi-Ahalkalaki railroad since it could enhance Kazakhstan's potential to ship goods to Europe and the Mediterranean region.[446] The number of Kazakh tourists visiting Turkey has also been increasing, with over 100,000 tourists

---

[442] American Chamber of Commerce in Kazakhstan, "Turkey, A Central Link In Eurasian Economic Integration," http://www.amcham.kz/article.php?article_id=578

[443] Roger McDermott, "Kazakhstan's Parliament Ratifies Strategic Partnership with Azerbaijan," Eurasia Daily Monitor, July 5, 2006, http://www.jamestown.org/edm/article.php?article_id=2371246

[444] President of the Republic of Kazakhstan, "In the Akorda Palace, President Nursultan Nazarbayev Meets with President of the Republic of Turkey Abdullah Gul Who Arrived in Kazakhstan on State Visit," December 13, 2007, http://www.akorda.kz/www/www_akorda_kz.nsf/4db47a8e8f1a638d4625723300323d1c/4e04df8d83959c4d462573b00058de8b?OpenDocument&Highlight=0,turkey.

[445] Marat Yermukanov, "Kazakhstan And Turkey Search For Common Ground," Eurasia Daily Monitor, May 04, 2005, http://www.jamestown.org/publications_details.php?volume_id=407&issue_id=3319&article_id=2369694.

[446] "Kazakhstan and Turkey Conducts Business Forum," RIA Oreanda, December 17, 2007.

visiting Turkey in 2005.[447] Turkey itself contains many ethnic Kazakhs, some of whom came from China's Xinjiang province.[448] Kazakh officials see Turkey as both a consumer of Kazakh energy exports as well as a potential transit country for Kazakh goods entering European and Mediterranean markets—a view that corresponds well with the vision of many American, European and Turkish analysts about Turkey's role as an emerging gateway between the Caspian region and Western markets.

Three bilateral accords signed in the 1990s continue to define the framework for economic relations between Kazakhstan and Turkey: the 1994 Agreement on Encouraging and Protecting Bilateral Investment; the 1996 Agreement on Preventing Double Taxation; and the 1998 Agreement on Encouraging and Protecting Bilateral Investments. The two governments are seeking ways to strengthen their economic ties still further. Kazakh and Turkish officials and business leaders see the potential for much greater interaction given that only a little over 1% of Turkey's trade now goes to Kazakhstan, despite the extensive cultural, personal, and other ties between their nationals.[449] In December 2007, Astana hosted a business forum that included representatives from over 100 Kazakh and 80 Turkish companies working in the fields of energy, telecommunications, transportation, construction, and other sectors.[450]

One mechanism Kazakh officials have sought to mobilize local support for regional economic processes independent of the great powers is by endorsing increased cooperation among Turkic-speaking nations. On November 17-18, 2006, the first summit of the leaders of Turkish-speaking countries in five years assembled in Turkey's Mediterranean resort city of Antalya. The presidents of Kazakhstan, Kyrgyzstan, and Azerbaijan attended along with

---

[447] "Kazakhstan, Turkey to Boost Tourism Cooperation, Open New Flights," Interfax-Kazakhstan News Agency, BBC Monitoring, April 28, 2006.

[448] Ozgecan, "Kazakh Refugees in Turkey—50th Anniversary, October 4, 2006, http://kazakhstan.neweurasia.net/2006/10/04/kazakh-refugees-in-turkey-50th-anniversary.

[449] Marat Yermukanov, "Kazakhstan and Turkey Spearhead Integration of Turkic Nations," Eurasia Daily Monitor, December 07, 2006, http://www.jamestown.org/publications_details.php?volume_id=414&issue_id=3947&article_id=2371713

[450] "Kazakhstan and Turkey Conducts Business Forum," RIA Oreanda, December 17, 2007.

high-level representatives from Turkmenistan and Uzbekistan. Turkey had regularly held such meetings in the 1990s, but the practice had fallen into abeyance by the end of the decade, when Ankara's gaze focused on Brussels. Turks' increasing frustration with their halting efforts to join the EU, however, has been stimulating their interesting in reaffirming ties with the Turkish-speaking nations of Central Asia. At the summit, Nazarbayev called for creating a Turkic parliamentary assembly. He nominated former Turkish president and Prime Minister Suleyman Demirel as its first chairman. Nazarbayev also endorsed the idea of creating a "Turkic commonwealth" in order to galvanize the region's "200 million Turks" into pursuing enhanced regional cooperation.[451]

Central Asian States

Afghanistan

Kazakh leaders are very eager to help restore political and economic stability to Afghanistan, given that the country's troubles have presented security threats and disrupted economic development throughout Kazakhstan's extended neighborhood.[452] As soon as Operation Enduring Freedom (OEF) began, Kazakhstan sold 15,000 metric tons of wheat to the USAID. The UN World Food Program then distributed the wheat to Afghans as emergency food assistance.[453] The Kazakh government also allowed coalition forces supporting Afghanistan through OEF to use Kazakhstan's air space and permits NATO warplanes to enjoy emergency landing and refueling rights. Kazakh officials have subsequently offered to help develop oil fields in

---

[451] Mevlut Katik, "Spirit of Cooperation Dominates Turkic Summit," Eurasia Insight, November 20, 2006,
http://www.eurasianet.org/departments/insight/articles/eav112006.shtml.
[452] Yerzhan Kh. Kazykhanov, "On Kazakhstan," *American Foreign Policy Interests*, vol. 28, no.3 (July 2006), p. 189.
[453] Alima Bissenova, "Nazarbayev, Seeking Oil Favor, Positions Himself as Central Asian Reformer," Eurasia Insight, January 4, 2002,
http://www.eurasianet.org/departments/business/articles/eav010402a.shtml.

northern Afghanistan. [454] Trade turnover between Kazakhstan and Afghanistan in 2006 amounted to $179.40 million. The commerce remains imbalanced. Afghanistan exported only $891,000 worth of goods to Kazakhstan, while importing $178.51 million worth of Kazakh merchandise. In the first half of 2007, the trade turnover between the two countries totaled to $79.62 million, continuing the trend of the previous year in terms of share of import and export of each country. Kazakhstan exported $79.31 million worth of goods and imported only $550,000. [455] In 2007, the two countries formed a joint intergovernmental commission to promote bilateral trade and economic cooperation. One of its tasks will be to make the trade more balanced as well as increase its aggregate volume.

A current Kazakh security priority regarding Afghanistan is to dampen the export of narcotics from that country. General Amangeldy Shabdarbayev, Chairman of Kazakhstan's National Security Committee, has warned that the wave of illicit drug trafficking sweeping through Central Asia—along the northern route extending from Afghanistan to Russia and Europe—threatens Kazakhstan's economic prosperity. [456] Kazakh officials have undertaken a vigorous domestic counternarcotics campaign as part of the government's "Astana without Drugs" program, but Shabdarbayev and other Kazakh officials have called for a multinational effort to revitalize the Afghan economy and provide alternative means of livelihood to the narcotics industry. In March 2007, for instance, Berik Imashev, the head of Kazakhstan's National Security Council, urged the international community "to work out concrete economic programs aimed at providing large-scale financial and economic aid to Afghanistan in order to 'de-narcotize'" its

---

[454] Julie A. Corwin, "Central/South Asia: Forum Examines Regional Trade Prospects," Radio Free Europe/Radio Liberty, April 5, 2006, http://www.rferl.org/featuresarticle/2006/04/F7BC6B94-E54B-447F-8729-35089CB109A3.html.

[455] Ministry of Foreign Affairs of Kazakhstan, "Sotrudnichestvo Respubliki Kazakhstan s Islamskoy Respublikoy Afghanistan," November 29, 2006, http://portal.mfa.kz/portal/page/portal/mfa/ru/content/policy/cooperation/asia_africa/21.

[456] Interview with Kazakhstan Today, March 2, 2007, cited in Embassy of Kazakhstan to the USA and Canada, "Kazakh Security Chief Says Drug Emergency Growing, International Cooperation Is Key to Defeating Scourge," Kazakhstan News Bulletin, March 11, 2007, http://www.kazakhembus.com/031407.html.

economy and stimulate conditions for exporting legal products from that country." Imashev said Kazakhstan was eager to contribute to such an endeavor, which he argued should involve both Afghanistan's neighbors and other countries.[457] Given that Eurasian narcotics trafficking is one of the region's most integrated transnational industries, the Kazakh government has stressed the need to improve integration of regional counternarcotics efforts, which presently involve a plethora of overlapping and poorly resourced national and multinational programs.

Kazakh officials share the belief of Afghan officials and other experts that Afghanistan's long-term economic viability depends on the development of improved transportation, communication, and other networks that would better integrate their country into regional economic processes. The Kazakh Foreign Ministry warns that, "Peace and security in the entire Central Asian region depend on stabilizing the situation in Afghanistan," but adds that Kazakhstan's support for regional integration will help solve the problems associated with "Afghanistan's transformation into a peaceful and constructive" country. [458] Afghanistan is well-situated to benefit from increased commerce between Europe and Asia, but only if rail, road, and pipeline construction extends throughout their territory.

As future chair of the OSCE, Kazakhstan likely will play a role in helping shape the OSCE's new initiative, launched at the 2007 Madrid summit, to help curb the trafficking of narcotics, weapons, and people across the border between Afghanistan and Tajikistan. For instance, the Ministerial Council decided to expand an OSCE project, which began earlier in November, to train anti-drug police in Afghanistan by allowing counternarcotics officers from Afghanistan's Central Asia neighbors to participate. The OSCE's current Chairman-in-Office, Spanish Foreign Minister Miguel Angel Moratinos, told a press conference at the end of the session that, "With this new contribution, this new involvement of the Organization in Afghanistan

---

[457] Embassy of Kazakhstan to the USA and Canada, "Kazakhstan Urges Financial, Economic Aid to Afghanistan," Kazakhstan News Bulletin, March 21, 2007, http://www.kazakhembus.com/032107.html.
[458] Ministry of Foreign Affairs of Kazakhstan, "Kazakhstan i Voprosy global'noi i regional'noy bezonasnocti uregulirovanie situatsii v Afganistane," "http://portal.mfa.kz/portal/page/portal/mfa/ru/content/policy/security/afganistan.

we hope to bolster our security and we acknowledge the link between OSCE countries and the problems and challenges which exist in Afghanistan."[459] Last year, Foreign Minister Tazhin indicated "it would be quite useful to combine the efforts" of the CICA, the CSTO, and especially the SCO with those of the OSCE "to solve the acute problems of Eurasia including [the] one of Afghanistan."[460]

Kyrgyzstan

Kazakhstan and Kyrgyzstan have established deep economic ties. Bilateral commerce amounts to some $400 million annually. Kazakhs provide the main source of foreign capital in Kyrgyzstan, with over $300 million invested in various projects.[461] Kazakh entrepreneurs have established hundreds of joint ventures in Kyrgyzstan in such sectors as banking, construction, and energy.[462] According to one estimate, Kazakh investors hold one third of the total equity of Kyrgyzstan banks.[463] Kyrgyzstan imports about one-fifth of its wheat from Kazakhstan.[464] In recent years, Kazakhstan's booming economy has led more Kyrgyz labor migrants to seek work in neighboring Kazakhstan than in more distant Russia. An estimated 200,000 Kyrgyz migrants work in Kazakhstan.[465]

---

[459] Organization of Security and Co-operation in Europe, "OSCE Ministers Agree Chairmanship Bids, Greater Engagement in Afghanistan," November 30, 3007, http://www.osce.org/item/28621.html.

[460] Marat Tazhin, "Kazakhstan in a Changing World," speech at U.S.-Kazakhstan Business Association dinner, Washington, D.C., May 8, 2007, http://www.kazakhembus.com/050907.html.

[461] Joanna Lillis, "Nazarbayev Flexes Diplomatic Muscle During Visit to Kyrgyzstan," Eurasia Insight, May 1, 2007, http://www.eurasianet.org/departments/insight/articles/eav050107.shtml.

[462] Embassy of Kazakhstan to USA and Canada, "Nazarbayev Visits Bishkek, Pledges Economic Investment," Kazakhstan News Bulletin, April 26, 2007, http://www.kazakhembus.com/042607.html.

[463] Meri Bekeshova, "Central Asia: A Kyrgyz-Kazakh Step Towards Regional Union," IPS, May 24, 2007, http://www.ipsnews.net/news.asp?idnews=37887.

[464] Bruce Pannier, "Central Asia: Kyrgyz President Returns from Astana with Wheat-Export Deal," Radio Free Europe/Radio Liberty, April 18, 2008, http://www.rferl.org/featuresarticle/2008/04/a6fc862a-649e-4cc3-acf4-57dc77effa9c.html.

[465] Erica Marat, "Nazarbayev Promises Economic Assistance, Urges Political Stability in Kyrgyzstan," Eurasia Daily Monitor, May 3, 2007,

During his April 25-26, 2007 visit to Kyrgyzstan, Nazarbayev indicated intent in principle to increase Kazakhstan's support substantially for Kyrgyzstan's economic development. He told his hosts that, under the right conditions, Kazakhs were "ready to invest billions of dollars in Kyrgyzstan's economy."[466] For example, Nazarbayev offered to support Kyrgyzstan's hydropower sector by helping finance its 1,900 MW Kambarata-1 and 240 MW Kambarata-2 power plants, despite the fact that Kazakhstan's own plants can generate electricity at cheaper prices than Kyrgyzstan.[467] Kazakh economists worry that their country lacks adequate generating capacity to meet the country's surging domestic demand for electricity. Investing in Kyrgyzstan's hydropower facilities—including the two Kambarata plans, whose combined projection costs could exceed $2 billion—would benefit Kazakhstan and other Central Asian countries, who share water and electricity.[468] Recognizing that the investment could take some time to materialize, Nazarbayev pledged $100 million in emergency humanitarian aid as well as wheat and fuel supplies.[469]

Yet, Nazarbayev bluntly warned that political instability and widespread corruption were discouraging Kazakh businessmen from investing in Kyrgyzstan, a view shared by the Asian Development Bank and other international financial experts.[470] "We propose Kazakhstan's experience of development and modernization, which only comes in conditions of stability.

---

http://jamestown.org/edm/article.php?volume_id=420&issue_id=4094&article_id=23721
41.
[466] Joanna Lillis, "Nazarbayev Flexes Diplomatic Muscle During Visit to Kyrgyzstan," Eurasia Insight, May 1, 2007,
http://www.eurasianet.org/departments/insight/articles/eav050107.shtml.
[467] Erica Marat, "Nazarbayev Promises Economic Assistance, Urges Political Stability in Kyrgyzstan," Eurasia Daily Monitor, May 3, 2007,
http://jamestown.org/edm/article.php?volume_id=420&issue_id=4094&article_id=23721
41.
[468] Joanna Lillis, "Central Asia: Water Woes Stoke Economic Worries," Eurasia Insight, April 28, 2009,
http://www.eurasianet.org/departments/insight/articles/eav042808.shtml.
[469] Lillis, "Nazarbayev Flexes Diplomatic Muscle."
[470] Some Western analysts have cited concerns about corruption and instability in Kazakhstan's legal structure (rather than political instability) as a factor impeding foreign investment in Kazakhstan; see for example Maureen S. Crandall, *Energy, Economics, and Politics in the Caspian Region: Dreams and Realities*, (Westport, Connecticut, London: Praeger Security International, 2006), pp. 85-92.

Investment does not come to an unstable country," Nazarbayev explained.[471] In an interview on Khabar and Kyrgyz state TV, Nazarbayev told listeners that all Kyrgyz political factions must peacefully negotiate a political compromise to their disputes and "use their power to establish order in the country in a democratic and lawful way." Otherwise, "Kyrgyzstan will be left with the alternative of being the same as Afghanistan was in its time: disturbances, anarchy . . . Kyrgyzstan will turn into an enclave of instability. . . .Does anybody really want this? I would rather not wish this on the Kyrgyz people." [472]

Another impediment has been cultural sensitivities, specifically Kyrgyz fears and resentment that their country could become a dependency of neighboring Kazakhstan.[473] Tensions have arisen in the way Kazakh authorities have deported Kyrgyz migrant laborers caught working illegally in Kazakhstan. In addition, popular protests have occurred after the Kyrgyz government ceded contested territories claimed by Kyrgyzstan to Kazakhstan. Even so, some influential Kyrgyz politicians are prepared to sacrifice some autonomy for the economic benefits of moving closer to Kazakhstan—confident that China and Russia will retain sufficient influence to avert any serious risk of their country's becoming overly dependent on their Kazakh neighbors.[474]

Kyrgyz leaders are particularly eager to use their ties with Kazakhstan to become more deeply involved in regional oil and gas projects. When President Kurmanbek Bakiyev traveled to Kazakhstan in April 2008, he lobbied Kazakh officials to help finance gas pipelines that would traverse Kyrgyz territory.[475] Kazakh officials also pledged to provide Kyrgyzstan's

---

[471] Lillis, "Nazarbayev Flexes Diplomatic Muscle."
[472] *Ibid.*
[473] Marat, "Nazarbayev Promises Economic Assistance."
[474] Meri Bekeshova, "Central Asia: A Kyrgyz-Kazakh Step Towards Regional Union," IPS, May 24, 2007, http://www.ipsnews.net/news.asp?idnews=37887.
[475] Bruce Pannier, "Central Asia: Kyrgyz President Returns from Astana with Wheat-Export Deal," Radio Free Europe/Radio Liberty, April 18, 2008, http://www.rferl.org/featuresarticle/2008/04/a6fc862a-649e-4cc3-acf4-57dc77effa9c.html.

underused refineries with over 300,000 tons of oil annually to help them meet domestic demand.[476]

One way Kazakhstan's influence over Kyrgyzstan has manifested itself has been support Kyrgyz leaders have given to Kazakh proposals for increased regional integration. In April 2007, Nazarbayev and Bakiyev signed an agreement to create a bilateral "International Supreme Council." Kazakh officials characterized the agreement as a step towards realizing Nazarbayev's goal of creating a wider Central Asian Union. Furthermore, the two presidents issued a joint statement pledging increased bilateral political and economic cooperation in such areas as countering terrorism, illegal migration, narcotrafficking, organized crime, and other threats to either country's "independence, sovereignty and territorial integrity." [477] In April 2008, Bakiyev committed to attend a conference the following year in Kazakhstan that would create a Central Asian union that, among other functions, would attempt to resolve disputes among Central Asian countries over how to distribute the region's energy and water resources.[478]

Mongolia

Kazakhstan and Mongolia established diplomatic relations in 1992. During Nazarbayev's visit to Ulaanbaatar the following year, the two governments signed basic documents establishing a basic legal and diplomatic framework for their bilateral economic relationship. [479] Since then, Kazakhstan and Mongolia have been striving to increase economic ties, which declined sharply in the mid-1990s due to the post-Soviet economic implosion in both countries. Trade has been increasing, but remains heavily skewed in favor of Kazakh exports to Mongolia. These include grain, petrochemicals, tobacco,

---

[476] "Kazakhstan Will Keep Kyrgyz Refineries Running," *Nezavisimaya Gazeta*, April 18, 2008,
http://enews.ferghana.ru/article.php?id=2365&PHPSESSID=be1b21f9220577cc82faa.

[477] Lillis, "Nazarbayev Flexes Diplomatic Muscle."

[478] Pannier, "Central Asia: Kyrgyz President Returns from Astana."

[479] Ministry of Foreign Affairs of Kazakhstan, "Sotrudnichestvo Respubliki Kazakhstan s Mongoliey," May 30, 2008,
http://portal.mfa.kz/portal/page/portal/mfa/ru/content/policy/cooperation/asia_africa/10.

and pipes, while Kazakhstan imports mostly meat, wool, and pear spar.[480] In 2006, the sales turnover between the two countries amounted to $67.4 million.[481] Economic ties are stronger between nearby regions. In particular, increasing trade between the East Kazakhstan Province and the western aymags of Mongolia has been a mutual priority.[482]

Besides a mutual desire to increase bilateral trade, the two governments have sought to increase the flow of Kazakh capital into Mongolia. Kazakhstan's political and business leaders have shown most interest in contributing to the development of Mongolia's mining industries. Mongolian leaders are eager to secure Kazakh contributions to developing their country's housing, construction, and other basic economic infrastructure. [483] To encourage Kazakh investments in Mongolia, the two governments have signed agreements that, for example, provide legal protections for Kazakh investment within Mongolia as well as exempt it from double taxation.[484] When Mongolian President Nambaryn Enkhbayar visited Kazakhstan from August 13-15, 2007, he participated in a business forum in Astana that sought to promote commercial cooperation in such areas as agriculture, construction, and mining. Representatives from Mongolia's twenty largest businesses showcased investment projects at the event.[485]

Another area of economic focus has been on improving the transportation networks connecting the two countries. Direct air flights do occur twice a week between East Kazakhstan and Mongolia.[486] Both sides agree on the

---

[480] "Mongolian President Travels to Kazakhstan on August 13-15," Kazakhstan General Newswire, August 9, 2007, BBC Monitoring.
[481] "Presidents of Kazakhstan and Mongolia Discussed Cooperation," Kazakhstan General Newswire, August 14, 2007, BBC Monitoring.
[482] Ministry of Foreign Affairs of Kazakhstan, "Sotrudnichestvo Respubliki Kazakhstan s Mongoliey," May 30, 2008, http://portal.mfa.kz/portal/page/portal/mfa/ru/content/policy/cooperation/asia_africa/10.
[483] "Kazakhstan, Mongolia Agree on Investment Projects," Interfax-Kazakhstan News Agency, August 14, 2007, BBC Monitoring.
[484] "Mongolia to Enhance Economic Cooperation with Kazakhtsan," Xinhua, November 13, 2006.
[485] "Mongolian President Travels to Kazakhstan on August 13-15," Kakzakhstan General Newswire, August 9, 2007, BBC Monitoring.
[486] "Kazakhstan, Mongolia to Negotiate Road Building Project with RF," August 14, 2007, BBC Monitoring.

desirability of expanding rail and road traffic between the two countries, but this process requires cooperating with the Russian Federation since Kazakhstan and Mongolia do not border each other. For example, driving Mongolian livestock on foot to Kazakhstan requires passage through the territory of Russia's Altay Republic. Representatives of Altay, Mongolia, and Kazakhstan are considering creating joint enterprises and other economic mechanisms to enhance trilateral cooperation. [487]

The presence of large numbers of ethnic Kazakhs in Mongolia also shapes bilateral relations between the two countries. During the 1930s, over a million ethnic Kazakhs sought to flee Soviet-era collectivization, which resulted in mass starvation among the traditionally nomadic Kazakh people, by migrating to other countries. An estimated 100,000 Kazakhs took refuge in Mongolia. Due to the weaker performance of the Mongolian economy as compared with that of Kazakhstan, many ethnic Kazakhs in Mongolia have experienced economic hardships. Kazakh officials have sought to ensure that these individuals "have all opportunities to preserve their ethnic identity, national language, culture and tradition." [488] The Astana government has provided Mongolia's Kazakhs with literary works in the Kazakh language, including school textbooks, and supported various cultural exchange programs. Tens of thousands of ethnic Kazakhs have moved from Mongolia to Kazakhstan, which has required Kazakh authorities to sponsor various educational, occupational retaining, and other assimilation programs.

Although Mongolia is not a member of the CIS, CSTO, or OSCE, it does have observer status within the SCO, which allows for some institutional interaction with Kazakhstan. In addition, Mongolia and Kazakhstan also cooperate on security issues. Mongolia participates in the Kazakh-led CICA process, supports the Central Asian Nuclear-Free-Zone, and has signed an agreement with Kazakhstan on averting and managing the consequences of

---

[487] Ministry of Foreign Affairs of Kazakhstan, "Sotrudnichestvo Respubliki Kazakhstan s Mongoliey," May 30, 2008,
http://portal.mfa.kz/portal/page/portal/mfa/ru/content/policy/cooperation/asia_africa/10.
[488] "Presidents of Kazakhstan and Mongolia Discussed Cooperation," Kazakhstan General Newswire, August 14, 2007, BBC Monitoring.

natural and man-made disasters.[489] Representatives of the two countries also interact in the United Nations and other large multinational organizations. Academic exchange programs allow students and scholars from Kazakhstan and Mongolia to enroll in each other's educational institutions.

Tajikistan

On January 13, 1993, the governments of Kazakhstan and Tajikistan signed an agreement defining the fundamental principles that govern their bilateral relations.[490] Until recently, however, interactions between Kazakhstan and Tajikistan remained marginal. From 1992-1996, Tajikistan was engulfed in a vicious civil war. Even after the 1997 peace accords, when Kazakhstan and other CIS members authorized the deployment of a CIS peacekeeping force in the region, the attention of the country's political and business elite remained focused inward.[491] During the early 2000s, Tajik leaders became preoccupied with managing relations with Afghanistan, Iran, and Russia.

It has only been in the last few years that bilateral relations with Kazakhstan have developed robustly. For example, bilateral trade turnover increased by 183.5% between January-March 2005 and January-March 2006, making Kazakhstan Tajikistan's third-largest trade partner after Russia and Uzbekistan among other CIS countries.[492] Kazakh-Tajik trade grew by a still respectable 57% between January-July 2007 over the same period of the previous year.[493] The trade is very imbalanced in Kazakhstan's favor. In 2007,

---

[489] Ministry of Foreign Affairs of Kazakhstan, "Sotrudnichestvo Respubliki Kazakhstan s Mongoliey," May 30, 2008,
http://portal.mfa.kz/portal/page/portal/mfa/ru/content/policy/cooperation/asia_afri ca/10.
[490] Ministry of Foreign Affairs of Kazakhstan, "Sotrudnichestvo Respubliki Kazakhstan s Respublikoy Tadzhikistan," February 22, 2008,
http://portal.mfa.kz/portal/page/portal/mfa/ru/content/policy/cooperation/CIS/04.
[491] Robert H. Donaldson and Joseph L. Nogee, *The Foreign Policy of Russia: Changing Systems, Enduring Interests*. 3rd ed. (Armonk, New York: M.E. Sharpe, 2005), pp. 197-198.
[492] Ministry of Foreign Affairs of Kazakhstan, "Sotrudnichestvo Respubliki Kazakhstan s Respublikoy Tadzhikistan," February 22, 2008,
http://portal.mfa.kz/portal/page/portal/mfa/ru/content/policy/cooperation/CIS/04.
[493] Gulnoza Saidazimova, "Kazakhstan: Nazarbaev's Regional Tour Shows Growing Economic Influence," Radio Free Europe/Radio Liberty, September 14, 2007,
http://www.rferl.org/featuresarticle/2007/09/5ae4b7b0-0cbc-4d60-8078-004574570ae1.html.

Tajikistan imported \$278.5 million worth of Kazakh goods, while exporting only \$27 million worth directly to Kazakhstan. Tajikistan's imports from Kazakhstan include 90% of its wheat and flour and 40% of combustive-lubricating materials.[494]

When President Nazarbayev visited Tajikistan in September 2007, he offered to help establish a special bilateral investment fund of \$100 million. "The Kazakh side will contribute its significant part. The fund will work for the benefit of the Tajik economy." [495] Besides pledging to provide 80% of the money for the joint fund, Nazarbayev offered to export grain to Tajikistan and help finance the construction of the Nurobod hydroelectric plant in the north of the country. [496] Some Kazakh investors are also interested in investing in the Tajikistan's Nurobod power plant, scheduled for commissioning in March 2009.[497] The existing Nurek hydroelectric power plant, Tajikistan's main energy source, has experienced debilitating water shortages recently. The growing demand for electricity in Kazakhstan and the rest of Central Asia has led the Eurasian Development Bank, a Russo-Kazakh venture, to explore providing financial support for the construction of Tajikistan's Rogun hydroelectric power station.[498]

Kazakhstan has also emerged recently as a leading provider of assistance to Tajikistan. For example, Astana made important contributions to international humanitarian relief efforts to help Tajikistan survive this winter's unusually cold weather. In February 2008, the Kazakh government offered 1,000 tons of fuel oil, food supplies, and other emergency assistance

---

[494] Ministry of Foreign Affairs of Kazakhstan, "Sotrudnichestvo Respubliki Kazakhstan s Respublikoy Tadzhikistan," February 22, 2008,
http://portal.mfa.kz/portal/page/portal/mfa/ru/content/policy/cooperation/CIS/04.
[495] Bruce Pannier, "Central Asia: Is The Region Entering a New Era of Cooperation?" Eurasia Insight, September 20, 2007,
http://www.rferl.org/featuresarticle/2007/09/8E31E2AA-C311-4216-925E-424DEB998442.html.
[496] Saidazimova, "Kazakhstan: Nazarbaev's Regional Tour."
[497] Joanna Lillis, "Central Asia: Water Woes Stoke Economic Worries," Eurasia Insight, April 28, 2009,
http://www.eurasianet.org/departments/insight/articles/eav042808.shtml.
[498] Ibid.

worth approximately $3 million.[499] In a gesture of appreciation, Tajik President Emomali Rakhmon said that Tajiks "regard Kazakhstan as a model."[500] Kazakh banks (e.g., Kazkommerzbank and BankTuranAlem) already have a strong presence in Tajikistan's financial sector.[501]

Turkmenistan

Kazakhstan and Turkmenistan signed a delimitation and demarcation agreement for their 379-km border on July 5, 2001.[502] Under Saparmurat Niyazov (a.k.a. Turkmenbashi, "the father of all Turkmen"), Turkmenistan's first president as an independent state, the country pursued an isolationist policy that limited contact with Kazakhstan and other countries. Although Niyazov and Nazarbayev met frequently, a recurring source of Kazakh-Turkmen tension was Niyazov's opposition to regional integration processes, which Nazarbayev normally championed. Niyazov followed a doctrine of "positive neutrality" regarding Central Asia's Russian-dominated international institutions such as the CIS, the CSTO, and the SCO.

Since Niyazov died unexpectedly on December 21, 2006, Nazarbayev and other Kazakh leaders have vigorously sought to engage Turkmenistan's new president, Gurbanguly Berdymukhamedov. At a minimum, they want to assess his plans for his country, especially its foreign policies. Ideally, they would like to pursue opportunities for mutually beneficial ties shunned by his predecessor. When Nazarbayev and Berdymukhamedov met at the end of May 2007, much of their attention focused on improving transportation links between their two countries. The meeting marked the renewal, on May 26, of direct air links between Ashgabat and Almaty. Nazarbayev and Berdymukhamedov discussed whether also to open direct bus connections

---

[499] "Chronicle of the Month: February 19, 2008," Asia-Plus, March 3, 2008, http://www.asiaplus.tj/en/news/61/28802.html.
[500] Embassy of Kazakhstan to the USA and Canada, "Kazakhstan Considers Tajikistan Important Partner in Central Asia," Kazakhstan's News Bulletin, September 19, 2007, http://www.kazakhembus.com/NB8-190907.html.
[501] Ministry of Foreign Affairs of Kazakhstan, "Sotrudnichestvo Respubliki Kazakhstan s Respublikoy Tadzhikistan," February 22, 2008, http://portal.mfa.kz/portal/page/portal/mfa/ru/content/policy/cooperation/CIS/04.
[502] Ministry of Foreign Affairs of Kazakhstan, "Sotrudnichestvo Respubliki Kazakhstan s Turkmenistanom," February 22, 2008, http://portal.mfa.kz/portal/page/portal/mfa/ru/content/policy/cooperation/CIS/03.

between Aktau and Turkmenbashi.[503] In any case, the two leaders committed to establishing a new road connecting Zhetybai in Kazakhstan with Turkmenbashi City, some 237 kilometers distant. The two governments envisage this road as constituting an element of the transnational ground corridor that will connect Astrakhan in Russia to Turkmenistan. They also agreed to reestablish a direct railway link that would enable commodities from Turkmenistan to proceed through Kazakhstan and Russia to European markets.[504]

When they met again in September 2007, Berdymukhamedov told Nazarbayev that, "One of the priority aspects of our cooperation is the further intensification of bilateral trade and economic relations." He added that the two countries "have great potential in the realization of large-scale projects in the field of trade, energy, transportation, and telecommunications."[505] Nazarbayev and Berdymukhamedov also discussed constructing a railroad that would connect Kazakhstan to Iran via Turkmen territory.[506] Bilateral trade was already growing robustly under Niyazov: in 2007, it increased by almost 44% as compared to 2006, amounting to $220.6 million.[507]

Berdymukhamedov has already demonstrated a more open attitude toward dealing with the SCO. Along with Afghan President Hamid Karzai, he was a "guest of honor" at the August 2007 SCO summit in Bishkek. The other SCO

---

[503] "Kazakhstan and Turkmenistan Underlined a Significant Potential in Bilateral Cooperation in Transport and Transit Spheres," Kazakhstan Today, May 29, 2007, http://eng.gazeta.kz/art.asp?aid=91732.

[504] "Kazakhstan/Turkmenistan: Resource-Rich Central Asian Duo Seeks Cooperation," Radio Free Europe/Radio Liberty, May 29, 2007, http://www.rferl.org/featuresarticle/2007/05/37aaf34c-7953-4d98-bf89-9042ef739cb5.html.

[505] Bruce Pannier, "Central Asia: Is the Region Entering a New Era of Cooperation?" Eurasia Insight, September 20, 2007, http://www.eurasianet.org/departments/insight/articles/eav112006.shtml.

[506] Gulnoza Saidazimova, "Kazakhstan: Nazarbaev's Regional Tour Shows Growing Economic Influence," Radio Free Europe/Radio Liberty, September 14, 2007, http://www.rferl.org/featuresarticle/2007/09/5ae4b7b0-0cbc-4d60-8078-004574570ae1.html.

[507] Ministry of Foreign Affairs of Kazakhstan, "Sotrudnichestvo Respubliki Kazakhstan s Turkmenistanom," February 22, 2008, http://portal.mfa.kz/portal/page/portal/mfa/ru/content/policy/cooperation/CIS/03.

members are eager to cooperate with Turkmenistan in the energy sector even if its government refrains from formally joining their organization. In the joint communiqué issued at the end of the Bishkek summit, the heads of the SCO member governments maintained that they would develop their energy coordination "according to the principle of openness for all interested states and organizations that share the goals and tasks of the SCO."[508] Cooperation with Turkmenistan would go far toward realizing Nazarbayev's ambitions to convert the SCO into an influential energy body. If Turkmenistan were to formally join the SCO, or merely coordinate its energy policies with its full members (China, Russia, and the other Central Asian countries) and formal observers (which include gas-rich Iran), the organization's weight in world energy affairs could increase dramatically.

Until now, the legacy of the USSR's integrated pipeline system has compelled Turkmenistan to rely on Soviet-era energy pipelines to reach world markets. The country's dependence on transit routes through Russia allowed Gazprom to buy Turkmen gas for lower than market prices—$65 per 1,000 cubic meters before August 2006; $100 per 1,000 cubic meters since then—and then resell it at much higher prices (recently around $250 per 1,000 cubic meters) to European customers.[509] While reaffirming a commitment to uphold long-term contractual obligations, which require Turkmenistan to continue shipping more than 50 billion cubic meters annually to Russia, the Berdymukhamedov administration has been exploring additional export routes, including eastward into China and southward toward Pakistan.

In addition, the governments of Turkmenistan and Kazakhstan are eager to diversify their energy export routes westward to supplement their deliveries through Russia, Iran, and to China. An obvious means to do so is shipping oil and gas to European markets via pipelines through the sectors of the Caspian seabed closest to Azerbaijan and Turkmenistan. Since the distance between their shores is the shortest route across the Caspian Sea, one or more Turkmenistan-Azerbaijan pipelines would present the most economically

---

[508] Shanghai Cooperation Organization, "Joint Communiqué of Meeting of Council of Heads of SCO Member States," August 16, 2007, http://www.sectsco.org/html/01721.html.
[509] Ilan Greenberg, "Russia to Get Central Asian Pipeline," *New York* Times, May 13, 2007, http://www.nytimes.com/2007/05/13/world/europe/13putin.html.

suitable route for exporting Turkmenistan's oil and natural gas to Europe via the South Caucasus.

The recent improvement in relations between Azerbaijan and Turkmenistan could help remove one major obstacle to the exploitation of Caspian Sea energy reserves. When Berdymukhamedov arrived in Baku on May 18, he became the first Turkmen president in over a decade to visit Azerbaijan. The two countries broke off relations in 1999 over an Azerbaijani decision to develop an oil and natural gas field that the Turkmenistan government also claimed.[510] During his recent visit, Berdymukhamedov stated that the two governments had agreed in principle on the need to resolve their long-standing differences regarding the Caspian Sea's legal status. He observed that a resolution to the dispute would create "favorable conditions" for exploiting its offshore oil and gas resources.[511]

Berdymukhamedov also underscored the strategic importance of the two countries in world energy markets. Not only do they possess important oil and gas reserves within their territories, but they are situated at both ends of the Caspian Sea, allowing them to function as potential gateways for Caspian energy exports to international oil and gas markets: "The advantageous geopolitical location of Turkmenistan and Azerbaijan, located at the intersection of Europe and Asia, offers the opportunity to use this fortunate location for the good of neighboring countries and for the interests of the two countries--and also for other countries in the West and in the East." [512] Although much uncertainty persists regarding the extent of Turkmenistan's natural gas reserves, which industry experts estimate at almost 3 trillion cubic meters but which may not prove adequate to meet all Turkmenistan's commitments to international purchasers, representatives of foreign governments and energy companies have flocked to the country during the last year.

---

[510] "Turkmen-Azeri Thaw Could Create New Caspian Axis," Institute for War & Peace Reporting, http://www.iwpr.net/?p=btm&s=b&o=344827&apc_state=henh.

[511] *Ibid.*

[512] Bruce Pannier, "Caspian: Azerbaijani-Turkmen Summit Marks Potentially Lucrative Thaw in Relations," Radio Free Europe/Radio Liberty, May 21, 2008, http://www.rferl.org/featuresarticle/2008/05/39c3e275-82e7-4750-ba2e-6769b6adffe5.html.

In October 2007, Nazarbayev, Berdymukhamedov and Putin agreed in principle to build a pipeline that would carry billions of cubic feet of Turkmenistan's natural gas through Kazakhstan along the Caspian shore. The gas would enter Russia's network of gas pipelines and, unless used for Russian domestic consumption, would then be transshipped to European customers.[513] Nazarbayev later made clear that he envisaged the gas deal as part of a larger arrangement to establish Kazakhstan's role as a leading transit nation for Eurasian commerce: "Kazakhstan is already building a modern structure in the Caspian zone that will become the central element in the establishment of an international Caspian energy and transport corridor from north to south, which follows up the agreement reached by Russia, Kazakhstan, and Turkmenistan to build a gas pipeline." [514] The parties confirmed the agreement on December 20, 2007, though they are still negotiating the details.[515]

Uzbekistan

Kazakh leaders see establishing good ties with neighboring Uzbekistan as essential for advancing their regional integration agenda. In March 2006, Nazarbayev observed, "The geopolitical situation in our region and the future of integration processes among our neighbors depends on Kazakh-Uzbek relations."[516] Kazakhstan and Uzbekistan are the two most influential of the "stans," having the largest land mass and population in Central Asia. Uzbekistan is also Kazakhstan's major trade partner within Central Asia. Since both countries became independent in 1991, their governments have

---

[513] "Russia to Get Central Asian Pipeline," *New York Times*, May 13, 2007, http://www.nytimes.com/2007/05/13/world/europe/13putin.html.
[514] "Central Asia: Kazakh, Russian Leaders Discuss Transport Corridor," Radio Free Europe/Radio Liberty, October 5, 2007, http://www.rferl.org/featuresarticle/2007/10/4482ab28-5ab9-4756-8386-48471d684d3f.html.
[515] Associated Press, "Russia, Kazakhstan and Turkmenistan sign Caspian gas pipeline deal," *International Herald Tribune*, December 20, 2007, http://www.iht.com/articles/ap/2007/12/20/news/Russia-Caspian-Pipeline.php.
[516] Mevlut Katik, "Kazakhstan, Uzbekistan Strive for Closer Cooperation," Eurasia Insight, March 27, 2006, http://www.eurasianet.org/departments/insight/articles/eav032706a.shtml.

signed approximately one hundred bilateral agreements. [517] The most important of these documents include the Program of the Economic Cooperation between Kazakhstan and Uzbekistan for 2006-2010 and the Strategy of the Economic Cooperation between Kazakhstan and Uzbekistan for 2007-2016.

Yet, relations between Uzbekistan and Kazakhstan have long been strained. Many of their bilateral agreements have been implemented partly, if at all. The two countries, along with their presidents, have become perennial competitors for regional primacy. Uzbekistan has the largest population (some 27 million compared with Kazakhstan's 15.4 million), but Kazakhstan has the richest natural resources (especially oil) and most successful economy (measured in terms of comparative growth rates and levels of foreign investment).

In addition, Uzbek President Islam Karimov has pursued confrontational policies with Kazakhstan and other neighboring states, often berating them for failing to oppose regional terrorist movements sufficiently. Uzbek authorities have unilaterally mined their borders, leading to the deaths of dozens of pedestrians annually in border regions. The Uzbek government has also periodically sealed border crossings, interrupting regional commerce and leading to shooting of Kazakh (and other) citizens seeking to visit relatives in neighboring Uzbek communities. Although some of these closures have aimed to disrupt international smuggling networks, Uzbek security bodies fear that terrorists and other regime opponents would exploit loosened border controls to infiltrate fighters and weapons into the country. [518]

Furthermore, some Uzbek nationalists have asserted claims to territories in southern Kazakhstan that once belonged to medieval Uzbek Khanates. [519] In 2000, Uzbek border guards unilaterally moved border markers deep into

---

[517] Gulnoza Saidazimova, "Uzbekistan/Kazakhstan: Summit Is a Sign of Changing Times," Radio Free Europe/Radio Liberty, March 18, 2006,
http://www.rferl.org/featuresarticle/2006/03/7234E505-1452-4508-9315-BCADE393B371.html.

[518] Ibragim Alibekov," Kazakhstan, Uzbekistan Clash over Border Policy," Eurasia Insight, September 29, 2003,
http://www.eurasianet.org/departments/insight/articles/eav092903a.shtml.

[519] Tom Bissell, *Chasing the Sea: Lost Among the Ghosts of Empire in Central Asia* (Westminister, Maryland: Knopf Publishing, 2003), p. 145.

Kazakhstan's territory. [520] Kazakhstan's contentious and difficult border demarcations with Uzbekistan were finalized only in August 2002. [521] Even so, in September 2003, the Kazakh Foreign Ministry issued a statement claiming that its border service had detected 1,127 border violations "by the Uzbek side" since the previous November. [522]

Kazakhstan has become Uzbekistan's major trading partner, accounting for 8.4% of its foreign trade. [523] According to Uzbek sources, trade between the two countries reached $1.193 billion in 2007, a 63.3% surge over 2006, but still below the level desired by the two countries. [524] (Kazakh sources cite a higher figure of $1.4 billion. [525]) Furthermore, Kazakh and Uzbek investors have established a number of joint business ventures. At present, 167 firms in Uzbekistan are financed in part though Kazakh capital, whereas 94 joint ventures in Kazakhstan involve Uzbek partners. [526] (Kazakh sources again cite a much higher number of 715 small and medium scale enterprises operating in Kazakhstan with some Uzbek investment. [527]) These joint ventures operate in such commercial sectors as food, pharmaceutics, construction, chemicals, and

---

[520] Rafis Abazov, "Kazakhstan's Security Challenges in a Changing World," in Michael Intriligator, Alexander Nikitin, and Majid Tehranian, eds., *Eurasia: A New Peace Agenda* (Amsterdam: Elsevier, 2005), pp. 229-231.

[521] Ministry of Foreign Affairs of Kazakhstan, "Aktual'nye Voprosy Vneshney Politiki Kazakhstana: Delimitatsiya i Demarkastsiya Gosudarstvennoy Granitsy," http://portal.mfa.kz/portal/page/portal/mfa/ru/content/policy/issues/delimitation.

[522] Ibragim Alibekov," Kazakhstan, Uzbekistan Clash over Border Policy," Eurasia Insight, September 29, 2003, http://www.eurasianet.org/departments/insight/articles/eav092903a.shtml.

[523] Erkin Akhmadov, "Uzbekistan: Central Asian Union Destined to Remain on Paper," *Central Asia-Caucasus Analyst*, April 30, 2008, http://www.cacianalyst.org/?q=node/4850.

[524] Press Service of the President of Uzbekistan, "President's Official Visit to Kazakhstan—'Fruitful and Effective," April 23, 2008, http://www.press-service.uz/en/mcontent.scm?sectionId=4489&contentId=15865.

[525] Ministry of Foreign Affairs of Kazakhstan, "Sotrudnichestvo Respubliki Kazakhstan s Respublikoy Uzbekistan," February 22, 2008, http://portal.mfa.kz/portal/page/portal/mfa/ru/content/policy/cooperation/CIS/02.

[526] Press Service of the President of Uzbekistan, "President's Official Visit to Kazakhstan—'Fruitful and Effective," April 23, 2008, http://www.press-service.uz/en/mcontent.scm?sectionId=4489&contentId=15865.

[527] Ministry of Foreign Affairs of Kazakhstan, "Sotrudnichestvo Respubliki Kazakhstan s Respublikoy Uzbekistan," February 22, 2008, http://portal.mfa.kz/portal/page/portal/mfa/ru/content/policy/cooperation/CIS/02.

manufacturing.[528] In Uzbekistan, Kazakh capital is currently concentrated in the cotton fiber, construction, and chemical industries.[529]

The southern regions of Kazakhstan traditionally rely on Uzbek natural gas, especially in winter, both for heating and for electricity generation. Under the terms of a recent deal, the Uzbek state energy company Uzbekneft has agreed to supply 5 billion cubic meters of natural gas to southern Kazakhstan in 2008.[530] The two countries are engaged in various multinational projects that would increase the flow of gas from and through their territories to Russia, China, and other countries.[531] Kazakh firms already use Uzbekistan's territory as a transshipment route for some non-energy exports.

Nonetheless, the similar economic profile of both countries, along with their excessive customs duties and border controls, unduly constrain their bilateral commerce. Kazakh business managers complain about an unwelcoming investment climate in Uzbekistan, especially compared with the opportunities offered Kazakh capital in other Eurasian countries. "Unlike Russia, Kyrgyzstan, and Georgia, where Kazakhstan's economic presence has been expanding, the Uzbek government is closed to its neighbor," says one Kazakh entrepreneur who has chosen to make his fortune in Bishkek rather than Tashkent.[532]

Another complication is the large number of illegal immigrants from Uzbekistan that work in Kazakhstan, especially at urban construction sites

---

[528] "Uzbekistan, Kazakhstan May be Crucial for Central Asian Stability," April 23, 2008, http://news.uzreport.com/aziya.cgi?lan=e&id=45228.

[529] Erkin Akhmadov, "Uzbekistan: Central Asian Union Destined to Remain on Paper," *Central Asia-Caucasus Analyst*, April 30, 2008, http://www.cacianalyst.org/?q=node/4850.

[530] "Kazakhstan Gears Up for Electricity Shortages," Reuters, April 22, 2008, http://www.reuters.com/article/rbssEnergyNews/idUSL2251073820080422.

[531] Gulnur Rakhmatullina, "Visit of President of Uzbekistan Islom Karimov to Kazakhstan," May 6, 2008, http://www.eurasianhome.org/xml/t/expert.xml?lang=en&nic=expert&pid=1548&qm onth=0&qyear=0.

[532] Cited in Erica Marat, "Karimov, Bakiyev React Differently To Nazarbayev's Central Asia Union," Eurasia Daily Monitor, April 25, 2008, http://www.jamestown.org/edm/article.php?article_id=2373006.

and in the cotton fields of southern Kazakhstan.[533] The two countries have also found it difficult to manage the Aral Sea, which borders both countries. Inefficient use of the Syrdarya and Amudarya rivers for fertilizing cotton production has led to a disturbing shrinkage in the sea's surface area, increasing harmful atmospheric dust. Nazarbayev has called for establishing a water energy consortium among Central Asian countries to help manage such problems. [534] On the other hand, Kazakhstan and Uzbekistan do share interests regarding the issue of regional water management. The two countries use Central Asian water supplies primarily to irrigate crops as well as for direct consumption. In contrast, Kyrgyzstan and Tajikistan seek to convert the region's water resources into electricity, some of which they can sell to neighboring countries.[535]

The interests of Kazakhstan and Uzbekistan seem to overlap most on issues of national security, especially countering threats from Muslim extremists. On April 23, 2008, Nazarbayev affirmed the commitment of both countries to "combine efforts in the fight against extremism and drug trafficking from Afghanistan."[536] During Nazarbayev's March 2006 state visit to Uzbekistan, he told his Uzbek hosts that they "defended the peace ... not only of Uzbeks, but also Kazakhs, Kyrgyz and Tajiks" by confronting "trained extremist groups" in Andijon the previous May. [537] A few hours after Karimov concluded his most recent visit to Kazakhstan, moreover, the Kazakh authorities arrested an asylum seeker whom the Uzbek government had

---

[533] Economist Intelligence Unit, "Country Profile 2007: Kazahhstan,"
[534] Office of the President of the Republic of Kazakhstan, "Today, President Nursultan Nazarbayev Meets President of the Republic of Uzbekistan Islam Karimov, Who Arrived in Astana for a Two Day Official Visit," April 22, 2008, http://www.akorda.kz/www/www_akorda_kz.nsf/news-open?OpenForm&idn=3&idno=4DCB67C0C6113A6806257434000FCEBF&lang=en.
[535] "Karimov's 'Once and For All' for Nazarbayev," *Journal of Turkish Weekly*, http://www.turkishweekly.net/news.php?id=54681.
[536] Quote from President Nursultan Nazarbayev, Kazakhstan, Uzbekistan will combine efforts in the fight against extremism, drug trafficking from Afghanistan, Interfax News Agency, April 23, 2008, http://www6.lexisnexis.com/publisher/EndUser?Action=UserDisplayFullDocument&orgId=574&topicId=100007185&docId=l:780585624&start=11.
[537] Mevlut Katik, "Kazakhstan, Uzbekistan Strive for Closer Cooperation," Eurasia Insight, March 27, 2006, http://www.eurasianet.org/departments/insight/articles/eav032706a.shtml.

accused of participating in the Andijan events.[538] Even so, Kazakhstan has not always followed Uzbekistan's lead on these issues. In March 2006, Kazakh authorities allowed one of Karimov's fiercest domestic opponents, dissident Imam Obidkhon Qori Nazarov, to leave Kazakhstan for asylum in Europe a few days before Nazarbayev visited Uzbekistan rather than accede to Uzbek extradition requests.[539]

During Nazarbayev's March 2006 visit, Kazakh and Uzbek officials signed cooperative agreements in a variety of sectors. They also agreed to establish a bilateral commission to regularize and improve economic, political, and security contacts. Nazarbayev told a March 2006 news conference that the commission "is to become a regular body for promptly solving all topical issues." He also called for expanding military and technical cooperation since "our special services and special agencies should work in an environment of complete trust to fight terrorism and drug trafficking and other actions by extremists in our region." Nazarbayev underscored the importance that improving Kazakh-Uzbek relations would have for his ambitions to increase wider regional political and economic cooperation: "The geopolitical situation in our region and the future of integration processes among our neighbors depends on Kazakh-Uzbek relations."[540]

In a March 2006 interview, Foreign Minister Tokaev also observed that, "We may have differences on a number of issues, but we are sincerely interested in friendly and predictable relations with Uzbekistan.... Kazakhstan is interested in political stability in Central Asia and the Caspian region. Good cooperation and stable relationships between Kazakhstan and Uzbekistan is, therefore, essential to ensure and sustain stability in the region."[541] Kazakh and Uzbek officials have recently coordinated their energy

---

[538] "Kazakhstan Detains Uzbek Wanted on Terror Charges," Reuters, April 23, 2008, http://www.reuters.com/article/latestCrisis/idUSL23749894.

[539] Gulnoza Saidazimova, "Uzbekistan/Kazakhstan: Summit Is a Sign of Changing Times," Radio Free Europe/Radio Liberty, March 18, 2006, http://www.rferl.org/featuresarticle/2006/03/7234E505-1452-4508-9315-BCADE393B371.html.

[540] Katik, "Kazakhstan, Uzbekistan Strive for Closer Cooperation."

[541] Mevlut Katik, "Kazakhstan Has 'Huge Plan' to Expand Energy Links With China," Eurasia Insight, March 13, 2006, http://www.eurasianet.org/departments/recaps/articles/eav031306.shtml.

polices to induce Russian firms to pay more for their oil and gas exports, which Russian middleman often resell to European consumers with a hefty markup.[542]

From April 22-23, 2008, President Karimov conducted his first official visit to Astana since September 2006. In a joint media appearance following his talks with Nazarbayev, Karimov observed that, "Kazakhstan and Uzbekistan may play a crucial role in solution of a number of principal matters, connected with the stability in the Central Asian region and prospects of its sustainable development." [543] The two leaders agreed to authorize their government to prepare a draft agreement on a bilateral free trade zone, which Karimov said would "increase volume of mutual trade significantly" by unifying customs duties and other trade practices of both countries.[544] Nazarbayev noted that, since he visited Uzbekistan two years earlier, bilateral commerce doubled. "Economic integration is growing," he added enthusiastically, "and it excites us."[545] A working group headed by the Kazakh and Uzbek Prime Ministers is now drafting the terms of the bilateral free trade zone and how it would integrate with the region's other multinational economic frameworks.[546]

Yet, Karimov again dismissed as premature the concept of a Central Asian Union, something Nazarbayev has long championed. Before the trip, Karimov observed that, "Seeking cheap popularity, some colleagues of mine make high-flown speeches on cooperation and come up with all sorts of

---

[542] Gulnoza Saidazimova, "Uzbekistan: President Karimov Meets with Close Ally Putin," Radio Free Europe/Radio Liberty, February 6, 2008, http://www.rferl.org/featuresarticle/2008/02/BADF8DB0-1DDD-414A-A603-82AB88A065D1.html.

[543] "Uzbekistan, Kazakhstan May be Crucial for Central Asian Stability," April 23, 2008, http://news.uzreport.com/aziya.cgi?lan=e&id=45228.

[544] Dina Yermaganbetova, "Kazakhstan and Uzbekistan to Create Free Trade Zone," *Kazinform*, April 22, 2008, http://www.inform.kz/showarticle.php?lang=eng&id=163528.

[545] "Kazakhstan and Uzbekistan May Play a Crucial Role in Insuring Security in the Region—Uzbek President," *Kazakhstan Today*, April 22, 2008, http://eng.gazeta.kz/art.asp?aid=108997.

[546] Erkin Akhmadov, "Uzbekistan: Central Asian Union Destined to Remain on Paper," *Central Asia-Caucasus Analyst*, May 2, 2007, http://www.cacianalyst.org/?q=node/4850.

slogans. Unfortunately, nothing at all is being done in practice."[547] Karimov
continued to employ rather undiplomatic language even during the trip: "As
far as Uzbekistan is concerned, this initiative is unacceptable. I'm saying it
right here and now to prevent any further speculations on the matter."[548]
Karimov justified his objection on socioeconomic rather than geopolitical
grounds: "In order to establish a union between the states, their
socioeconomic development level and potential should be comparable,"
Karimov told the media. "Secondly, policy and directions the countries'
leaders work at should be comparable as well."[549] Karimov also argued that,
"Unfortunately, we have too many matters to address yet... all and any
alliances are therefore untimely." [550]

Furthermore, Karimov insisted that Uzbekistan provided more favorable
conditions for international business than Kazakhstan, a claim reflecting the
often fierce competition between the two countries for foreign investment
and international business opportunities. [551] According to Karimov,
"international rating agencies place Uzbekistan above Kazakhstan from the
standpoint of business," adding that "no other post-Soviet country could
match the preferences businesses enjoy in Uzbekistan."[552] Kazakhstan and
Uzbekistan are now both maneuvering to become the preeminent transit

[547] "President of Uzbekistan Islam Karimov is on a Two-Day Official Visit to Astana,
Kazakhstan," Ferghanu.ru, April 22, 2008,
http://www.turkishweekly.net/news.php?id=54659.
[548] "Uzbek President's Visit to Astana Exposed Existence of a Serious Obstacle on the
Road to a Central Asian Alliance," May 5, 2008,
http://enews.ferghana.ru/article.php?id=2373.
[549] "Uzbekistan, Kazakhstan May be Crucial for Central Asian Stability," April 23,
2008, http://news.uzreport.com/aziya.cgi?lan=e&id=45228.
[550] "Uzbek President's Visit to Astana Exposed Existence of a Serious Obstacle on the
Road to a Central Asian Alliance," May 5, 2008,
http://enews.ferghana.ru/article.php?id=2373.
[551] "Uzbekistan Grants More Favorable Terms for Making Business, than in
Kazakhstan—Karimov," *Kazakhstan Today*, April 23, 2008,
http://eng.gazeta.kz/art.asp?aid=109074.
[552] "Karimov's 'Once and For All' for Nazarbayev," *Journal of Turkish Weekly*,
http://www.turkishweekly.net/news.php?id=54681.

country for pan-Eurasian commercial and transportation networks (including a possible Europe-Asian highway).[553]

Karimov's pessimism regarding Nazarbayev's Union of Central Asian States may reflect the difficulties the two countries experienced after they agreed to establish a bilateral customs union in 1994. Karimov recalled during his April 2008 trip to Astana that problems with this structure led the two governments to join additional regional economic structures (e.g., the Central Asian Cooperation Organization and the Eurasian Economic Community), which also proved largely ineffective. [554] We've been through it already," he remarked to journalists.[555]

But Karimov's opposition also reflects longstanding Uzbek aversion to Kazakh-led regional integration initiatives, which Uzbek leaders perceive as efforts to strengthen and legitimize Kazakhstan's primacy in Central Asia. In June 2002, Karimov boycotted the first Summit of the Heads of States and Heads of Governments associated with the Conference on Interaction and Confidence-Building in Asia (CICA), the Kazakh-led effort to enhance regional security through non-military security initiatives. The Uzbek envoy sent in his place lacked the authority to sign the "Almaty Document" and "The CICA Declaration about the Elimination of Terrorism and Promotion of Dialogue between Civilizations," the two main products of the summit.[556]

---

[553] Frederick Starr, "Introduction," in S. Frederick Starr, ed., *The New Silk Roads: Transport and Trade in Greater Central Asia* (Washington, D.C.: Central Asia-Caucasus Institute, 2007), pp. 8, 21.

[554] Press Service of the President of Uzbekistan, "President's Official Visit to Kazakhstan—'Fruitful and Effective," April 23, 2008, http://www.press-service.uz/en/mcontent.scm?sectionId=4489&contentId=15865.

[555] "Karimov's 'Once and For All' for Nazarbayev."

[556] "Uzbek President's Visit to Astana Exposed Existence of a Serious Obstacle on the Road to a Central Asian Alliance," May 5, 2008, http://enews.ferghana.ru/article.php?id=2373.

South Caucasus States

Armenia

Although both Kazakhstan and Armenia are former Soviet republics, they have not developed the close ties Kazakhstan has achieved with Azerbaijan or Georgia. Both Kazakhstan and Armenia are members of the CIS and the CSTO, which ensures that their government leaders meet at their various summits. Nevertheless, Armenia's involvement with the CSTO has not been as great as that of the other members and Armenia is not a member of the SCO. Within the framework of the CIS, the two countries in January 1993 signed the Treaty of Fundamentals of Relations between the Republic of Kazakhstan and Republic of Armenia in January 1993, and the Treaty of Friendship and Cooperation during President Kocharian's official visit to Astana in early September 1999.[557] During Nazarbayev's May 2001 visit to Yerevan, the two governments signed additional political and legal agreements regarding intergovernmental obligations in the areas of standardization, security, criminality, expansion of parliamentary ties, and legal cooperation.[558]

Kazakh-Armenian economic ties have lagged behind. Bilateral commerce and investment have remained relatively limited despite the presence of some 25,000 Armenians in Kazakhstan, who could in principle help promote ties between the two nations.[559] In September 1999, the two governments signed a Free Trade Agreement, which came into effect in December 2001. Besides eliminating mutual tariffs, the agreement created an Intergovernmental

---

[557] Ministry of Foreign Affairs of Kazakhstan, "Sotrudnichestvo Respubliki Kazakhstan s Respublikoy Armeniya," November 29, 2006, http://portal.mfa.kz/portal/page/portal/mfa/ru/content/policy/cooperation/CIS/09.

[558] "Increase Cooperation Dynamic," *Kazakh Pravda*, May 25, 2001, http://www.kazpravda.kz/index.php?uin=1152243624&act=archive_date&day=25&month=5&year=2001.

[559] Public Radio of America, "Armenia and Kazakhstan Willing to Develop Bilateral Relations," July 11, 2007, http://armradio.am/news/?part=off&id=10200.

Commission for Economic Cooperation to promote bilateral economic ties, but it did not meet until 2005.[560]

It was only in November 2006, when President Robert Kocharian visited Kazakhstan, that the two governments signed such fundamental economic agreements as those curtailing double taxation, providing for the mutual protection of investments, and others aimed at establishing a basis for expanding commercial exchanges. In his remarks, Kocharian acknowledged Armenia's laggard position with respect to its commercial relations with Kazakhstan: "Recently Kazakhi businesses pay more attention to the countries of the South Caucasus. We welcome your presence in Georgia and hope that your presence in Armenia will be more substantial than it is now."[561]

Following Kocharian's visit, Kazakhstan Investment Promotion Center (KAZINVEST) established a special delegation to explore potential opportunities for Kazakh capital in Armenia.[562] In addition, the Kazakh government upgraded its diplomatic presence in Armenia and opened a formal embassy complex in Yerevan.[563] In December 2007, the Kazakh Charge d'Affairs in Yerevan, Yerlan Kubashev, announced that Kazakhstan would hold an exposition of Armenian goods in 2008. He also stated that the members of the bilateral Intergovernmental Economic Cooperation Commission would meet, for only its second time, in Kazakhstan later in 2008.[564]

During his April 2008 visit to Yerevan for the inauguration of the newly elected president, Mukhambet Kopeev, the Vice President of the Senate of

---

[560] "Free Trade Agreement Between Armenia and Kazakhstan," September 2, 1999, www.worldtradelaw.net/fta/agreements/cisfta.pdf.

[561] President of the Republic of Armenia, "Official Visit of President Robert Kocharian to The Republic of Kazakhstan," November 6, 2007, http://news.president.am/eng/?sub=official&id=155&from=0&year=2006.

[562] American Chamber of Commerce in Kazakhstan News Release, "Armenian President Visits Astana," November 7, 2006, http://www.amcham.kz/article.php?article_id=534.

[563] "Kazakhstan Opens Embassies in Armenia, Qatar," Kazakhstan Today, December 15, 2006, http://eng.gazeta.kz/art.asp?aid=84699.

[564] "Armenian-Kazakh Relations Enhancing," ARKA News Agency, December 11 2007, http://www.arka.am/eng/economy/2007/12/11/7363.html.

Kazakhstan, indicated that he sought to further strengthen inter-parliamentary cooperation through the establishment of a parliamentary cooperation group. He also expressed gratitude for Armenia's support for Kazakhstan's aspirations to chair the OSCE. [565] Armenian backing for Kazakhs' OSCE aspirations arises not only from their existing political-military ties—which operate both bilaterally and through the CIS and the CSTO—but also because many Armenians hope that Kazakhstan's OSCE chairmanship will enhance that institution's ability to resolve the Armenia-Azerbaijani conflict over Nagorno-Karabakh.

Kazakh officials have expressed their hope for a resolution of the Karabakh conflict as well as an improvement in Armenia's relations with Azerbaijan. Kubashev alluded to the harmful effects of the conflict on the regional economies when he lamented how "unsettled conflicts in Eurasia affect the region's development." [566] Kazakhstan, like the rest of Eurasia, is adversely affected by the Nagorno-Karabakh conflict. As long as it threatens to flare up again, some foreign investors will shun the region. Perhaps more seriously, the trade barriers imposed on Armenia for its occupation of Azerbaijani territory has excluded realization of potentially valuable Trans-Caspian trade and transportation routes that would traverse the conflict region.

Kazakh officials have sought to avoid taking sides over the Nagorno-Karabakh conflict. The Kazakh government abstained in the voting on the March 2008 UN General Assembly resolution that called for the immediate, complete, and unconditional withdrawal of Armenian troops from all occupied territories of Azerbaijan. "I want to reassure you that there are friendly relations between our countries and these relations are more important than any resolution," the new Kazakh Ambassador to Azerbaijan, Serik Primbetov, told the local media. "We have always supported Azerbaijan's territorial integrity and our position will remain unchanged. On

---

[565] "Vice President of the Kazakh Senate in the National Assembly," Official Press Release of the Armenian National Assembly, April 10 2008.
http://www.parliament.am/chairman.php?id=meetings&NewsID=2719&month=04&year=2008&lang=eng.

[566] "Kazakhstan for Resolution of Armenian-Turkish Problem through Direct Dialogue," ARKA News Agency, August 29 2007,
http://library.aua.am/library/news/archive/2007_08-28.htm

the other hand, we support peaceful settlement of conflict. We keep friendly relations with both Armenia and Azerbaijan. I will do my best for much more improvement of relations between Azerbaijan and Kazakhstan."[567]

Despite the problems resulting from the unsettled Karabakh conflict, the robust performance of the economies of Armenia and Kazakhstan in recent years has established a good basis for future economic cooperation. Two-way trade turnover rose to $191.3 million in January-October 2007, a 62.4% increase compared with the corresponding period of the previous year.[568] Bilateral trade, which is very imbalanced in Kazakhstan's favor, mainly consists of Kazakh sales of grain, oil, and refined petroleum products in exchange for imports of Armenian beverages, chemical products, as well as machinery and equipment.

Azerbaijan

The governments of Azerbaijan and Kazakhstan have cooperated most comprehensively in the energy sector. Early on, they collaborated with the United States to defeat terrorist threats to Caspian energy infrastructures. In addition, Kazakh and Azerbaijani officials sought to resist Iranian efforts to delay developing underground hydrocarbon resources along their Caspian coasts pending the adoption of a new convention defining the Caspian Basin's legal status. Whereas Tehran wants to divide the sea into equal shares and provide for multilateral management of undersea mining activities, Astana and Baku have sought to divide the sea's underwater resources in proportion with the size of their coastal zones. During a November 2001 CIS summit in Moscow, their presidents signed an agreement delimitating the surface of the

---

[567] "Kazakhstan Supports Friendly Relations with Azerbaijan and Armenia— Ambassador," TrendNews, March 18, 2008, http://news.trendaz.com/index.shtml?show=news&newsid=1159028&lang=EN.
[568] "Kazakhstan Interested in Armenia's energy sector," ARKA News Agency, December 11, 2007, http://www.arka.am/eng/energy/2007/12/11/7365.html.

Caspian Sea.[569] Along with Russia, Kazakhstan and Azerbaijan agreed to partition the northern sector of the Caspian Sea into three unequal shares.[570]

More recently, Kazakh and Azerbaijani officials have sought to explore opportunities for Kazakh energy and other exports to transit Azerbaijan en route to European and Mediterranean markets. Kazakhstan currently ships as much as 5 million tons of oil by tanker between terminals in Kazakhstan and Azerbaijan. The oil then moves via the Baku-Tbilisi-Ceyhan (BTC) pipeline to the Mediterranean.[571] Previously, Kazakh exporters did ship a few million tons of oil to Baku by tanker from the port of Aktau, but then the oil was moved to Georgia's Black Sea coast by rail.[572]

In September 2005, Azerbaijan President Ilham Aliyev created a special government commission to address issues related to facilitating the transportation of Kazakh oil through Azerbaijani territory.[573] Thanks in part to the commission's work, the two governments signed a transportation cooperation agreement in June 2006 to support the BTC pipeline.[574] The accord provided Kazakhstan with a third export route for its oil, supplementing the existing northern route through Russian-controlled Atyrau-Samara and KTK pipelines and the newer eastward route to China through the Atasu-Alashankou pipeline. The two countries' national energy companies subsequently signed a memorandum on implementing their Trans-Caspian project. The memo covers joint use of Azerbaijan's oil and gas infrastructure and other issues relating to implementing the agreement signed

---

[569] Ministry of Foreign Affairs of Kazakhstan, "Sotrudnichestvo Respubliki Kazakhstan s Azerbaydzhanskoy Respublikoy," July 26, 2006, http://portal.mfa.kz/portal/page/portal/mfa/ru/content/policy/cooperation/CIS/10.

[570] Ibid.

[571] Marat Tazhin, "Kazakhstan in a Changing World," speech at U.S.-Kazakhstan Business Association dinner, Washington, D.C., May 8, 2007, http://www.kazakhembus.com/050907.html.

[572] Ibragim Alibekov, "While Russia Watches, Kazakhstan and Azerbaijan Explore New Ties," Eurasia Insight, March 3, 2004, http://www.eurasianet.org/departments/business/articles/eav030304.shtml.

[573] Sevindzh Abdullayeva and Viktor Shulmann, "Kazakhstan Oil Transit via Azerbaijan Territory Planned," TASS, September 14, 2005.

[574] G. G. Rakhmatulina, "Kazakhstan's Joining to the 'Baku-Tbilisi—Ceyhan' Project," Kazakhstan Institute of Strategic Studies, July 4, 2006, http://www.kisi.kz/site.html?id=847.

by Nazarbayev and Aliyev in June 2006.[575] On May 29, Nazarbayev signed into law a bill ratifying the treaty allowing Kazakh oil to use the BTC pipeline. The BTC is currently transporting one million barrels of oil per day; this total should rise to 1.6 million barrels daily by 2013 once Kazakh oil joins that from Azerbaijan's own fields.[576]

Although long-term proposals to construct pipelines under the Caspian Sea remain under consideration, legal and environmental impediments have led Kazakh policy makers to focus their near-term plans on developing a Kazakhstan Caspian Transport System (KCTS). Following construction of an oil terminal at Kuryk, ships will be able to load as much as 500,000 barrels of crude oil daily and transport it across the Caspian to Azerbaijan, where their cargo will be unloaded and channeled into the BTC pipeline. On January 24, 2007, major oil companies including Chevron, ExxonMobil, LUKarco, Agip, Total as well as KazMunaiGs (KMG) signed a memorandum of understanding launching the KCTS consortium, which will work directly with the Azerbaijani and Kazakh governments.[577] Although Russian policy makers have expressed unease at the creation of a direct connection between Kazakhstan and Azerbaijan, an oil executive involved said that the Nazarbayev administration and KMG are now fully behind the project.[578] In January 2008, KazMunaiGaz announced plans to send oil from the fields at Tengiz and Kashagan (which, barring further delays, should be producing large quantities of oil by then) to Kuryk for tanker shipment to Azerbaijan and the BTC starting in 2012.[579] Observers expect that, should the tanker system produce poor results, Azerbaijan and Kazakhstan might

---

[575] Embassy of Kazakhstan to the USA and Canada, "Kazakhstan and Azerbaijan Sign Documents on Oil and Gas Cooperation," Kazkahstan's News Bulletin, August 15, 2007, http://www.kazakhembus.com/NB3_081507.html.

[576] "Kazakhstan Ratifies Oil Transit Treaty with Azerbaijan," Kazinform, May 30, 2008, http://www.inform.kz/showarticle3.php?lang=eng&id=165101.

[577] Embassy of Kazakhstan to the USA and Canada, "New Export Route for Kazakh Oil Gets Closer to Reality," Kazkahstan's News Bulletin, January 25, 2007, http://www.kazakhembus.com/012507.html.

[578] James Delly, "Kazakhstan Eyes New Oil Export Route via Caspian Sea," Eurasia Insight, April 11, 2007, http://www.eurasianet.org/departments/insight/articles/eavo41107.shtml.

[579] Joanna Lillis, "Kazakhstan: Astana Set to Make an Energy Export Break with Russia," Eurasia Insight, May 2, 2008, http://www.eurasianet.org/departments/insight/articles/eavo50208.shtml.

commit to construct an undersea pipeline that would feed oil directly into the BTC.[580]

Azerbaijani and Kazakh officials are now seeking ways to deepen other economic exchanges between their countries, which have two of the most rapidly growing economies of the Caspian region. In early April 2007, Kazakh Prime Minister Karim Masimov visited Azerbaijan. In Baku, he marked the launch of a terminal that stores and processes Kazakh grain shipped across the Caspian from the Kazakh port of Aktau.[581] The Baku Grain Terminal is a joint venture between Planeta L of Azerbaijan and the Food Corporation of Kazakhstan. The facility, which cost $6 million to construct, grew out of the 2004 visit to Kazakhstan by Azerbaijan President Ilham Aliyev. The terminal has a capacity to process up to 800,000 tons of grain annually; some of this is for domestic Azerbaijan consumption, but the terminal also aims to supply Georgia, Turkey, and North Africa.[582] When Azerbaijani President Ilham Aliyev visited Astana in August 2007, he told Kazinform, the main Kazakh news agency, that he was eager to involve Kazakh investors in the construction of the Baku-Tbilisi-Kars railway.[583] An Azerbaijani-Kazakh intergovernmental commission is actively considering new joint commercial projects.

In addition to their economic cooperation, the two countries have collaborated to enhance maritime security in the Caspian Sea. When Azerbaijani President Ilham Aliyev visited Kazakhstan in early March 2004, the two countries signed a military cooperation agreement aimed at

---

[580] "Chevron to Help Kazakhstan Skirt Russia with Pipeline," Bloomberg News, June 6, 2008, http://www.chron.com/disp/story.mpl/business/energy/5822320.html.

[581] Embassy of Kazakhstan to the USA and Canada, "PM Massimov Visits Azerbaijan and Georgia Talking Oil Transportation and Trade," Kazakhstan's News Bulletin, April 5, 2007, http://www.kazakhembus.com/040507.html.

[582] "Kazakhstan Has Resumed Grain Supplies for Azerbaijan," Azerbaijan Business Center, May 25, 2008, http://abc.az/cgi-bin/wnews_one.cgi?nid=24398&lang=eng.

[583] Kazinform, "President Aliyev: Azerbaijan's Border Remains Open for Resources Transportation to Europe," Kazakhstan's News Bulletin, August 15, 2007, http://www.kazakhembus.com/NB3_081507.html.

enhancing collaboration between their Caspian Sea flotillas.[584] Some Kazakh officials share Azerbaijani concerns about Iranian efforts to contest control of Caspian Sea resources. The U.S. Caspian Guard initiative has aimed to strengthen the capabilities of both countries to counter security threats to Caspian countries and commerce from regional terrorist groups.[585]

Georgia

A series of high-level political visits made relations between Kazakhstan and Georgia especially prominent in 2005. At the beginning of June, Kazakh Prime Minister Danial Akhmetov visited Georgia to discuss commercial exchanges with Georgian Prime Minister Zurab Nogaideli. They conducted a joint excursion to Georgia's Black Sea ports of Poti and Batumi. In October, Nazarbayev visited Georgia and spoke enthusiastically about deepening economic ties between the two countries. Kazakh-Georgian commercial exchanges, which were already on the upswing after the 2003 Rose Revolution increased political stability in Georgia while decreasing corruption, grew substantially after the visits. "We are grateful to Kazakhstan because the first investment to Georgia in the most difficult time for us came from Kazakhstan," Georgian President Mikheil Saakashvili remarked at a joint news conference with Nazarbayev in Astana in March 2007. "When we started, Kazakhstan was the first to believe in Georgia, and today we are seeing investments from this country ranging in billions."[586]

Kazakhs hope to benefit from Georgia's potential as a key transit state for goods exchanged between Kazakhstan and Western markets via the Black Sea region, including through energy pipelines and by rail and other surface transportation. When Saakashvili visited Astana in March 2007, Nazarbayev told him that, "The Caucasus corridor to Europe and the Mediterranean is

---

[584] Ibragim Alibekov, "While Russia Watches, Kazakhstan and Azerbaijan Explore New Ties," Eurasia Insight, March 3, 2004, http://www.eurasianet.org/departments/business/articles/eav030304.shtml.
[585] Roger McDermott, "Kazakhstan's Parliament Ratifies Strategic Partnership with Azerbaija," Eurasia Daily Monitor, July 5, 2006, http://www.jamestown.org/edm/article.php?article_id=2371246
[586] Embassy of Kazakhstan to the USA and Canada, "Kazakhstan Will Pursue Large Scale Diverse Investments in Georgia," Kazakhstan's News Bulletin, March 9, 2007, http://www.kazakhembus.com/030907.html.

becoming very important for us, and Georgia is our very active partner" in this endeavor.[587] Kazakh investors also praise the Georgian government for creating an attractive investment climate by offering favorable tax conditions and by making it easy for investors, foreign and domestic, to start new businesses. The two governments have signed over 70 agreements designed to establish a favorable legal framework for bilateral economic relations. These include an agreement for the promotion and reciprocal protection of investments; an accord to avoid double taxation, and a free trade agreement.

Since 2005, Kazakh firms have invested over $1 billion in various projects in Georgia.[588] According to Georgian sources, during the first three quarters of 2006, Kazakh investments approximated $142 million in Georgia.[589] Kazakhs are very active in Georgia's tourism and real estate markets. For example, Kazakhstan's Turan Alem Bank is financing the construction and renovation of a number of luxury hotels in Tbilisi, Batumi, and other Georgian cities.[590] Kazakh banks have also participated in privatizing Georgia's communication and power industries. Two of the most important Kazakh investments in recent years are KazTransGas' $12.5 million purchase of Tbilisi gas distributor Tbilgazi and Bank TuranAlem's $90 million purchase of a controlling share in United Telecom of Georgia, the country's largest telephone company.[591]

Trade turnover between Kazakhstan and Georgia has increased considerably in recent years. In 2005, Kazakhstan imported $9.80 million worth of Georgian goods and exported $11.55 million. In 2006, Kazakh imports from Georgia rose to $15.43 million, while exports soared to $25.4 million.[592] Kazakh

---

[587] Diana Petriashvili, "Georgia Pins Investment Hopes on Kazakhstan," Eurasia Insight, April 17, 2007,
http://www.eurasianet.org/departments/insight/articles/eav041707a.shtml.
[588] Erica Marat, "Nazarbayev Promises Economic Assistance, Urges Political Stability in Kyrgyzstan," Eurasia Daily Monitor, May 3, 2007,
http://jamestown.org/edm/article.php?volume_id=420&issue_id=4094&article_id=23721
41.
[589] Dinara Salieva and Asset Matayev, "Kazakh Invests in Georgian Market," *Brosse Street Journal*,
May 30 2007, http://www.bsj.ge/newspaper/2007/05/30/EElEyFklZAYyGwtrwH.
[590] Petriashvili, "Georgia Pins Investment Hopes on Kazakhstan."
[591] *Ibid.*
[592] Ministry of Foreign Affairs of Georgia, "Relations between Georgia and the Republic of Kazakhstan," http://www.mfa.gov.ge/index.php?sec_id=445<_id=ENG.

and Georgian officials hope these record figures will increase even further as Kazakh investment continues to help develop Georgia's transportation network and other infrastructure. The Georgian government wants natural gas from Kazakhstan to be transported through the Trans-Caspian gas pipeline and hopes that Kazakh investors will support the Baku-Tbilisi-Kars railway.[593] Kazakh Transportation and Communications Minister Serik Akhmetov indicated that Kazakh businesses aim to ship at least 10 million tons of cargo annually via the Baku-Akhalkalaki-Kars railway, which is scheduled to become operational in 2010. Private Kazakh companies are constructing an oil refinery plant at Batumi and a wheat storage terminal at Poti in anticipation of its opening.[594] The Poti terminal will establish a Caspian network by interconnecting with the grain terminals in Aktau and Baku. When he visited Georgia in early April 2007, Kazakh Prime Minister Karim Masimov inspected both facilities and participated in a meeting of the Kazakh-Azerbaijani-Georgian high-level working group on transportation issues.[595]

Despite its close political ties with Russia, Astana has not followed Moscow's negative line toward Tbilisi. For example, this March, the Russian Foreign Ministry announced that the Russian government had unilaterally lifted financial, trade, transport, and other economic sanctions on Abkhazia imposed as a collective decision of the CIS Council of Heads of State on January 19, 1996.[596] In addition to explicitly blaming Georgia's supposedly unconstructive approach towards its separatist regions as warranting the reversal, the Foreign Ministry called on other CIS countries to follow its example. David Bakradze, then acting Georgian foreign minister,

---

[593] *Ibid.*

[594] Petriashvili, "Georgia Pins Investment Hopes on Kazakhstan."

[595] Embassy of Kazakhstan to the USA and Canada, "PM Massimov Visits Azerbaijan and Georgia Talking Oil Transportation and Trade," *Kazakhstan's News Bulletin,* April 5, 2007, http://www.kazakhembus.com/040507.html.

[596] Ministry of Foreign Affairs, "Russian Federation Withdraws from Regime of Restrictions Established in 1996 for Abkhazia," March 6, 2008, http://www.mid.ru/brp_4.nsf/e78a48070f128a7b43256999005bcbb3/79c58f476caec4e8c32 574040058934c?OpenDocument.

subsequently thanked Kazakhstan for declining to follow this advice.[597] Kazakh officials have always opposed separatism, especially within the SCO, but also in the case of Georgia.

---

[597] N. Kirtskhalia, "Georgia Thanks Azerbaijan, Kazakhstan & Ukraine for their Support – Foreign Minister," TrendNews, April 8, 2008, http://news.trendaz.com/index.shtml?show=news&newsid=1171467&lang=EN.

Conclusion

Eurasian international politics could well experience major discontinuities in coming years. None of the most important historical forces shaping Kazakhstan's neighborhood are necessarily linear. It is unclear whether Eurasia is experiencing a democratic wave or crest. The transformation of Islamic extremism continues with no visible end. The fate of WMD proliferation now lies at a tipping point, with the cases of Iran and North Korea still very much in doubt. The potential contribution of the region's energy resources to global markets also remains uncertain until Afghanistan becomes more stable. Major ambiguities surround the future policies of Russia, China, and the other countries and institutions engaged in Eurasia. Besides sudden geopolitical shifts, cases of abrupt regime collapse are also possible, as seen in Kyrgyzstan.[598] Even the biologically inevitable transition to a new generation of Central Asian leaders as the current cohort of elderly strongmen fade from the scene is fraught with uncertainty.[599] Central Asian political systems are so tightly controlled by their leaders and their immediate circles that sweeping policy transformations could easily ensue from turnover at the top.

Kazakhstan's ability to achieve its regional objectives will depend on several factors, including the state of the Eurasian economies, Kazakhstan's success in transitioning to a post-Nazarbayev era of political leaders, the effectiveness of Astana's stewardship of the OSCE, and the policies of the other important

---

[598] In January 2007, then U.S. Director of National Intelligence, John D. Negroponte, warned about the risks of the collapse of state authority resulting from competition among regions or clans for power, which he feared could open a vacuum for criminal and terrorist activities ("Annual Threat Assessment and U.S. National Security Challenges," Statement for the Record to the Senate Select Committee on Intelligence, January 11, 2007), http://www.state.gov/s/inr/rls/79065.htm.

[599] For an outline of several possible succession paths for post-Niyazov Turkmenistan—a process that is still occurring—that could easily apply to other Central Asian regimes see International Crisis Group, *Repression and Regression in Turkmenistan: A New International Strategy* (November 4, 2004), pp. 21-22.

countries engaged in Central Asia and the Caspian region—above all China and Russia, but also the United States.

Kazakhstan's tremendous economic growth largely explains its emergence as a major force in the new international politics of Eurasia. Thanks in particular to the recovery of world oil prices during the last decade, Kazakh citizens have been able to enjoy a rising standard of living as well as acquire the capital to exploit investment opportunities in neighboring states. These nations in turn have eagerly sought to bolster trade and other economic ties with Kazakhstan—including by supporting Kazakh efforts to chair the OSCE and assume other leadership roles within Eurasia.

Any sustained slowdown in Kazakhstan's economic development would weaken Astana's claims to regional leadership. In the near-term, the main challenge is the potentially disruptive effects of the world financial crisis, which has threatened the viability of many banks and lowered stock prices and growth rates throughout the world. Most experts expect that Kazakhstan should be able to weather the current storm due to its strong banking sector and growing revenue from surging prices for its oil exports.

Ironically, this very oil revenue presents a double long-term danger to the Kazak economy. A collapse of world oil prices, as occurred a decade ago and regularly before then, could derail Kazakhstan's economic prospects. Alternately, the country might fall victim to the same kind of "oil curse" that has afflicted Nigeria and other energy exporting countries, where easy profits from the sale of natural resources have undermined entrepreneurship and stoked corruption. The present leadership seems committed to pursuing vertical as well as horizontal market diversification, but its successor might prove more susceptible to the resource curse.

This consideration raises the question of which individual, group, or regime will replace Nazarbayev as Kazakhstan's chief policy maker when the president leaves the scene. Nazarbayev's inevitable departure could present a major transition crisis for a political system that, since its creation with Kazakhstan's independence in 1991, has known only his stewardship. Even were a successor able to consolidate as much power as Nazarbayev, it is unlikely that the new regime would pursue the same set of policies, with the same skill, as the current president.

Kazakhstan's chairmanship of the OSCE in 2010 will also affect the country's aspirations to regional leadership. Kazakh officials are characterizing this long-sought prize as an international endorsement of their country's successful economic and political reforms, Kazakhstan's leading role in Eurasia, and their contribution as a bridge between the former Soviet republics and other OSCE members. Many of the OSCE's most ardent supporters are counting on Kazakhstan's diplomats to restore the institution's prestige and influence in the former Soviet republics. There is also hope that, in preparing for the OSCE chairmanship, Kazakh officials will liberalize their own political practices to better conform to OSCE principles. Yet, fears are also widespread that Astana will prove reluctant to confront the governments of Russia or other member countries should they continue to violate OSCE norms regarding elections and civil rights.

On the other hand, Kazakhstan's regional leadership could also be challenged should the country's OSCE chairmanship prove highly successful and the country's economy continue to surge ahead of many of its neighbors. One reason for Kazakhstan's emergence as the most important driver of regional integration within Central Asia and the Caspian Sea region has been the country's powerful but not overwhelming attributes of state power. Thus far, Kazakhstan has lacked the economic and military foundations to aspire to regional hegemony, though even now multiple membership categories are emerging within Eurasec, the CIS, and the SCO that reflect participants' diverging economic and military progress. A widening gap between Kazakhstan and its Central Asian neighbors could reinforce the already visible resentment in Kyrgyzstan and especially Uzbekistan about Astana's progress, and might lead other Eurasian governments to seek countervailing ties with Beijing, Moscow, Washington, or even Tehran. Heightened geopolitical competition could in turn weaken the regional integration processes most sought by Kazakh leaders.

The same consequence would ensue should Central Asia again emerge as a region of active great power rivalry. Kazakhstan has striven to maneuver between China, Russia, and the United States by pursuing a "multi-vector" foreign policy that cultivates good relations with all these countries (and others) while eschewing alignment with any particular bloc. Astana would find it hard to resist a sustained effort by Beijing and Moscow to establish a condominium within Central Asia, even with Washington's help. Likewise, managing growing difference between Beijing and Moscow, an equally likely scenario, would require considerable diplomatic skill.

Acronyms

ADB	Asian Development Bank
ALA	Almaty International Airport
BTC	Baku-Tbilisi-Ceyhan pipeline
BWC	Biological Weapon's Convention
CANWFZ	Central Asian Nuclear-Weapon-Free Zone
CAREC	Central Asia Regional Economic Cooperation
CASFOR	Caspian Force
CENTCOM	U.S. Central Command
CENTRASBAT	Central Asian Peacekeeping Battalion
CFE	Conventional Forces in Europe
CICA	Conference on Interaction and Confidence-Building in Asia
CIS	Commonwealth of Independent States
CNCP	Chinese National Petroleum Corporation
CPC	Caspian Pipeline Consortium
CRDF	Collective Rapid Deployment Force
CSCE	Conference on Security and Cooperation in Europe
CST	Collective Security Treaty
CSTO	Collective Security Treaty Organization
CTR	Cooperative Threat Reduction
EAPC	Euro-Atlantic Partnership Council
EEC/Eurasec	Eurasian Economic Community
ENP	European Neighborhood Policy
EU	European Union

GICNT	Global Initiative to Combat Nuclear Terrorism
GNEP	Global Nuclear Energy Partnership
HEU	highly enriched uranium
IAEA	International Atomic Energy Agency
IAG	Implementation and Assessment Group
IMF	International Monetary Fund
IMU	Islamic Movement of Uzbekistan
IOC	Indian Oil Corporation
INOGATE	Interstate Oil and Gas Transport to Europe
IPAP	Individual Partnership Action Plan
ISAF	International Security Assistance Force
KAZINVEST	Kazakhstan Investment Promotion Center
KAZBAT	Kazakhstan Peacekeeping Battalion
KCTS	Kazakhstan Caspian Transport System
KMG	KazMunaiGs
LEU	low-enriched uranium
NATO	North Atlantic Treaty Organization
NPT	Nuclear Nonproliferation Treaty
NWFZ	Nuclear-Weapon-Free-Zone
ODIHR	Office of Democratic Institutions and Human Rights
OEF	Operation Enduring Freedom
ONGC	India's Oil and Natural Gas Corporation
OSCE	Organization for Security and Cooperation in Europe
PAP-T	Partnership Action Plan on Terrorism
PARP	Planning and Review Process
PCA	Partnership and Cooperation Agreement
PFP	Partnership for Peace

PLA   Chinese People's Liberation Army

RATS   Regional Anti-Terrorism Structure

RC07   Regional Cooperation 2007

RFCA   Regional Financial Center of Almaty

SCO   Shanghai Cooperation Organization

TAP   Trans-Afghan Pipeline

TAPI   Turkmenistan-Afghanistan-Pakistan-India gas pipeline

TIFA   Trade and Investment Framework Agreement

TRACECA   Transportat Corridor Europe, Caucasus, Asia

USJFCOM   U.S. Joints Forces Command

WTO   World Trade Organization